# Fodor's 93
# Chicago

.45
.50
2.00

Fodor's Travel Publications, Inc.
New York • Toronto • London • Sydney • Auckland

## Fodor's Chicago

**Editor:** Suzanne De Galan
**Editorial Contributors:** Paul A. Camp, Elizabeth Gardner, Dominic A. Pacyga, Marcy Pritchard, Barbara Shortt, Doris L. Taub, Phil Vettel
**Creative Director:** Fabrizio La Rocca
**Cartographer:** David Lindroth
**Illustrators:** Joseph Sipri, Karl Tanner
**Cover Photograph:** Brooks/Masterfile

**Design:** Vignelli Associates

## Special Sales

# Contents

**Maps**

# Foreword

The Chicago most visitors see first is the commercial and cultural heart of the city, the Downtown and Near North areas that contain the world-famous architecture, the impressive skyline, the department stores, major hotels, and fine restaurants that together define a great American city. This Chicago is the primary focus of the present guide, which takes a close look at the town, gives extensive information on places to stay, and provides reviews of more than 130 recommended places to eat throughout the city.

Yet there is another, equally interesting Chicago, a vibrant Chicago of the neighborhoods and their distinctive populations, and this guide takes the reader into some of those neighborhoods and shows how the tides of immigration have led to change, development, and curious ethnic juxtapositions. Quite a few of the restaurants recommended here are located in those neighborhoods, too.

*Fodor's Chicago '93*, through its walking tours and essays, examines the two Chicagos—the downtown and the neighborhoods—and tries to suggest the greater political and human entity that is the foremost city of the American Middle West.

While every care has been taken to assure the accuracy of the information in this guide, the passage of time will always bring change, and consequently the publisher cannot accept responsibility for errors that may occur.

All prices and opening times quoted here are based on information supplied to us at press time. Hours and admission fees may change, however, and the prudent traveler will avoid inconvenience by calling ahead.

Fodor's wants to hear about your travel experiences, both pleasant and unpleasant. When a hotel or restaurant fails to live up to its billing, let us know and we will investigate the complaint and revise our entries where the facts warrant it.

Send your letters to the editors of Fodor's Travel Publications, 201 East 50th Street, New York, NY 10022.

# Highlights'93 and Fodor's Choice

# Highlights '93

Unfortunately for its boosters, the city's biggest story in 1992 was the **Great Chicago Flood,** which paralyzed the city's heart for weeks and cost $800 million in property damage and lost business. It happened in April, when workers accidentally punctured an old railway tunnel beneath the city, causing millions of gallons of Chicago River water to roar into the gap. City engineers worked furiously to plug the leak before the water rose to street level, but they weren't able to stop flooding in Loop basements and two subway lines (miraculously, no one was killed or seriously hurt). Happily for visitors, little visible evidence remains of the Great Chicago Flood, although officials continue to wrangle over who's to blame, and the topic is still a favorite among residents.

The flood turned attention away, at least temporarily, from two of Mayor Richard M. Daley's projects: a **third airport** for Chicago and a casino-gambling complex somewhere near downtown. Although the state legislature last year voted down the mayor's plan for a new airport at Lake Calumet, on the southeast side near the Indiana border, some observers think the proposal may be revived. Residents of the area, who face displacement if the airport is built, are watching particularly closely.

**Casino gambling** is another hot topic among residents and politicians. Up to now, the only forms of gambling allowed on Illinois land were horse-race betting, the state lottery, and bingo. (Riverboat gambling is legal on the Mississippi and Joliet rivers, but low bet-limits make the boats unsuitable for Vegas-style high rollers.) Daley must enlist the help of Republican Governor Jim Edgar (normally an opponent) to make casino gambling legal. The mayor is touting the casino as a draw for conventions that would otherwise go to Las Vegas, although a local business-newspaper survey showed that managers of the country's 100 largest conventions are largely indifferent to the idea.

Episodes of looting and vandalism marred the city's frenzied victory celebration when the **Chicago Bulls** won their second national basketball championship in a row, in June 1992, beating the Portland Trailblazers in six exciting games. Roving gangs of Bulls fans broke store windows on the south and west sides of town as well as on Michigan Avenue, and 1,000 people were arrested, mostly for burglary and looting. Superstar Bull player Michael Jordan has become the hottest property on the advertising endorsement circuit, and coach Phil Jackson isn't far behind. Bulls fever is likely to burn bright again this year.

The **Museum of Broadcast Communications** has moved into new quarters at the Chicago Public Library Cultural Center, at the corner of Randolph Street and Michigan Avenue. The former home of the five-year-old museum, on South Wells Street, was off the beaten track for most visitors. Visitors to the new million-dollar quarters can watch old sitcoms, documentaries, variety shows, and dramas, and browse among old television sets and memorabilia from early TV and radio days. Admission is free.

The **hotel-building** spree that added more than 5,000 rooms to the city's supply between 1987 and 1992 seems to have stopped. Although a few companies are flirting with the idea of building new properties, particularly in the still under-served River North area, none has committed itself to schedules or opening dates. Currently, the average occupancy for the city's 25,000-odd rooms is about 62%, but that means more than half the rooms stand empty when there's no big convention at McCormick Place to take up every spot in town. Tourists should be able to pick from more deals than ever during slow periods.

The recession took its toll on Chicago retailers, as numerous STORE FOR LEASE signs in all parts of town attest. Venerable **I. Magnin** closed the doors of its classy, gray, Michigan Avenue store. But there are signs of hope: Right next door, at 840 North Michigan Avenue, a new, vaguely Parisian-looking structure has gone up to house toy merchants **FAO Schwarz & Co.** The store is scheduled to open in fall 1992. Down the street are two newcomers to the category of store-as-shrine. **Sony**'s sumptuous new **showroom** (663 N. Michigan Ave.) has every imaginable gadget, exhibited in a style reminiscent of the Terra Museum across the way. Next door, at 669, **Nike Town** glorifies athletic wear in a way that will thrill, repel, or amuse you, depending on your attitude toward participant sports. Try on "surf shoes" while standing on a surface of video screens that show rock-bound coastline, or watch tropical fish glide around the wall-size aquarium. Use the mini basketball court on the second level to test your Air Jordans. Niketown's murals, life-size sculptures, and bas reliefs of athletes in action are done in a style similar to the "socialist realism" of the 1930s—ironic for this quintessential capitalist venture.

The oldest section of Chicago's **elevated train** celebrated its 100th anniversary in 1992 amid doubts about the El's ultimate viability. Routine maintenance of its 46 miles of track costs about $800,000 per mile per year, and a Chicago Transit Authority (CTA) study estimates it would cost $22 million per mile to give the system a structural overhaul that would last into the next century. A few of the alternatives: move the tracks to existing railroad right-of-ways, substitute express buses, construct a new El similar to systems in Washington and San Francisco, or build light-rail trolleys on surface streets. Neighborhood groups are protesting any proposal to eliminate the El.

Meanwhile, the CTA is contemplating adoption of a **fare structure** even more confusing than the one it has now. Currently, Chicagoans can buy passes that allow them unlimited rides on trains and buses. One proposed change would cut the prices of those passes, but make pass-holders pay 25¢ per ride. Even more daunting, particularly for tourists, is the proposal to eliminate the 30¢ transfers that let riders switch between trains and buses. Nothing's been decided at this writing, but travelers to Chicago in 1993 shouldn't be surprised if the CTA costs more than our first chapter says it does.

Travelers can expect torn-up roads all over the Chicago area no matter when they visit. A long-term project to resurface the **Kennedy Expressway** is likely to stretch into 1993, slowing the trip to and from O'Hare Airport and making it difficult to get to the northwestern suburbs. Repair work on other roads is sporadic. If recent road construction is any indication, the new roads are worth the trouble: Driving on North Lake Shore Drive has become a treat since a total overhaul in 1991 resurfaced all eight lanes and added a landscaped median strip.

# Fodor's Choice

No two people will agree on what makes a perfect vacation, but it's fun and helpful to know what others think. We hope you'll have a chance to experience some of Fodor's Choices yourself while visiting Chicago. For detailed information about each entry, refer to the appropriate chapters in this guidebook.

## Activities

Watching the animals in a "thunderstorm" in the rain forest at the Brookfield Zoo

Singing "Take Me Out to the Ballgame" during the seventh-inning stretch at Wrigley Field

Exploring the tomb of Unis-ankh in "Inside Ancient Egypt" at the Field Museum of Natural History

## Turn-of-the-Century Architecture

Fisher Building

Robie House

The Rookery

## Modern Architecture

Northwestern Atrium Center

State of Illinois Center

333 North Wacker Drive

## Moments

Feeding time at the coral reef of the John G. Shedd Aquarium

The winter orchid show at the Chicago Botanic Garden

The skylit sculpture court at the Art Institute

## Sights

Chicago River from the Michigan Avenue Bridge

Chicago skyline from Olive Park

Chicago skyline from South Lake Shore Drive

The panoramic view of the city from the top of the John Hancock Building

**Hotels**

The Drake (*Very Expensive*)

The Four Seasons (*Very Expensive*)

Chicago Hilton and Towers (*Expensive*)

The Raphael (*Moderate–Expensive*)

**Restaurants**

Everest (French, *Very Expensive*)

Spiaggia (Italian, *Very Expensive*)

Charlie Trotter's (American, *Expensive–Very Expensive*)

Yoshi's Cafe (French, *Expensive–Very Expensive*)

Arun's (Thai, *Expensive*)

Morton's of Chicago (Steakhouse, *Expensive*)

Vivere (Italian, *Expensive*)

Frontera Grill (Mexican, *Moderate*)

Taylor St. Bistro (French, *Moderate*)

Ed Debevic's (American 1950s, *Inexpensive*)

Lou Mitchell's (American, *Inexpensive*)

# Chicago

800W · Crosby · Kingsbury · North Branch Chicago · Larrabee · Hudson · 400W · Walton · Locust · Chestnut · Institute Pl. · 001W · 001E · Rush · John H. Bu · Tower

Chicago · Superior · Huron · Erie · Ontario St. · Orleans · Franklin · Wells · La Salle · Clark St. · Dearborn · State St. · Wabash · Rush

Ohio · Grand · Ohio St. · River · Grand · Ontario St. · Ohio St. · Grand

Illinois · Hubbard · Kinzie · Wrigle Buildin

400N · Kinzie · Milwaukee

O'HARE INTERNATIONAL AIRPORT · Union · Fulton · W. Wacker Dr. · Wate

Lake · Lake

Randolph · Washington · Madison · John F. Kennedy Expwy. · Desplaines · Jefferson · Clinton · Canal · S. Wacker Dr. · Franklin · Wells · La Salle · Clark St. · Dearborn · State Street Mall

State of Illinois Building · Daley Center · Washington · THE LOOP · Madison · Monroe · Marsha Field & · Wabash · Carson Pirie Scott & Co.

Peoria · Green · Halsted · 90 94 · Monroe · Adams · Jackson Blvd. · Adams · Sears Tower · Quincy · Orchest He

400S · Van Buren · 290 · Eisenhower Expwy. · Chicago Board of Trade · Van Buren · Harold Washington Library Center · Congress Pkwy. · Aud Thee

Harrison · Dan Ryan Expwy. · South Br. · Wells · Financial · La Salle · Federal · Plymouth Ct. · Harrison · Harrison · State St.

800S · 800W · 500W · Polk · Chicago River · Polk · 8th S · Wabash

Taylor · Taylor · 9th St. · 11th St. · 001W · 001E

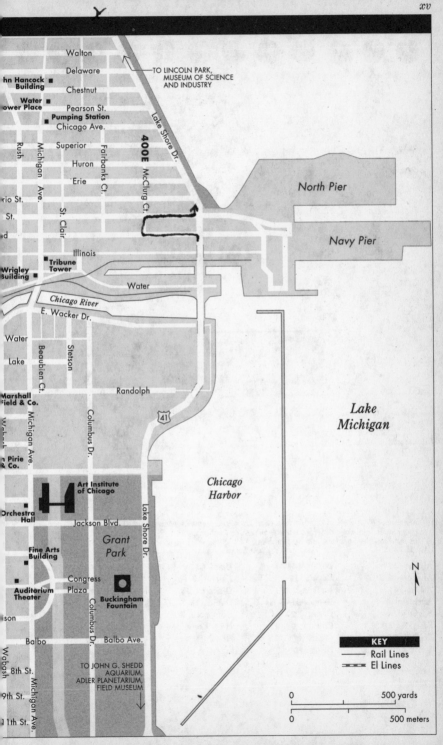

Walton

Delaware

hn Hancock
Building

Chestnut

Water
ower Place

Pearson St.

**Pumping Station**

Chicago Ave.

TO LINCOLN PARK,
MUSEUM OF SCIENCE
AND INDUSTRY

Rush

Michigan Ave.

Superior

Fairbanks Ct.

400E

McClurg Ct.

Lake Shore Dr.

Huron

rio St.

St. Clair

Erie

North Pier

St.

Navy Pier

d

Illinois

**Tribune
Tower**

**Wrigley
Building**

Water

*Chicago River*

E. Wacker Dr.

Water

Beaubien Ct.

Stetson

Lake

**Marshall
Field & Co.**

Michigan Ave.

Columbus Dr.

Randolph

41

*Lake
Michigan*

n Pirie
& Co.

**Art Institute
of Chicago**

*Chicago
Harbor*

Orchestra
Hall

Jackson Blvd.

Lake Shore Dr.

**Fine Arts
Building**

*Grant
Park*

**Auditorium
Theater**

Congress
Plaza

Columbus Dr.

**Buckingham
Fountain**

ison

Balbo

Balbo Ave.

8th St.

Michigan Ave.

TO JOHN G. SHEDD
AQUARIUM,
ADLER PLANETARIUM,
FIELD MUSEUM

9th St.

Wabash

N

1th St.

**KEY**

—— Rail Lines

▭▭ El Lines

0                    500 yards

0                    500 meters

# World Time Zones

MONDAY
SUNDAY

International Date Line

+12 +13 -9 -10 -11 -10 +11 +12

-7 -4 -3 -5 -4 -3:30 -7 -8 -6 -4 -5 -4 -3 -3 25

+11 +12 -11 -10 -9 -8 -7 -6 -5 -4 -3 -2

Numbers below vertical bands relate each zone to Greenwich Mean Time (0 hrs.).
Local times frequently differ from these general indications,
as indicated by light-face numbers on map.

| | | | |
|---|---|---|---|
| Algiers, **29** | Berlin, **34** | Delhi, **48** | Istanbul, **40** |
| Anchorage, **3** | Bogotá, **19** | Denver, **8** | Jerusalem, **42** |
| Athens, **41** | Budapest, **37** | Djakarta, **53** | Johannesburg, **44** |
| Auckland, **1** | Buenos Aires, **24** | Dublin, **26** | Lima, **20** |
| Baghdad, **46** | Caracas, **22** | Edmonton, **7** | Lisbon, **28** |
| Bangkok, **50** | Chicago, **9** | Hong Kong, **56** | London (Greenwich), **27** |
| Beijing, **54** | Copenhagen, **33** | Honolulu, **2** | Los Angeles, **6** |
| | Dallas, **10** | | Madrid, **38** |
| | | | Manila, **57** |

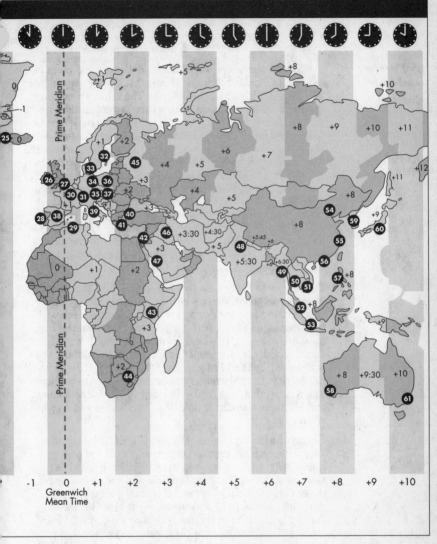

-1    0    +1    +2    +3    +4    +5    +6    +7    +8    +9    +10
Greenwich
Mean Time

# Introduction

By Elizabeth
Gardner

Elizabeth
Gardner grew up
in what is now
Chicago's Oak
Park Historic
District.

**A** few years ago, the *Chicago Tribune* ran a piece in its Sunday magazine about what Chicago would be like without Lake Michigan. The artist's rendering showed a one-street town with a tumbleweed in the foreground. In many ways, Chicago *is* Lake Michigan. Whereas some cities radiate from a central hub, Chicago flattens out along the lakeshore like a string bean. On sunny summer weekends the whole city heads to the lakefront parks to swim (yes, you can swim in the lake, although the water could be cleaner), to sunbathe, to bicycle, to roller-skate, to stroll, to jog, and just to soak up the atmosphere. Whatever the summer weather, it's always "cooler near the lake." In winter, many fleeting snowfalls come from the "lake effect," when cold clouds hit the warmer air above the water. The lake's moods range from glassy calm to roiling tempest, and the population reacts accordingly.

The city owes its origins to Lake Michigan. Chicago was born as a shipping center when it was discovered that a series of rivers and one portage could connect the lake with the Mississippi River. Any water traffic between the east coast and the country's heartland had to pass through this damp, marshy land, christened Checagou or "place of the wild onion" by local Indians. In 1833 Chicago officially became a city. In 1836 ground was broken to turn the portage into a canal that was finally finished in 1848. The Illinois and Michigan Canal still links the Des Plaines and Illinois rivers.

People who like cities generally love Chicago. To urbanites, it's got everything: architectural wonders old and new, gracious parks, cultural institutions that rival the world's finest, outstanding restaurants, classic and avant-garde theater, music from heavy metal to weary blues, nightlife, streetlife, urban grit, and urban sophistication. Because the city is not as large or famous as New York, many Chicagoans suffer from "Second City" complex, a fear that out-of-towners won't appreciate their city's charms. But they're worrying needlessly, for the charms—from the stunning sweep of the skyline to the elegance of Michigan Avenue's shops to the tree-lined streets of the outlying neighborhoods—are hard to miss.

A number of events have left their mark on the city's history. The Great Fire of 1871 razed nearly every building in the city, making it a virtual blank canvas on which architects could design (*see* "The Builders of Chicago" in Chapter 2). Such giants as Louis Sullivan and Daniel H. Burham began experimenting with the steel frames that even today define the term "skyscraper." In these architects wake came droves of carpenters, masons, and other laborers,

who flocked here to build the new Chicago. Their arrival
was nothing new to Chicago, which welcomed successive
waves of German's, Swedes, Poles, Irish, Jews, and Italians
throughout the 19th and early 20th centuries.

Many of these immigrants came to work in the burgeoning
industries here, and their eventual uprising against
wretched labor conditions had a profound impact upon the
city—and the country. When Upton Sinclair published his
landmark novel *The Jungle*, describing the lives of
Chicago's stockyard and meatpacking workers, the public
outcry was so great that it led to the 1906 passage of the
federal Pure Food and Drug Act. The Haymarket Riot of
May 4, 1886, began as a demonstration by workers in sympathy with strikers at the McCormick Reaper plant and
ended with a bomb explosion and a melee that killed four
workers and seven policemen. The Haymarket became a
rallying point for the world labor movement when eight
"anarchists" were convicted of the bombing in a blatantly
unjust trial, and four were executed. (Governer John P.
Altgeld pardoned the others in 1893, committing political
suicide in the process.)

The lawless era of Prohibition will forever be linked
with Chicago in people's minds. Today's city hall
would like people to forget the notorious criminals
who subverted the police and courts and terrorized ordinary citizens here. The tourism council's "brief history" of
the city breathes not a word about gangsters. But Al
Capone and John Dillinger are more famous than Chicago
luminaries Frank Lloyd Wright and Ludwig Mies van der
Rohe (at least, they've had more movies made about them).
According to a history of the city published in 1929, mur-
ders in Cook County rose from 190 in 1920 to 399 in 1928,
and felony convictions fell almost 50%. And almost 24,000
felony charges were dropped or modified in 1923 alone, due
primarily to "friendly" judges. If it didn't actually create
the term "racketeer," Chicago played a key role in defining
it.

Like so many American cities, Chicago saw its middle class
flee to the suburbs during the postwar prosperity of the
1950s and the turbulence of the 1960s. Some neighborhoods
turned from rich to poor, although many ethnic enclaves on
the northwest and southwest sides remained relatively stable. But in the 1970s, young "urban pioneers" began to
creep back to the city, picking up run-down properties for a
song and renovating them into showplaces. Meanwhile,
new groups of immigrants—Vietnamese, Thai, Cambodi-
an, Hmong, Russian Jews—were finding their riches in the
city. Today each of Chicago's dozens of neighborhoods has a
distinct character: the wealthy socialite Gold Coast, "lakefront liberal" Lincoln Park and Lakeview, white-ethnic
Bridgeport, Ukranian Village and Blue Island, black
middle-class South Shore, integrated Hyde Park and Bev-

erly, and battle-scarred ghettos such as North Lawndale and Austin. Black people and white people, divided as often by an economic abyss as by skin color, coexist with caution, although overt hatred has in many cases been replaced by the pragmatic need to get along in a city where neither group predominates. (Black and white each account for about 40% of Chicago's 2.6 million people.)

**N**onetheless, factions abound. The North Side and the South Side are two different worlds. You're a White Sox fan or a Cubs fan, not both (unless one of the teams is down to the wire in a serious pennant race—a once-in-a-blue-moon event that sucks in even the nonfan). The conflicts on the city council, although currently muted, are legendary. Even in a city chronically strapped for cash, don't try to suggest closing an under-used public school or cutting service to a redundant El stop, except over the ward alderman's dead body.

It's true that Chicagoans can be contentious, territorial, and possessive. Although the city's official motto is "Urbs in Horto" (City in a Garden), its unofficial one is "Ubi est Meus?" (Where's Mine?). But to visitors, Chicagoans are as friendly and open as big-city dwellers can be. Perhaps the one thing that unites many of them is unparalleled civic chauvinism. Don't be shy about asking directions or questions; people will probably tell you more than you really want to know. You'll find the city straightforward and unpretentious: For every club imported from the coast where your outfit has to pass muster with the doorman, there are a hundred corner bars where you'll be welcome in anything from a tux to a T-shirt. To meet the real Chicago, try to get away from downtown a little and venture into the 'hoods, preferably with a local guide. (*See* Chapter 3 for some of our favorites.) And if you get lost, just remember the one Chicago rule: The lake is east.

# 1 Essential Information

# Before You Go

## Visitor Information

For information on the city, contact the **Chicago Office of Tourism** (806 N. Michigan Ave., Water Tower in the Park, Chicago, IL 60611, tel. 312/280–5740 or 800/487–2446).

If you plan on traveling outside Chicago, contact the **Illinois Bureau of Tourism** (310 S. Michigan Ave., Chicago, IL 60601, tel. 312/793–2094 or 800/233–0121) for a free packet of brochures on travel in the state of Illinois.

Foreign travelers may wish to contact the **International Visitors Center** (520 N. Michigan Ave., Chicago, IL 60611, tel. 312/645–1836).

## Tips for British Travelers

**Passports**  You will need a valid 10-year passport. You do not need a visa if you are staying 90 days or less, have a return ticket, or are flying with a participating airline and complete visa waiver form I–94W, available at the airport or on the plane. There are some exceptions, so check with your travel agent or with the **United States Embassy** (Visa and Immigration Department, 5 Upper Grosvenor St., London W1A 2JB, 071/499–3443).

No vaccinations are required for entry into the United States.

**Customs**  Returning to Britain, you may bring home (1) 200 cigarettes or 100 cigarillos or 50 cigars or 250 grams of tobacco; (2) 2 liters of table wine and, in addition, (a) 1 liter of alcohol over 22% by volume (most spirits) or (b) 2 liters of alcohol under 22% by volume (fortified or sparkling wine) or (c) two more liters of table wine; (3) 60 milliliters of perfume and 250 milliliters of toilet water; and (4) other goods up to a value of £32, but not more than 50 liters of beer or 25 mechanical lighters.

**Insurance**  We recommend that you insure yourself to cover health and motoring mishaps with **Europ Assistance** (252 High St., Croydon CR0 1NF, tel. 081/680–1234). Their excellent service is all the more valuable when you consider the possible costs of health care in the United States.

**Airfares**  We suggest that you explore the current scene for budget flight possibilities; check the small ads in daily and Sunday newspapers. Be warned, however, that these cut-rate flights are fiendishly hard to come by, so be sure to book well in advance. Check, also, on APEX and other money-saving fares, because, quite frankly, only business travelers who don't have to watch the price of their tickets fly full price these days—and find themselves sitting right beside an APEX passenger!

**Tour Operators**  Among the many tour operators who offer packages to Chicago, you may like to consider some of these as you plan your trip:

**British Airways Holidays** (Atlantic House, Hazelwick Ave., Crawley, West Sussex RH10 1NP, tel. 0293/611611).
**Kuoni Travel** (Kuoni House, Dorking, Surrey RH5 4AZ, tel. 0306/742222).
**North American Vacations** (Acorn House, 172/174 Albert Rd., Jarrow, Tyne & Wear NE32 5JA, tel. 091/483–6226).

**Information**  Contact **United States Travel and Tourism Administration** (Box
1EN, London W1A 1EN, tel. 071/495–4466).

## When to Go

Chicago promises activities and attractions to keep any visitor
busy at any time of year. Travelers whose principal concern is
to have comfortable weather for touring the city may prefer
spring or fall, when moderate temperatures can make it a
pleasure to be out and about, and the city's cultural institutions
are well into their seasons. Late fall has a special dividend for
children of all ages in the lavish Christmas decorations in the
stores of the Magnificent Mile and the State Street Mall.

Summertime brings many opportunities for outdoor recreation. Yet the temperatures will climb to the 90s in hot spells,
and the humidity can be uncomfortably high. In more normal
times the presence of Lake Michigan has a moderating effect on
the city's weather, keeping it several degrees cooler in summer, a bit warmer in winter.

Those winters can see very raw weather and occasionally the
news-making blizzard, and temperatures in the teens are to be
expected; wintertime visitors should come prepared for the
cold. Yet mild winters, with temperatures in the 30s, are common, too. There are January sales to reward those who venture
out, and many indoor venues let one look out on the cold in
warm comfort.

**Climate**  What follows are the average daily maximum and minimum
temperatures for Chicago.

| Jan. | 32F | 0C | May | 65F | 18C | Sept. | 73F | 23C |
|------|-----|------|------|-----|-----|-------|-----|------|
|      | 18  | – 8  |      | 50  | 10  |       | 58  | 14   |
| Feb. | 34F | 1C   | June | 75F | 24C | Oct.  | 61F | 16C  |
|      | 20  | – 7  |      | 60  | 16  |       | 47  | 8    |
| Mar. | 43F | 6C   | July | 81F | 27C | Nov.  | 47F | 8C   |
|      | 29  | – 2  |      | 66  | 19  |       | 34  | 1    |
| Apr. | 55F | 13C  | Aug. | 79F | 26C | Dec.  | 36F | 2C   |
|      | 40  | 4    |      | 65  | 18  |       | 23  | – 5  |

Current weather information for foreign and domestic cities
may be obtained by calling The Weather Channel Connection at
900/WEATHER from a touch-tone phone. In addition to the
weather report, The Weather Channel Connection offers local
time and travel tips as well as hurricane, foliage, and ski re-
ports. The call costs 95¢ per minute.

## Festivals and Seasonal Events

Chicagoans love celebrations. They find occasions for them in
anniversaries and events, and when those don't come up often
enough, they will hold a celebration for no particular reason at
all. Spring and summer are the festival seasons. The **International Theatre Festival** arrives in April during even-numbered
years and stays for a month, presenting selections by talented
writers and theater groups from around the world. Summer
brings a multitude of art fairs, including the outstanding juried
**Hyde Park Art Fair** during the first weekend in June. Parades
and neighborhood ethnic, cultural, and food fairs are almost
weekly occurrences, capped by the granddaddy of them all,

**A Taste of Chicago,** during the week of July 4. Columbus Drive between Jackson and Randolph is closed to traffic for the duration, and half a million people or more each day flock to sample the culinary offerings of scores of local purveyors. The 4th of July weekend is also the occasion for a splendid coordinated celebration by the Grant Park Symphony Orchestra and the City of Chicago: The city sets off an awesome fireworks display on the lakefront, providing the cannon sound effects for the Symphony's rendition of Tchaikovsky's *1812 Overture*.

The **James C. Petrillo Bandshell,** in Grant Park, is the site of outdoor music all summer, beginning with the **Blues and Gospel festivals** in mid-June, continuing with four performances weekly by the **Grant Park Symphony Orchestra and Chorus** in late June through the end of August, and ending with a week-long **Jazz festival.** Labor Day brings the *Chicago Tribune's* **Ribfest,** with some 500 avid barbecuers and their families and friends pitching grills, nursing briquettes, marinating slabs in secret concoctions, and generating a dense, aromatic cloud of hickory smoke seasoned with beer that hovers over the central city and the marchers in the **Labor Day parade.** Fall brings **Oktoberfest** to the Berghoff Restaurant downtown and to neighborhood watering holes around the city, providing a delightful way to end an evening spent at the **Chicago International Film Festival,** a three-week showing at the Music Box and Biograph theaters of distinguished new American and foreign films.

Celebrations move indoors for the winter. The Museum of Science and Industry mounts a **Christmas Around the World** show that displays trees decorated in the traditional styles of more than 40 countries. February chills are dispelled by the warmth of celebrations honoring **Black History Month,** with special exhibitions and music and dance performances at the Museum of Science and Industry, the DuSable Museum, the Chicago Cultural Center, and other institutions.

The following is a small sampling of the many events that Chicagoans and visitors alike enjoy each year. For precise dates and details, contact the Chicago Tourism Council (Historic Water Tower-in-the-Park, 806 N. Michigan Ave., Chicago, IL 60611, tel. 312/280–5740) or consult one of these excellent calendars of events for the weekend and the upcoming week: *The Reader*, and *New City*, two free weekly newspapers distributed on Thursday in many stores in Hyde Park, the Loop, and the North Side; the Friday section of the Friday *Chicago Tribune;* and the "Weekender" section of the Friday *Chicago Sun-Times*.

**Month of Feb. Black History Month** celebrations at the Museum of Science and Industry (57th St. and Lake Shore Dr., tel. 312/684–1414), the DuSable Museum (740 E. 56th Pl., tel. 312/947–0600), the Chicago Cultural Center (78 E. Washington St., tel. 312/269–2900), the Field Museum (Roosevelt Rd. at Lake Shore Dr., tel. 312/922–9410), the Art Institute of Chicago (Michigan Ave. at Adams St., tel. 312/443–3600) and other Chicago cultural institutions include arts and crafts exhibitions and theater, music, and dance performances.
**Mid-Feb.–Early Mar. Azalea and Camellia Show** at Lincoln Park Conservatory (2400 N. Stockton Dr., tel. 312/294–4770).
**Mid-Feb. Chicago International Auto Show** previews the complement of next year's domestic and imported models (McCormick Pl., 2300 S. Lake Shore Dr., tel. 312/698–6630).

**Late Feb.–mid-Mar. Medinah Shrine Circus** at Medinah Temple (600 N. Wabash Ave., tel. 312/266–5000).

**Mar. 17.** The Chicago River is dyed green, and the center stripe of Dearborn Street is painted the color of the Irish for a **St. Patrick's Day parade** from Wacker Drive to Van Buren Street.

**Late Mar.–early Apr. Spring and Easter Flower Show** blooms at the Lincoln Park Conservatory.

**Mid-May. International Art Exposition** in Donnelley International Hall at McCormick Place (2300 S. Lake Shore Dr., tel. 312/787–6858).

**Mid-May.** See masterpieces by Frank Lloyd Wright and other Prairie School architects on the **Wright Plus House Walk,** Oak Park (tel. 708/848–1978).

**Late May. Festival of Illinois Film and Video Artists,** a two-day visual arts display, has events at various theaters (tel. 312/663–1600).

**Memorial Day. Buckingham Fountain,** in Grant Park, is turned on. Shows daily; colored lights nightly, 9–10, through Labor Day.

**Early June. Body Politic Street Festival** takes over the 2200 North block of Lincoln Avenue with food and theatrics (tel. 312/348–7901).

**Early June. 57th Street Art Fair** (Ray School yard, 57th St., and Kimbark Ave.), one of the major juried art fairs in the Midwest, selects exhibitors from applicants from all over the country. Offerings include both the decorative and the utilitarian: paintings, sculpture, jewelry, ceramics, and clothing and textiles (tel. 312/744–3315).

**Mid-June. Printer's Row Book Fair,** a two-day multimedia event that takes place in the historic Printer's Row District, is built around books and the printer's and binder's arts. Clowns, jugglers, and food vendors weave their way through displays from major and specialty booksellers and craftspeople demonstrating book-related arts (Dearborn St. between Harrison St. and Polk St., tel. 312/663–1595).

**Mid-June. Chicago Blues Festival** in Grant Park, a three-day, three-stage event featuring blues greats from Chicago and around the country.

**Mid-June. The Boulevard–Lakefront Bicycle Tour** brings 5,000 cyclists to the city's fabled network of boulevards and parks for a 35-mile ride (tel. 312/427–3325).

**Late June. Grant Park Symphony Orchestra and Chorus** give four concerts weekly through mid-August (tel. 312/819–0614).

**Late June—early Sept. Ravinia Festival,** Highland Park, hosts a variety of classical and popular musical artists in a pastoral setting north of the city (tel. 312/728–4642).

**All summer. Noontime music and dance performances** are held outdoors weekdays at the Daley Plaza Civic Center (Washington St. between Dearborn and Clark Sts.) and at the First National Bank of Chicago Plaza (Dearborn St. at Madison St.).

**July 4. Evening fireworks** along the lakefront; bring a blanket and a portable radio to listen to the *1812 Overture* from Grant Park.

**Early July. Taste of Chicago** (Columbus Dr. between Jackson and Randolph) feeds 4 million hungry visitors with specialties from scores of restaurants in the Chicago area.

**Late July. Air and water show** along the Near North lakefront at North Avenue features precision flying teams and displays of antique and high-tech aircraft going through their paces.

**Late July. Chicago to Mackinac Island Boat Race** originates at

Belmont Harbor under the auspices of the Chicago Yacht Club (Monroe St. Harbor, tel. 312/861–7777).

**Mid-Aug. Chicago International Sky Nights** features two nights of fireworks and boats festooned with lights (Monroe St. Harbor, Grant Park, tel. 312/744–3315).

**Late Aug. Chicago Triathlon** participants plunge in at Oak Street Beach for a one-mile swim, followed by a 10-kilometer run and a 25-mile bike race on Lake Shore Drive.

**Labor Day. Chicago Federation of Labor Parade** on Dearborn Street, from Wacker Drive to Congress Street. *Chicago Tribune* Ribfest in Grant Park (tel. 312/222–3232).

**Labor Day weekend. Chicago Jazz Festival,** Grant Park.

**Mid-Sept. International New Art Forms Exposition** comes to Navy Pier (tel. 312/787–6858).

**Mid-Sept. Viva Chicago,** a festival of Latin music, comes to Grant Park (tel. 312/280–5740).

**Late Sept.–early Oct. Oktoberfest** brings out the best in beer and German specialties at the Berghoff Restaurant (17 W. Adams St., tel. 312/427–3170) and Chicago area pubs.

**Columbus Day. Columbus Day Parade** on Dearborn Street from Wacker Drive to Congress Street.

**Mid-Oct. International Antiques Show,** Navy Pier (tel. 312/787–6858).

**Late Oct. Chicago Marathon** starts at Daley Bicentennial Plaza (337 E. Randolph St.) and follows a course through the city (tel. 312/951–0660).

**Late Oct.–early Nov. Chicago International Film Festival** brings outstanding new American and foreign films to the Music Box and Biograph theaters. Some Music Box intermissions feature a live organist performing in restored 1920s movie palace grandeur (tel. 312/644–3400).

**Thanksgiving Weekend.** Friday marks the illumination of **Chicago's Christmas tree** in the Daley Center Plaza (Washington St. between Dearborn and Clark Sts.). The **Christmas parade,** with balloons, floats, and Santa bringing up the rear, travels down Michigan Avenue on Saturday.

**Late Nov.–Dec. Christmas Around the World** display at the Museum of Science and Industry (57th St. and Lake Shore Dr., tel. 312/684–1414) features trees decorated in the traditional styles of more than 40 countries.

**Early Dec.** The Goodman Theatre (200 S. Columbus Dr., tel. 1312/443–3800) presents *A Christmas Carol,* and *The Nutcracker* is performed at the Arie Crown Theatre at McCormick Place (2300 S. Lake Shore Dr., tel. 312/791–6000).

**Late Dec.–early Jan. Christmas Flower Show** at Lincoln Park Conservatory.

## What to Pack

Pack light, because porters and luggage carts are hard to find. Luggage allowances on domestic flights vary slightly from airline to airline. Most allow two or three checked pieces and two carryons. Check-in luggage cannot weigh more than 70 pounds per piece or be larger than 62 inches (length + width + height). Carry-on luggage cannot be larger than 72 inches (length + width + height) and must fit under the seat, in a storage closet, or in the overhead luggage compartment.

Be prepared for cold, snowy weather in the winter and hot, sticky weather in the summer. Jeans (shorts in summer) and T-

shirts or sweaters and slacks are fine for sightseeing and informal dining. Men will need jackets and ties, women dresses, for
expensive restaurants. In the winter take boots or a sturdy
pair of shoes with nonslip soles for icy sidewalks, and a hat to
protect your ears from the numbing winds that buffet Michigan
Avenue. In the summer, bring a swimsuit for Lake Michigan
swimming or sunning.

## Getting Money from Home

**Cash Machines**  When possible, use automated-teller machines (ATMs) to withdraw money from your checking account with a bank card, or,
though it's more expensive, advance cash with your credit card.
Before leaving home ask your local bank for a Personal Identification Number (PIN) for your bank and credit cards. Also find
out the fees for withdrawals or cash advances overseas, limits
on these transactions within given time periods, and a list of af-
filiated cash-machine networks—such as **Cirrus** and **Plus**. (For
locations, tel. 800/4–Cirrus or 800/THE–PLUS.) Cash advances can also be made through bank tellers. Either way, you
pay interest from the day of posting, and some banks tack on an
extra service charge.

**Bank Transfers**  Just call your local bank and have money sent to a bank in the
area you're visiting. It's easiest to transfer money between like
branches; otherwise, the process may take longer and cost
more.

**American Express**  The company's Express Cash system links your U.S. checking
**Cardholder**  account to your Amex card. You can withdraw up to $1,000 in a
**Services**  seven-day period (more if your card is gold or platinum). For
each transaction there's a 2% fee (minimum $2, maximum $6).
Call 800/227–4669 for information.

Cardholders can also cash personal or counter checks at any
American Express office for up to $1,000, of which $500 may be
claimed in cash and the balance in traveler's checks carrying a
1% commission.

**Wiring Money**  You don't have to be a cardholder to have an **American Express
MoneyGram** sent to you. Just have a friend at home fill out a
MoneyGram for up to $10,000 at an American Express
MoneyGram agency (call 800/543–4080 for locations). Payment
of up to $1,000 may be made with a credit card (AE, D, MC, V);
the balance must be in cash. Your friend then telephones you
with a reference number and the MoneyGram agent authorizes
a funds transfer to the participating office nearest you. Present
proper I.D. and the reference number for payment. Fees are
roughly 5% to 10%, depending upon the amount and method of
payment.

If there are no American Express offices nearby, you can use
**Western Union** (tel. 800/325–6000). A friend at home can bring
cash or a check to the nearest Western Union office or pay over
the phone with a credit card. Delivery usually takes two business days, and fees are roughly 5%–10%.

## Traveling with Film

If your camera is new, shoot and develop a few rolls of film before leaving home. Pack some lens tissue and an extra battery
for your built-in light meter. Invest about $10 in a skylight fil-

ter and screw it onto the front of your lens. It will protect the lens and also reduce haze.

On a plane trip, never pack unprocessed film in check-in luggage; if your bags get X-rayed, say good-bye to your pictures. Always carry undeveloped film with you through security and ask to have it inspected by hand. (It helps to isolate your film in a plastic bag, ready for quick inspection.) Inspectors at American airports are required by law to honor requests for hand inspection; abroad, you'll have to depend on the kindness of strangers.

The old airport scanning machines—still in use in some Third World countries—use heavy doses of radiation that can turn a family portrait into an early morning fog. The newer models— used in all U.S. airports—are safe for anything from 5 to 500 scans, depending on the speed of your film. The effects are cumulative; you can put the same roll of film through several scans without worry. After five scans, though, you're asking for trouble.

If your film gets fogged and you want an explanation, send it to the **National Association of Photographic Manufacturers** (550 Mamaroneck Ave., Harrison, NY 10528). They will try to determine what went wrong. The service is free.

## Traveling with Children

Publications   *Family Travel Times* is an eight- to twelve-page newsletter published 10 times a year by TWYCH (Travel with Your Children, 45 W. 18th St., 7th Floor Tower, New York, NY 10011, tel. 212/206–0688). Subscription includes access to back issues and twice-weekly opportunities to call in for specific advice.

*Great Vacations with Your Kids: The Complete Guide to Family Vacations in the U.S.*, by Dorothy Ann Jordon and Marjorie Adoff Cohen (E.P. Dutton, 375 Hudson St., New York, NY 10014, $12.95), details everything from city vacations to adventure vacations to child-care resources.

*Chicago Parent News Magazine* (141 S. Oak Park Ave., Oak Park, IL 60302, tel. 708/386–5555) is a monthly publication with events and resource listings available free at locations throughout the city. You can call and ask for an issue to be sent before your trip.

Hotels   **The Ritz-Carlton** (160 E. Pearson St., Chicago, IL 60611, tel. 312/266–1000 or 800/621–6906) provides many children's services, from complimentary strollers to a children's menu, and kids stay free in their parents' room. **The Drake** (140 E. Walton Place, Chicago, IL 60611, tel. 312/787–2200) allows kids under 18 to stay in their parents' room at no extra charge and provides a children's menu in the restaurant. Most **Days Inn** hotels (tel. 800/325–2525) charge only a nominal fee for children under 18 and allow kids 12 and under to eat free (many offer efficiency-type apartments, too). Many other Chicago hotels offer family plans in which kids stay free or at nominal cost in their parents' room (*see* Chapter 7); be sure to inquire when making reservations.

Home Exchange   Exchanging homes is a surprisingly low-cost way to enjoy a vacation in another part of the country. **Vacation Exchange Club, Inc.** (Box 820, Haleiwa, HI 96712, tel. 800/638–3841), specializes in domestic home exchanges. The club publishes directories in January, March, July, and September each year and updated late listings throughout the year. Membership is $50 per year, for which you receive one listing, a newsletter, and copies of all publications. **Loan-a-Home** (2 Park La., 6E Mount Vernon, NY 10552, tel. 914/664–7640) is popular with academics on sabbatical and businesspeople on temporary assignment. There's no annual membership fee or charge for listing your home; however, one directory and a supplement costs $35.

**Getting There** On domestic flights, children under two not occupying a seat travel free. Various discounts apply to children 2 to 12 years of age. Regulations about infant travel on airplanes are in the process of changing. Until they do, however, if you want to be sure your infant is secured in his/her own safety seat, you must buy a separate ticket and bring your own infant car seat. (Check with the airline in advance; certain seats aren't allowed. Or write for the booklet "Child/Infant Safety Seats Acceptable for Use in Aircraft," from the **Federal Aviation Administration,** APA–200, 800 Independence Ave., SW, Washington, DC 20591, tel. 202/267–3479.) Some airlines allow babies to travel in their own safety seats at no charge if there's a spare seat on the plane available; otherwise, safety seats will be stored and the child will have to be held by a parent. If you opt to hold your baby on your lap, do so with the infant outside the seatbelt, so he or she won't be crushed in case of a sudden stop.

Also inquire about special children's meals or snacks. See the February 1990 and 1992 issues of *Family Travel Times* (*see above*) for "TWYCH's Airline Guide," which contains a rundown of the children's services offered by 46 airlines.

**Baby-sitting** Make child-care arrangements with the hotel concierge or
**Services** housekeeper or through **American Registry for Nurses and Sitters** (3921 N. Lincoln Ave., Chicago, IL 60613, tel. 312/248–8100) and **Art Resource Studio** (537 W. Diversey Pkwy., Chicago, IL 60614, tel. 312/975–1671), with weekday craft workshops and drop-off care on weekends. Call ahead, as hours vary.

## Hints for Disabled Travelers

**The Information Center for Individuals with Disabilities** (Fort Point Pl., 1st floor, 27–43 Wormwood St., Boston, MA 02210–1606, tel. 617/727–5540) offers useful problem-solving assistance, including lists of travel agents that specialize in tours for the disabled.

**Moss Rehabilitation Hospital Travel Information Service** (1200 W. Tabor Rd., Philadelphia, PA 19141, tel. 215/456–9600; TDD 215/456–9602) provides information for a small fee on tourist sights, transportation, and accommodations in destinations around the world.

**Mobility International USA** (Box 3551, Eugene, OR 97403, tel. 503/343–1284) has information on accommodations, organized study, etc., around the world.

**The Society for the Advancement of Travel for the Handicapped** (347 5th Ave., Suite 610, New York, NY 10016, tel. 212/447–7284) offers access information. Annual membership costs $45, or $25 for senior travelers and students. Send a stamped, self-addressed envelope.

***The Itinerary*** (Box 2012, Bayonne, NJ 07002, tel. 201/858–3400) is a bimonthly travel magazine for the disabled.

**Greyhound/Trailways** (tel. 800/752–4841; TDD 800/345–3109) will carry a disabled person and companion for the price of a single fare. **Amtrak** (tel. 800/USA–RAIL) requests 24-hour notice to provide redcap service and special seats. All handicapped passengers are entitled to a 15% discount on the lowest available fare.

**Access Living** (310 S. Peoria, Suite 201, Chicago, IL 60607, offers personal-attendant referrals for disabled travelers.

**Travel Industry and Disabled Exchange** (TIDE, 5435 Donna Ave., Tarzana, CA 91356, tel. 818/368–5648) is an industry-based organization with a $15 per person annual membership fee. Members receive a quarterly newsletter and information on travel agencies and tours.

## Hints for Older Travelers

**The American Association of Retired Persons** (AARP, 601 E St. NW, Washington, DC 20049, tel. 202/434–2277) has two programs for independent travelers: (1) The Purchase Privilege Program, which offers discounts on hotels, airfare, car rentals, and sightseeing; and (2) the AARP Motoring Plan, provided by Amoco, which offers emergency aid and trip routing information for an annual fee of $33.95 per couple. The AARP also arranges group tours through **AARP Travel Experience from American Express** (400 Pinnacle Way, Suite 450, Norcross, GA 30071, tel. 800/927–0111). AARP members must be 50 or older. Annual dues are $5 per person or per couple.

When using an AARP or other identification card, ask for a reduced hotel rate at the time you make your reservation, not when you check out. At participating restaurants, show your card to the maitre d' before you're seated, since discounts may be limited to certain set menus, days, or hours. When renting a car, remember that economy cars, priced at promotional rates, may cost less than cars that are available with your ID card.

**Elderhostel** (75 Federal St., Boston MA 02110, tel. 617/426–7788) is an innovative program for people 60 and older. Participants live in dorms on some 1,600 campuses around the world. Mornings are devoted to lectures and seminars; afternoons, to sightseeing and field trips. The all-inclusive fee for two- to three-week international trips, including room, board, tuition, and round-trip transportation, is $1,800–$4,500.

**National Council of Senior Citizens** (1331 F St. NW, Washington, DC 20004, tel. 202/347–8800) is a nonprofit advocacy group with some 5,000 local clubs across the country. Annual membership is $12 per person or per couple. Members receive a monthly newspaper with travel information and an ID card for reduced-rate hotels and car rentals.

**Mature Outlook** (6001 N. Clark St., Chicago, IL 60660, tel. 800/336–6330), a subsidiary of Sears Roebuck & Co., is a travel club for people over 50, with hotel and motel discounts and a bimonthly newsletter. Annual membership is $9.95 per couple. Instant membership is available at participating Holiday Inns.

**Golden Age Passport** is a free lifetime pass to all parks, monuments, and recreation areas run by the federal government.

People 62 and over should pick them up in person at any national park that charges admission. A driver's license or other proof of age is required.

## Further Reading

In *Fabulous Chicago* Emmett Dedmon provides an interesting look at the city. Studs Terkel's *Division Street* contains interviews with people in and around Chicago.

Saul Bellow's novel *The Adventures of Augie March* follows the life of the son of Russian Jewish immigrants. Andrew M. Greeley's *Lord of the Dance* is a drama about an Irish Catholic family. His Monsignor Ryan mysteries are set in Chicago, as are Sara Paretsky's V. I. Warshawski novels.

Other Chicago titles include *Maud Martha*, by Gwendolyn Brooks; *Studs Lonigan*, by James T. Farrell; *Dandelion Wine*, by Ray Bradbury; *The Coast of Chicago*, a collection of short stories by Stuart Dybek; and Richard Wright's explosive story of black ghetto life, *Native Son*.

A librarian in Chicago recommends *The Gorilla of Chicago*, by Mary Parker; *The Story of Eva*, by Will Paine; *The Second Generation*, by James Linn; *Purple Peeks*, by John Driver; and Susan Glaspell's *The Glory of the Conquered*. Lois Wille's *Forever Open, Clear and Free* is a superb history of the fight to save Chicago's lakefront parks.

# Arriving and Departing

## By Plane

Every national airline, most international airlines, and a number of regional carriers fly into Chicago. The city has two national airports and one regional airport. **O'Hare International Airport,** one of the world's busiest, is some 20 miles from downtown, in the far northwestern corner of the city.

**Midway Airport,** on Chicago's Southwest Side, about 7 miles from downtown, is distinguished by its relative lack of crowds and confusion and its smaller scale. **Meigs Field,** on the lakefront just south of Downtown, serves commuter airlines with flights to downstate Illinois and Wisconsin.

Smoking   Smoking is banned on all scheduled routes within the 48 contiguous states; within the states of Hawaii and Alaska; to and from the U.S. Virgin Islands and Puerto Rico; and on flights of less than six hours to and from Hawaii and Alaska. The rule applies to the domestic legs of all foreign routes, but does not affect international flights.

On a flight on which smoking is permitted, you can request a nonsmoking seat during check-in or when you book your ticket. If the airline tells you there are no seats available in the nonsmoking section on the day of the flight, insist on one: Department of Transportation regulations require U.S. carriers to find seats for all nonsmokers, provided they meet check-in time restrictions.

Carry-on Luggage   Passengers aboard major U.S. carriers are usually limited to two carry-on bags. For a bag you wish to store under the seat, the maximum dimensions are 9″ × 14″ × 22″, for a total of 45″. For bags that can be hung in a closet or on a luggage rack, the maximum dimensions are 4″ × 23″ × 45″, for a total of 72″. For bags you wish to store in an overhead bin, the maximum dimensions are 10″ × 14″ × 36″, for a total of 60″. Your two carry-ons must each fit one of these sets of dimensions, and any item that exceeds the specified dimensions will generally be rejected as a carry-on and handled as checked baggage. Keep in mind that an airline can adapt these rules to circumstances; don't be surprised when you are allowed only one carry-on bag on an especially crowded flight.

The rules list eight items that may be carried aboard in addition to the two carry-ons: a handbag (pocketbook or purse), an overcoat or wrap, an umbrella, a camera, a reasonable amount of reading material, and crutches, a cane, braces, or other prosthetic device upon which the passenger is dependent. Infant/child safety seats may also be brought aboard if parents have purchased a ticket for the child or if there is space in the cabin.

Note that these regulations are for U.S. airlines only. Foreign airlines generally allow one piece of carry-on luggage in tourist class, in addition to handbags and bags filled with duty-free goods. Passengers in first and business class are also allowed to carry on one garment bag. It is best to check with your airline in advance to learn its rules regarding carry-on luggage.

**Checked Luggage**  U.S. airlines allow passengers to check two or three suitcases whose total dimensions per piece (length + width + height) do not exceed 62″ and whose weight per piece does not exceed 70 pounds.

Rules governing foreign airlines vary among carriers, so check with your travel agent or the airline itself before you go. All airlines allow passengers to check two bags. In general, expect the weight restriction on the two bags to be not more than 70 pounds each, and the size restriction to be not more than 62″ total dimensions on each bag.

**Lost Luggage**  Airlines are responsible for lost or damaged property only up to $1,250 per passenger on domestic flights; $9.07 per pound (or $20 per kilo) for checked baggage on international flights; and $400 per passenger for unchecked baggage on international flights. When you carry valuables, either take them with you on the airplane or purchase additional insurance for lost luggage. Some airlines will issue additional luggage insurance when you check in, but many do not. One that does is American Airlines. Rates are $2 for every $100 valuation, with a maximum of $5,000 per passenger. Hand luggage is not included.

Insurance for lost, damaged, or stolen luggage is available through travel agents or from various insurance companies. Two that issue luggage insurance are Tele-Trip, a subsidiary of Mutual of Omaha, and The Travelers Insurance Corporation.

**Tele-Trip** (tel. 800/228–9792) operates sales booths at airports and issues insurance through travel agents. Tele-Trip will insure checked luggage for up to 180 days; rates vary according to the length of the trip.

**The Travelers Insurance Corporation** (Ticket and Travel Dept., 1 Tower Sq., Hartford, CT 06183–5040, tel. 203/277–0111 or 800/243–3174) will insure checked or hand luggage for $500 to $2,000 valuation per person, for a maximum of 180 days. For one to five days, the rate for a $500 valuation is $10; for 180 days, $85.

The two companies offer the same rates on both domestic and international flights. Consult the travel pages of your Sunday newspaper for the names of other companies that insure luggage. Before you travel, itemize the contents of each bag in case you need to file an insurance claim. Be certain to put your home address on each piece of luggage, including carry-on bags. If your luggage is stolen and later recovered, the airline will deliver the luggage to your home free of charge.

**From the Airport to Downtown Chicago** *By Public Transit* You can reach the Chicago Transit Authority's rapid transit station at O'Hare Airport from the baggage claim level without going outdoors. When you're heading to the North Side or Downtown and you don't have much luggage, this is the cheapest ($1.50) way to get from the airport to the city. Travel time is 40–60 minutes. The first stop in the Loop (downtown) is Washington and Dearborn streets. From here you can take a taxi to your hotel or change to other rapid transit lines. There is no convenient public transportation downtown from Midway Airport.

*By Bus* **Continental Airport Express** (tel. 312/454–7799) coaches provide express service from both airports to major downtown and Near North hotels; the coaches leave every half hour. The trip downtown from O'Hare takes an hour or longer, depending on traffic conditions and your point of debarkation; the fare is $13.00. (When taking the coach to O'Hare to catch a departing flight, be sure to allow at least 1½ hours.) The trip downtown from Midway takes about half an hour; the fare is $9.50.

**CW Limo** (tel. 312/493–2700) offers moderately priced express van service from both airports to locations in Hyde Park and the South Side. Vans leave O'Hare about every 45 minutes, and the travel time to Hyde Park is about an hour (more when traffic is heavy); the fare is $9.75. CW serves Midway with five vans daily, at Midway's traffic peaks; the fare is $8.00. If you're going from the South Side to Midway, call 24 hours in advance.

*By Taxi* Metered taxicab service is available at both O'Hare and Midway airports. Expect to pay about $28–$32 plus tip from O'Hare to Near North and Downtown locations, about $14 plus tip from Midway. Some cabs participate in a share-a-ride program that combines two or three individuals going from the airport to Downtown; the cost per person is substantially lower than the full rate.

*By Rental Car* On leaving the airport, follow the signs to I–90 east to Chicago. This is the Kennedy Expressway, which merges with I–94, the Edens Expressway. Take the eastbound exit at Ohio Street for Near North locations, the Washington or Madison Street exits for Downtown. After you exit, continue east about a mile to get to Michigan Avenue.

## By Car

Travelers coming from the east can pick up the Indiana Toll Road (I–80/90) westbound for about 30 miles to the Chicago Skyway (also a toll road), which runs into the Dan Ryan Expressway (I–90/94). Take the Dan Ryan north (westbound) just past the turnoff for I–290 to any of the Downtown eastbound exits (Monroe, Madison, Washington, Randolph, Lake) and drive east about a mile to reach Michigan Avenue. If you are heading to the Near North, take the Ohio Street exit eastbound and continue straight through local streets for about a mile to reach Michigan Avenue.

Travelers coming from the south should take I–57 northbound to the Dan Ryan Expressway.

Travelers from the west may follow I–80 eastbound across Illinois to I–55, which is the major artery from the southwest. Continue east on I–55 to Lake Shore Drive. Those coming from areas due west of Chicago may prefer to pick up I–290 eastbound, which forks as it nears the city, heading to O'Hare in one direction (where it meets I–90) and to downtown Chicago in the other (where it ends).

Travelers from the north will need to be on I–90 eastbound, which merges with I–94 south (eastbound) to form the Kennedy Expressway (I–90/94) about 10 miles north of Downtown. (I–90/94 is called the Kennedy Expressway north of I–290 and the Dan Ryan Expressway south of I–290).

## By Train

**Amtrak** (800/USA–RAIL) offers nationwide service to Chicago's Union Station (Jackson and Canal Sts., tel. 312/558–1075). Some trains travel overnight, and you can sleep in your seat or book a roomette at additional cost. Most trains have attractive diner cars with acceptable food, but you may prefer to bring your own. Excursion fares, when available, may save you nearly half the round-trip fare.

## By Bus

**Greyhound/Trailways** (630 W. Harrison St., tel. 312/408–5971) has nationwide service to its main terminal in the Loop and to its neighborhood bus stations: on the South Side at the 95th Street and Dan Ryan Expressway CTA station; on the northwest side at the Cumberland CTA station, 5800 North Cumberland Avenue, near O'Hare Airport. The Harrison Street terminal is nowhere near anywhere you're likely to be staying, so plan on another bus or a cab from the station to your hotel.

**Indian Trails, Inc.** (tel. 312/928–8606 for 95th St. terminal or 312/408–5971 for Harrison St. terminal), serves Chicago from Indiana and Michigan, sharing Greyhound's terminal facilities at 630 West Harrison Street and at 95th Street and the Dan Ryan Expressway.

# Staying in Chicago

## Important Addresses and Numbers

Tourist Information The main **Tourist Information Center** is housed in the Historic Water Tower, in the middle of the Magnificent Mile (806 N. Michigan Ave., tel. 312/280–5740).
The **Mayor's Office of Special Events General Information and Activities** (121 N. La Salle St., tel. 312/744–3315) will tell you about city-sponsored events of interest. Call 312/744–3370 for a taped announcement.
The **State of Illinois Office of Tourism** (310 S. Michigan Ave.,

tel. 312/793–2094) maintains a **Tourism Hotline** (tel. 800/223–0121).

**Emergencies**  **Police, fire, ambulance** (tel. 911).

*Hospitals*  In the Near North or north, **Northwestern Memorial Hospital** (Superior St. at Fairbanks Ct., tel. 312/908–2000). In the Loop, **Rush Presbyterian St. Luke's** (1753 W. Congress Pkwy., tel. 312/942–5000). In Hyde Park and the South Side, **Humana Michael Reese Hospital** (Lake Shore Dr. at 31st St., tel. 312/791–2000), or the **Bernard Mitchell Hospital at the University of Chicago** (5841 S. Maryland Ave., tel. 312/702–1000). Humana Michael Reese and other hospitals sponsor storefront clinics for fast treatment of minor emergencies. Call the hospitals for information, or check the Chicago Consumer Yellow Pages under "Clinics."

*Dentists*  The **Chicago Dental Society Emergency Service** (tel. 312/726–4321) makes referrals at all hours.

*24-Hour Pharmacies*  **Osco** (call 800/654–6726 for nearest location). **Walgreen's** (757 N. Michigan Ave., at Chicago Ave., tel. 312/664–8686).

## Opening and Closing Times

**Banks** are generally open 8:30–3; a few banks open for a half day on Saturday and close on Wednesday. Many banks in the Loop and Near North stay open until 5 PM.

The main **U.S. Post Office** (433 W. Van Buren St., tel. 312/765–3210) is open weekdays until 9, Saturday until 5, closed Sunday. The post office at O'Hare International Airport is open daily 24 hours.

The **Kluczynski** and **Dirksen federal buildings** (230 S. Dearborn St., 219 S. Dearborn St.) are open weekdays 8–4, closed on federal holidays.

The **State of Illinois Building** (100 W. Randolph St., tel. 312/793–3500) is open weekdays, closed on state holidays.

**Chicago City Hall** (121 N. La Salle St., tel. 312/744–6873) is open weekdays, closed on city holidays.

**Stores**  Most department stores, except those in Water Tower Place, are open Monday–Saturday 9:45–5:30 or 9:45–6, Thursday until 7. Sunday hours at Magnificent Mile department stores are usually noon–5. Loop department stores are closed Sunday except once a month (designated Super Sunday); the newspapers announce the specific day. Lord & Taylor and Marshall Field at the Water Tower are open Monday–Saturday 10–8 and Sunday noon–6.

## Getting Around

Chicago's planners followed a grid pattern in laying out the city's streets. Madison Street is the baseline for streets and avenues that run north/south; Michigan Avenue (for example) is North Michigan Avenue above Madison Street, South Michigan Avenue below it. House numbers start at 1 at the baseline and climb in each direction, generally by 100 a block. Thus the Fine Arts Building at 410 South Michigan Avenue is four blocks south of Madison Street. Even-numbered addresses are on the west side of the street, odd numbers on the east side.

For streets that run east–west, State Street is the baseline; 18th Street (for example) is East 18th Street east of State Street and West 18th Street west of State Street. House numbers start at 1 at the baseline and rise in each direction, east and west. Even-numbered addresses are on the north side of the street, odd numbers on the south side.

The Loop is a common Chicago term denoting the section of downtown that is roughly encircled by the el tracks, although the Loop boundaries actually exceed the tracks. They are Michigan Avenue on the east, Wacker Drive on the north and west, and Congress on the south.

The **Chicago Consumer Yellow Pages** has a complete guide to Chicago street locations and zip codes in the white pages in the center of the book.

**By Train and Bus** Chicago's extensive public transportation network includes buses and rapid transit trains, both subway and elevated. The **Chicago Transit Authority (CTA)** publishes an excellent map of the transit system, available on request from the CTA, Merchandise Mart, Chicago, IL 60654. The **RTA Travel Information Center** (tel. 312/836–7000) will provide information on how to get about on city rapid transit and bus lines, suburban bus lines, and commuter trains.

In 1990 the CTA restructured its fares to make a 25¢ fare increase more palatable to Chicagoans, but the result is likely to confuse the uninitiated. The basic fare is $1.50 for rapid transit trains; this fare also applies to buses during morning and afternoon rush hours (at other times, the bus fare is $1.25). Tokens (which can be used for full fare on either buses or rapid transit trains) offer a substantial discount over the regular fare: a roll of 10 tokens costs $12. Tokens can be bought at currency exchanges, some rapid transit stations, and Jewel and Dominick's supermarkets. Transfers, which must be bought when you board the bus or train, cost an extra 25¢; they can be used twice within a two-hour time period but not twice on the same route. Children ages 7–11 travel for less than half fare (65¢ at this writing). Children under 7 travel free. Several different weekly and monthly passes are available, but tokens are the most economical option for those staying in the city for only a short time.

Most, but not all, rapid transit lines operate 24 hours; some stations are closed at night. (In general, late-night CTA travel is not recommended.) To transfer between Loop's elevated ("el") lines and subway lines, or between rapid transit and bus service, you must use a transfer; be sure to *buy the transfer when you board the first conveyance*. Buses generally stop on every other corner northbound and southbound (on State Street they stop at every corner). Eastbound and westbound buses generally stop on every corner. The Loop is a terminus for most north–south buses that serve it: Buses generally run either south from the Loop or north from the Loop. Principal transfer points are on Michigan Avenue at the north side of Randolph Street for northbound buses, Adams and Wabash for westbound buses and the el, and State and Lake streets for southbound buses.

**By Car** Chicago's extensive network of buses and rapid transit rail, as well as the availability of taxis and limousine services (often priced competitively with metered cabs) make having a car in

Chicago unnecessary, particularly for those whose visit is confined to the Loop, Near North, and Lakefront neighborhoods. If your business or interests take you to the suburbs, you may want to rent a car for that part of your trip. Like most major cities today, Chicago traffic is often heavy, on-street parking is nearly impossible to find, parking lots are expensive, congestion creates frustrating delays, and other drivers may be impatient with those who are unfamiliar with the city and its roads. During the 1990s, extensive repair work is planned for several of the city's major arteries, including Lake Shore Drive and the Kennedy Expressway (I–90/94). Similar work on the Dan Ryan Expressway in 1988–1989 caused a nightmare of snarled traffic during rush hours. In these circumstances, the visitor to Chicago may find a car to be a liability rather than an asset.

If business or pleasure obliges you to rent a car, however, you will have no trouble finding vendors to serve you. National companies, most with airport, as well as downtown, locations, include **Alamo Rent-A-Car** (tel. 800/327–9633), **Amerex Rent-A-Car** (tel. 800/843–1143), **Avis** (tel. 800/331–1212), **Budget** (tel. 800/527–0700), **Dollar** (tel. 800/800–4000), **Hertz** (tel. 800/654–3131), **National** (tel. 800/227–7368), and **Sears** (tel. 800/527–0770). Budget and Sears also have numerous suburban locations. Local and lower-cost companies include **Airways** (tel. 708/678–2300), **Fender Benders** (tel. 312/569–2678), and **Rent-a-Wreck** (tel. 800/421–7253 or 800/535–1391).

Make your car arrangements before you leave home, and do some comparison shopping before making a reservation. Costs vary greatly among companies, depending on the number of days you expect to need the car, whether you need it for weekend or weekday use, and whether you expect to do a lot of driving or a little, and car rental advertisements can be misleading. Be sure to ask about add-on charges for insurance coverage (collision, personal injury), gasoline (some companies include gas in their daily rate, others in their mileage fees, others make a separate charge for gas, and still others leave the gas up to you), and drop-off at a location other than the one where you picked up the car (surcharges here can be substantial).

Find out what the collision damage waiver (usually an $8–$12 daily surcharge) covers and whether your corporate or personal insurance already covers damage to a rental car (if so, bring along a photocopy of the benefits section). Companies are holding renters responsible for theft and vandalism if they don't buy the CDW. In response, many credit card and insurance companies are extending their coverage to rental cars. Check the insurance coverage provided by your credit card company or insurance carrier. When you've decided on the company and reserved a car, *be sure to get a reservation number*. Remember, if the company doesn't have the car you reserved when you arrive to pick it up, the company must provide a comparable or better car at the price you reserved.

**By Taxi**  Chicago taxis are metered, with fares beginning at $1.20 for the first ⅑ mile and 20¢ for each additional ⅑ mile (or each minute of waiting time). A charge of 50¢ is made for each additional passenger between the ages of 12 and 65. A charge of 25¢ per bag may be levied when luggage is bulky. Expect to pay $28–$30, including tip, between O'Hare Airport and downtown and about half that amount for a trip to or from Midway Airport. Taxi drivers expect a 15% tip. The principal taxi companies are

**American United Cab Co.** (tel. 312/248–7600), **Yellow Cab Co.** (tel. 312/829–4222), and **Checker Cab Co.** (tel. 312/829–4222).

## Guided Tours

**Orientation Tours**
*By Land*

**Chicago Motor Coach Co.** Double-decker buses take visitors on one-hour narrated tours of Chicago landmarks. Climb on at the Sears Tower (Jackson Blvd. and Wacker Dr.), the Field Museum (Lake Shore Dr. at E. Roosevelt Rd.), Orchestra Hall (220 S. Michigan Ave.), or the Water Tower (Michigan Ave. at Pearson St.). *Tel. 312/922–8919. Daily 10–4. Cost: $7 adults, $5 senior citizens.*

**American Sightseeing.** The North tour along State Street and North Michigan Avenue includes the John Hancock Center, Water Tower Place, and the Lincoln Park Conservatory. The South tour covers the financial district, Grant Park, the University of Chicago, the Museum of Science and Industry, and Jackson Park. Tours leave from the Congress Hotel (530 S. Michigan Ave.), or you can arrange to be picked up at your hotel. *Tel. 312/427–3100. Cost: $15 adults, $7.50 children 5–14. For a combined 4-hour tour of north and south: $23 adults, $11.50 children 5–14. Two-hour tours leave daily 9:30, 11:30, 1:30, and 3:30 during the summer, 10 and noon in winter.*

*By Boat*

Touring Chicago by boat offers a different kind of sightseeing and travel experience. Schedules vary by season; be sure to call for exact times and fares.

**Wendella Sightseeing Boats** (400 N. Michigan Ave., tel. 312/337–1446). Guided tours traverse the Chicago River to south of the Sears Tower and through the locks; on Lake Michigan, they travel between the Adler Planetarium on the south and Oak Street Beach on the north. Available April–October. Ninety-minute tours at 10, 11:30, 1:15, 3 and 7:30; cost: $8 adults, $7 senior citizens, $4 children 11 and under. Two-hour evening tours at 7:30; cost: $10 adults, $5 children 11 and under. Wendella also offers an unscheduled, but fairly frequent, one-hour tour on Lake Michigan only; cost: $6 adults, $3 children. At press time a 5:30 cocktail cruise was being planned. All Wendella tours leave from lower Michigan Avenue at the foot of the Wrigley Building on the north side of the river.

**Mercury Skyline Cruises** (tel. 312/332–1353 for recorded information or 312/332–1368). A 90-minute river and lake cruise departs at 10, 11:30, 1:15, 3:15, and 7:30; cost: $8 adults, $4 children under 12. A two-hour sunset cruise costs $9 adults, $4.50 children under 12. Tickets can be obtained one hour before departure time. One-hour lakefront cruises, not prescheduled, are available evenings: daily 5–9 PM and weekends at 9:30, 10, and 11 PM. A one-hour Chicago River cruise begins at noon, weekends only, June–August; cost: $6 adults, $3 children under 12. All Mercury cruises leave from Wacker Drive at Michigan Avenue (the south side of the Michigan Avenue bridge).

**Shoreline Marine** (tel. 312/222–9328). Half-hour boat trips on Lake Michigan are offered daily between Memorial Day and Labor Day. Tours leave from the Adler Planetarium (1800 S. Lake Shore Dr.) at quarter past the hour daily, 12:15–9:15; from the Shedd Aquarium 11:15–5:15; and in the evening from Buckingham Fountain, 6:15–11:15. Cost: $5 adults, $2 children.

**Interlude Enterprises** (tel. 312/641–7245). Cruises with an architectural narrative leave from the southeast corner of Wabash Avenue and Wacker Drive, lower level, by the Wabash Avenue bridge, Monday–Saturday, every two hours from 9:30 AM to 7:30 PM. Tours run from mid-April to early November, depending on the weather. Reservations can be made from one week in advance to 10 AM the day of the tour. The boat travels on the Chicago River through the Loop and the locks, and into Lake Michigan and Monroe Harbor. Cost: $6 for the tour plus $5.50 for lunch, or you can bring your own.

**Special-Interest Tours** **Pumping Station** (806 N. Michigan Ave., tel. 312/467–7114). Tour the facility at the historic Water Tower and see a multimedia show about the city, *Here's Chicago!* Shows begin every half hour Monday–Thursday 10–5:30, Friday and Saturday 10–6:30. Cost: $5.75 adults, $4.50 children.

**Newspaper Tours.** The *Chicago Tribune* offers free weekday tours of its Freedom Center production facility (777 W. Chicago Ave., tel. 312/222–2116) to individuals and groups of up to 30, age 10 and older. Reservations must be made in advance of your visit.

**Chicago Mercantile Exchange** (30 S. Wacker Dr., tel. 312/930–8249). The visitors' gallery, which offers a view of the often frenetic trading floor, is open 7:30–3:15. Tours are given to groups of 15 or more by advance reservation on weekday mornings. Individuals can join prereserved groups when space is available.

**Walking Tours** The **Chicago Architecture Foundation** gives core tours, such as a walking tour of Loop architecture and tours of historic houses, on a regular daily or weekly schedule, depending on the season. It also offers many tours on an occasional, seasonal, or prescheduled basis. They include Graceland Cemetery; Frank Lloyd Wright's Oak Park buildings; and bicycle tours of Lincoln Park and Oak Park. Tour departure times vary; prices run about $5–$10 per person. For information, write or call the foundation at Glessner House (1800 S. Prairie Ave., tel. 312/326–1393), where the house tours begin, or at the Archicenter (224 S. Michigan Ave., tel. 312/922–8687), where most other tours originate.

**Friends of the Chicago River** (407 S. Dearborn St., Chicago 60605, tel. 312/939–0490) offers walking tours along the river April–July, September, and October, Saturday at 10 AM. The tours last two hours and cost $5. There are seven different tours; call in advance to find out which tour is being offered and where it starts. The organization also has maps of the routes available for a small donation.

# 2 Portraits of Chicago

# Chicago

By Studs Terkel

*A writer, a broadcaster, and of late a film actor, Studs Terkel has come to be a virtual symbol of Chicago. His newest collection of oral histories is* The Great Divide: Second Thoughts on the American Dream.

**J**anus, the two-faced god, has both blessed and cursed the city-state Chicago. Though his graven image is not visible to the naked eye, his ambiguous spirit soars atop Sears, Big Stan, and Big John. (Our city is street-wise and alley-hip of the casually familiar. Thus the Standard Oil Building and the John Hancock are, with tavern gaminess, referred to as Big Stan and Big John. Sears is simply that; never mind Roebuck. Ours is a one-syllable town. Its character has been molded by the muscle rather than the word.)

Our double-vision, double-standard, double-value, and double-cross have been patent ever since—at least, ever since the earliest of our city fathers took the Pottawattomies for all they had. Poetically, these dispossessed natives dubbed this piece of turf *Chikagou*. Some say it is Indian lingo for "City of the Wild Onion"; some say it really means "City of the Big Smell." "Big" is certainly the operative word around these parts.

Nelson Algren's classic *Chicago: City on the Make* is the late poet's single-hearted vision of his town's doubleness. "Chicago . . . forever keeps two faces, one for winners and one for losers; one for hustlers and one for squares . . . One face for Go-Getters and one for Go-Get-It-Yourselfers. One for poets and one for promoters. . . . One for early risers, one for evening hiders."

It is the city of Jane Addams, settlement worker, and Al Capone, entrepreneur; of Clarence Darrow, lawyer, and Julius Hoffman, judge; of Louis Sullivan, architect, and Sam Insull, magnate; of John Altgeld, governor, and Paddy Bauler, alderman. (Paddy's the one who some years ago observed, "Chicago ain't ready for reform." It is echoed in our day by another, less paunchy alderman, Fast Eddie.)

Now, with a new kind of mayor, whose blackness is but one variant of the Chicago norm, and a machine—which like the old gray mare ain't what it used to be—creaking its expected way, all bets are off. Race, though the dominant theme, is but one factor.

It is still the arena of those who dream of the City of Man and those who envision a City of Things. The battle appears to be forever joined. The armies, ignorant and enlightened, clash by day as well as night. Chicago is America's dream, writ large. And flamboyantly.

---

*This essay is drawn from Studs Terkel's* Chicago, *which was originally published in 1986, when the late Harold Washington was mayor of Chicago.*

It has—as they used to whisper of the town's fast wo-man—a reputation.

Elsewhere in the world, anywhere, name the city, name the country, Chicago evokes one image above all others. Sure, architects and those interested in such matters mention Louis Sullivan, Frank Lloyd Wright, and Mies van der Rohe. Hardly anyone in his right mind questions this city as the architectural Athens. Others, literary critics among them, mention Dreiser, Norris, Lardner, Algren, Farrell, Bellow, and the other Wright, Richard. Sure, Mencken did say something to the effect that there is no American litera-ture worth mentioning that didn't come out of the palati-nate that is Chicago. Of course, a special kind of jazz and a blues, acoustic rural and electrified urban, have been called Chicago style. All this is indubitably true.

Still others, for whom history has stood still since the Democratic convention of 1968, murmur: Mayor Daley. (As our most perceptive chronicler, Mike Royko, has pointed out, the name has become the eponym for city chieftain; thus, it is often one word, "Maredaley.") The tone, in distant quarters as well as here, is usually one of awe; you may interpret it any way you please.

An English Midlander, bearing a remarkable resemblance to Nigel Bruce, encounters me under London's Marble Arch: "Your mayor is my kind of chap. He should have bashed the heads of those young ruffians, though he did rather well, I thought." I tell him that Richard J. Daley died several years ago and that our incumbent mayor is black. He finds this news somewhat startling.

"Really?" He recovers quickly: "Nonetheless, I do like your city. I was there some thirty-odd years ago. Black, is he?"

Yeah, I tell him, much of the city is.

He is somewhat Spenglerian as he reflects on the decline of Western values. "Thank heavens, I'll not be around when they take over, eh?"

I nod. I'm easy to get along with. "You sound like Saul Bel-low," I say.

"Who?"

"Our Nobel laureate. Do you realize that our University of Chicago has produced more Nobel Prize winners than any other in the world?"

"Really?"

"Yeah."

He returns to what appears to be his favorite subject: gumption. "Your mayor had it. I'm delighted to say that our lady prime minister has it, too."

I am suddenly weary. Too much Bells Reserve, I'm afraid. "So long, sir. I'll see you in Chicago."

"Not likely; not bloody likely."

In Munich, a student of the sixties, now somewhat portly and balding, ventures an opinion. Not that I asked him. Chicago does that to strangers as well as natives.

"Your Mayor Daley vas bwutal to those young pwotesters, vasn't he?"

Again I nod. Vat could I say?

But it isn't Daley whose name is the Chicago hallmark. Nor Darrow. Nor Wright. Nor is it either of the Janes, Addams or Byrne. It's Al Capone, of course.

In a Brescian trattoria, to Italy's north, a wisp of an old woman, black shawl and all, hears where I'm from. Though she has some difficulty with English (far less than I have with Italian), she thrusts both hands forward, index fingers pointed at me: *Boom, boom,* she goes. I hold up my hands. We both laugh. It appears that Jimmy Cagney, Edward G. Robinson, and Warner Brothers have done a real job in image making.

Not that Al and his colleagues didn't have palmy days during what, to others, were parlous times. Roaring Twenties or Terrible Thirties, the goose always hung high for the Boys. I once asked a casual acquaintance, the late Doc Graham, for a résumé. Doc was, as he modestly put it, a dedicated heist man. His speech was a composite of Micawber and Runyon:

"The unsophisticated either belonged to the Bugs Moran mob or the Capone mob. The fellas with talent didn't belong to either one. We robbed both."

Wasn't that a bit on the risky side?

"Indeed. There ain't hardly a one of us survived the Biblical threescore and ten. You see this fellow liquidated, that fellow—shall we say, disposed of? Red McLaughlin was the toughest guy in Chicago. But when you seen Red run out of the drainage canal, you realized Red's *modus operandi* was unavailing. His associates was Clifford and Adams. They were set in Al's doorway in his hotel in Cicero. That was unavailing."

Was it a baseball bat Al used?

"You are doubtless referring to Anselmi and Scalisi. They offended Al. This was rare. Al Capone usually sublet the matter. Since I'm Irish, I had a working affiliate with Bugs Moran. Did you know that Red and his partners once stole the Checker Cab Company? They took machine guns, went up, and had an election. I assisted in that operation."

What role did the forces of law and order play?

"With a bill, you wasn't bothered. If you had a speaking acquaintance with Mayor Thompson, you could do no wrong. Al spoke loud to him." . . .

Chicago is not the most corrupt of cities. The state of New Jersey has a couple. Need we mention Nevada? Chicago, though, is the Big Daddy. Not more corrupt, just more theatrical, more colorful in its shadiness.

It's an attribute of which many of our Respectables are, I suspect, secretly proud. Something to chat about in languorous moments. Perhaps something to distract from whatever tangential business might have engaged them.

Consider Marshall Field the First. The merchant prince. In 1886, the fight for the eight-hour day had begun, here in Chicago. Anarchists, largely German immigrants, were in the middle of it for one reason or another.

There was a mass meeting; a bomb was thrown; to this day, nobody knows who did it. There was a trial. The Haymarket Eight were in the dock. With hysteria pervasive—newspaper headlines wild enough to make Rupert Murdoch blush—the verdict was in. Guilty.

Before four of them were executed, there was a campaign, worldwide, for a touch of mercy. Even the judge, passionate though he was in his loathing of the defendants, was amenable. A number of Chicago's most respected industrialists felt the same way. Hold off the hooded hangman. Give 'em life, what the hell. It was Marshall Field I who saw to it that they swung. Hang the bastards. Johnny Da Pow had nothing on him when it came to power.

Lucy Parsons, the youngest widow of the most celebrated of the hangees, Albert—an ex-soldier of the Confederacy—lived to be an old, old woman. When she died in the forties and was buried at Waldheim Cemetery, my old colleague Win Stracke sang at the services. Though Parsons sang "Annie Laurie" on his way to the gallows, Win sounded off with "Joe Hill." It was a song, he said, that Lucy liked. When I shake hands with Win, I shake hands with history. That's what I call continuity.

The Janus-like aspect of Chicago appeared in the being of John Peter Altgeld. One of his first acts as governor of Illinois in 1893 was an 18,000-word message, citing chapter and verse, declaring the trial a frame-up. He pardoned the three survivors. The fourth had swallowed a dynamite cap while in the pokey.

Though it ended his political life. Altgeld did add a touch of class to our city's history. He was remembered by Vachel Lindsay as Eagle Forgotten. Some kid, majoring in something other than business administration or computer programming, might come across this poem in some anthology. Who knows? He might learn something about eagles.

Eagles are a diminished species today, here as well as elsewhere. On occasion, they are spotted in unexpected air pockets. Hawks, of course, abound, here as well as elsewhere. Some say this is their glory time. So Dow-Jones tells us. Observe the boys and girls in commodities. Ever ride the La Salle Street bus? Bright and morning faces; *Wall Street Journals* neatly folded. The New Gatsbys, Bob Tamarkin calls them. Gracelessness under pressure.

Sparrows, as always, are the most abundant of our city birds. It is never glory time for them. As always, they do the best they can. Which isn't very much. They forever peck away and, in some cock-eyed fashion, survive the day. Others—well, who said life was fair? They hope, as the old spiritual goes, that His eye is on all the sparrows and that He watches over them. And you. And me . . .

On a hot summer day, the lake behaves, the beach is busy, and thousands find cool delight. All within sight of places where ads are created telling you Wendy's is better than Burger King, where computers compute like crazy, and where billions of pages are Xeroxed for one purpose or another, or for no purpose at all. All within one neighborhood. It's crazy and phenomenal. No other city in the world has a neighborhood like this. Visitors, no matter how weary-of-it-all and jaded, are always overawed. You feel pretty good; and, like a spoiled débutante, you wave a limp hand and murmur: It *is* rather impressive, isn't it? . . .

But those damn bridges. Though I haven't searched out any statistics, I'll bet Chicago has more bridges than Paris. When up they go and all traffic stops, you lean against the railing and watch the boats: pulp paper from Canada for the *Trib* and *Sun-Times*, and ore from where?—the Mesabi iron range?—and all sorts of tugs easing all sorts of lake vessels, bearing all sorts of heavy stuff, big-shouldered stuff. You may not feel particularly chesty, yet there's a slight stirring, a feeling of Chicago's connection with elsewhere.

However—and what an infuriating however—when a lone sailboat comes through with two beautiful people sporting Acapulco or Palm Beach tan, she in a bikini and he in Calvin Klein shorts, and the two, with the casualness and vast carelessness of a Tom and Daisy Buchanan, wave at the held-up secretaries, file clerks, and me, I look around for a rock to throw, only to realize I'm not Walter Johnson, and I settle for a mumbled *sonofabitch* and I'm late for lunch. *Sonofabitch.*

There's no other city like this, I tell you.

And taxi drivers.

When, in eighth-grade geography, Miss O'Brien, her wig slightly askew, quizzed you ferociously on populations of the world's great cities, you had to, with equal ferocity, look them up in the atlas. Thanks to Third World hackies, you can save an enormous amount of time and energy.

You peek up front toward the driver and you see the name Ahmed Eqbal. Naturally, you ask him what's the population of Karachi and he tells you. With great enthusiasm. If his surname is Kim, you'll find out that Seoul is close to seven million. If the man driving at an interesting speed is Marcus Olatunji, you might casually offer that Ibadan is bigger than Lagos, isn't it? If his name has as many syllables as a Welsh town's, you simply ask if Bangkok has changed much; has its population really experienced an exponential growth?

Of course, all short cuts to knowledge have their shortcomings. Sometimes he'll whirl around, astonished, and in very, very precise British English ask, "How do you *know* that?" A brief cultural exchange ensues as suddenly you cry out, Watch out! We missed an articulated bus with a good one-tenth of an inch to spare. If it's a newspaper circulation truck, God help the two of us.

Chicago's traffic problem is hardly any problem at all—if you forget about storms, light rains, accidents, and road construction—when compared with other great cities. In contrast to New York's cacophony of honks and curses, ours is the song of the open road. Mexico City is not to be believed. Ever been to Paris where the driver snaps his fingers, frustrated, as you successfully hop back onto the curb? Need we mention the Angeleno freeway? . . .

S o we're reminiscing about one thing or another, Verne and I. Vernon Jarrett knocks out a *Sun-Times* column: reflections of black life in Chicago and elsewhere. I can't get that Jubilee Night, '38, out of my mind. He tells me of that same celebratory moment in Paris, Tennessee, along the IC tracks. Hallelujah and hope. We see our reflections in the mirror behind the bar and neither of us looks too hopeful. Hallelujah for what?

"The ghetto used to have something going for it," he says. "It had a beat, it had a certain rhythm and it was all hope. I don't care how rough things were. They used to say, If you can't make it in Chicago, you can't make it anywhere. You may be down today; you're gonna be back up tomorrow."

The lyric of an old blues song is rolling around in my head like a loose cannonball:

*I'm troubled in mind, baby, I'm so blue,*
*But I won't be blue always*
*You know the sun, the sun gonna shine*
*In my back door someday.*

"You had the packinghouses going, you had the steel mills going, you had secondary employment to help you 'get over.'"

Oh, there's still a Back of the Yards, all right, but where are the yards? And Steeltown. Ever visit South Chicago these days? Smokestacks with hardly an intimation of smoke. A town as silent, as dead as the Legionnaires' fortress in *Beau Geste*. Where the executioner's ax fell upon Jefferson and Johnson as upon Stasiak, Romano, and Polowski.

"Now it's a drag," says Verne. "There are thousands of people who have written off their lives. They're serving out their sentences as though there were some supreme judge who said, 'You're sentenced to life imprisonment on earth and this is your cell here.' What do you do if you've got a life sentence? You play jailhouse politics. You hustle, you sell dope, you browbeat other people, you abuse other cellmates, you turn men into weaklings, and girls you overcome.

"If I'm feeling good and want to have my morale lowered, all I have to do is drive out Madison Street on a bright, beautiful day and look at the throng of unemployed young guys in the weird dress, trying to hang on to some individuality.' Can't read or write; look mean at each other. You see kids hating themselves as much as they hate others. This is one thing that's contributed to the ease with which gangs kill each other. Another nigger ain't nothin'."

**I**s it possible that ol' Hightower, the pub-crawling buddy of Dude and me during those Jubilee hours on a June night so long ago, has a signifying grandson among the wretched and lost on some nonsignified corner somewhere on the West Side?

From the year one we've heard Lord Acton cited: Power corrupts and absolute power corrupts absolutely. You're only half right, Your Lordship, if that. In a town like Chicago, Johnny Da Pow and a merchant prince and, in our day, a Croatian Sammy Glick run much of the turf because of another kind of corruption: the one Verne Jarrett observed. Powerlessness corrupts and absolute powerlessness corrupts absolutely. You see, Lord A knew nothing of Cabrini-Green. Or—*memento mori*—47th and South Parkway, with exquisite irony renamed Martin Luther King, Jr., Drive. Mine eyes haven't seen much glory lately.

However—there's always a however in the city Janus watches over . . .

Somethin's happenin' out there not covered by the six-o'clock news or a Murdoch headline. There is a percolating and bubbling in certain neighborhoods that may presage unexpected somethings for the up-againsters. A strange something called self-esteem, springing from an even stranger something called sense of community.

Ask Nancy Jefferson. It happened at the Midwest Community Council on the West Side. She's director of this grass-roots organization. "This morning I had a young man. He had taken some money from us. I didn't think I'd see him again. I spread the warning: 'Watch out; he's a bad egg.' Today, out of the clear blue sky, he walked into my office. He says, 'I want to pay back my debt at fifty dollars a month. I've gotten a job. I didn't want to see you until I got a job.' I didn't know what made him come back. Was it the spirit of the community?"

In South Chicago, a bit to the southeast, Fast Eddie is finding out about UNO. That's the United Neighborhood Organization. While the alderman was busy giving Harold a hard time, his Hispanic constituents in the Tenth Ward were busy giving Waste Management, Inc., a hard time. The multinational toxic dumper was about to dump some of the vile stuff in the neighborhood. Hold off, big boy, said Mary Ellen Montez, a twenty-six-year-old housewife. So far, she and her neighbors are doing a far better job than Horatio ever did at the bridge.

UNO's grassroots power is being felt in Pilsen, too, where rehabs are springing up without the dubious touch of gentrification. The community folk are there because they're there and that's where they intend to stay. No shoving out in these parts. And no yuppies need apply.

Farther west, the South Austin Community Council, when not challenging joblessness and street crime, has sent housewives and suddenly redundant steelworkers to Springfield as well as to City Hall to lobby for the Affordable Budget, so that gas and electric bills don't destroy those whom God has only slightly blessed with means. They're not waiting for the hacks to fight for it; they're do-it-yourselfers.

Talk about fighting redundancy, the Metro Seniors are among the most militant. Never mind the wheelchairs, crutches, tea, and sympathy. They bang away everywhere, with or without canes and walkers: Keep your grubby hands off Medicare and Social Security. Ever hear of the time they marched into official sanctums with a cake: Cut the cake but not the COLA (cost-of-living adjustment)? The hacks ate that cake more slowly and thoughtfully than ever. There are 7,500 such scrappers in town, the youngest sixty-five. They may not have heard "Me and Bobby McGee," but they sure know the lyric: "Freedom's just another word for nothin' left to lose."

All sorts of new people from Central America and Southeast Asia, together with the more settled have-nots, are at it in Uptown with ONE (Organization of the North East). Tenants' rights, lousy housing, ethnic identity—name it; if it's an elementary right, they're battling for it.

And let's not forget all those nimble neighborhood organizers coming out of Heather Booth's Midwest Academy. Their style is sixties hipness, Saul Alinsky's Actions (politi-

cal jujitsu, he called it), and eighties hard-earned aware-
ness. They're all over town, astirring.

This is house-to-house, block-by-block, pavement-pound-
ing, church-meeting, all-kinds-of-discussion stuff that
may, as we wake up some great gettin'-up morning, reveal a
new kind of Chicago. Nick Von Hoffman, who for a time was
Alinsky's right arm, said it: "You who thought of yourself,
up to that moment, as simply being a number, suddenly
spring to life. You have that intoxicating feeling that you
can make your own history, that you really count."

Call it a back-yard revolution if you want to. It will sure as
hell confute the Johnny Da Pows of our day, the merchant
princes and the Fast Eddies. And, incidentally, lay the
ghost of Lord Acton: less powerlessness that corrupts and
more power than may ennoble.

Perhaps mine eyes may yet see the glory.

# Neighborhoods of the Southwest Side

*By Dominic A.
Pacyga*

*An urban
historian who
teaches at
Columbia College
in Chicago,
Dominic A.
Pacyga is the
coauthor of*
Chicago: City of
Neighborhoods.

Chicago is proud of its ethnic neighborhoods. The "City of the Big Shoulders" is also the city of the blues and the polka, the jig and the tarantella. Tacos, kielbasa, Irish meat pies, and soul food are the sustenance of Chicago beyond the Loop and the high-rise towers of the lakefront. On Chicago streets newspapers in Polish, Lithuanian, Arabic, Spanish, German, and Greek are sold alongside the better-known English-language dailies, and a black newspaper, the *Chicago Defender*, makes its voice heard throughout the city. Many of the churches whose spires dot the cityscape can trace their origins to the arrival in Chicago of a particular national group. Schools, hospitals, museums, monuments, even street names (Emerald Avenue, King Drive, Lituanica Street, Pulaski Road) speak to the influence of ethnic groups on the city's history and political life.

As the city grew along with the Industrial Revolution of the 19th century, its neighborhoods became mazes of railroads, mills, factories, and packinghouses that reached across the Illinois prairie. The huge industrial complexes attracted workers from all over the United States, Europe, and Asia. Every major wave of migration that affected the United States after 1825 had a part in transforming Chicago. In recent years Arab, Vietnamese, Mexican, and Chinese immigrants have joined the descendants of the Germans, Irish, Swedes, Poles, Jews, Italians, and black Americans who made earlier journeys in search of peace and prosperity. And each group has left its mark on the city: Hispanic and Vietnamese cultural centers and museums have now joined the long-established Polish Museum on the Northwest Side, the Balzekas Museum of Lithuanian Culture on the Southwest Side, and the DuSable Museum of African American Culture on the South Side.

Chicago's communities have not always lived in harmony. Clashes between white ethnic groups have marked the history of the city, and relationships between whites and blacks exploded in a calamitous race riot in 1919. Although much has changed over the last 30 years, Chicago is still known as the nation's most segregated city. Yet its pluralism remains intact and healthy. Polish, Hmong, Greek,

*The areas of the communities described in this essay are shown in the Chicago Neighborhoods map. A note following the essay gives directions and suggestions for visiting these neighborhoods, which are not covered in the tours of the Exploring Chicago chapter.*

# South Chicago Neighborhoods

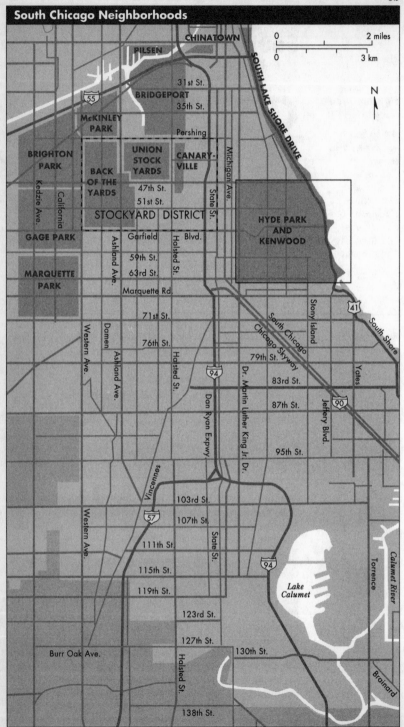

CHINATOWN

PILSEN

0       2 miles
0       3 km

N

31st St.

BRIDGEPORT

35th St.

55

McKINLEY
PARK

Pershing

SOUTH LAKE SHORE DRIVE

BRIGHTON
PARK

UNION
STOCK
YARDS

CANARY-
VILLE

Michigan Ave.

BACK
OF THE
YARDS

47th St.

51st St.

Kedzie Ave.

California

State St.

STOCKYARD DISTRICT

HYDE PARK
AND
KENWOOD

GAGE PARK

Garfield        Blvd.

59th St.

Ashland Ave.

Halsted St.

63rd St.

MARQUETTE
PARK

Marquette Rd.

71st St.

Stony Island

41

Western Ave.

Damen

Ashland Ave.

76th St.

South Chicago Skyway

South Shore

79th St.

Halsted St.

94

83rd St.

Yates

Dr. Martin Luther King Jr. Dr.

87th St.

90

Jeffery Blvd.

Dan Ryan Expwy

95th St.

Vincennes

103rd St.

57

107th St.

111th St.

State St.

Western Ave.

115th St.

94

119th St.

Lake
Calumet

Torrence

Calumet River

123rd St.

127th St.

Burr Oak Ave.

130th St.

Halsted St.

Brainard

138th St.

Arabic, and other languages mix freely with English, and summer in Chicago is a time when ethnic and community street fairs attract crowds.

The neighborhoods that lie like a fan to the southwest of the meeting of State Street and Archer Avenue have seen a succession of working-class ethnic populations. Archer Avenue, which runs roughly parallel to the South Branch of the Chicago River and the Chicago Sanitary and Ship Canal, is part of a huge transportation corridor that includes rail lines and the Stevenson Expressway (I–55). On this corridor much of the industrial history of the city took place.

Father Jacques Marquette and the explorer Louis Jolliet, who first arrived in the area in 1673, suggested the construction of a canal to connect Lake Michigan with the Illinois River. Begun in 1836, the monumental task took 12 years to complete. The Illinois–Michigan Canal gave Chicago commercial transportation to the hinterlands, and the canal and the river soon teemed with barges, docks, and factories. The activity quickly brought the railroads as well to the Archer Avenue corridor. By the turn of the century, the larger Chicago Sanitary and Ship Canal had also been constructed.

Irish workers made up a large portion of those who came to dig the Illinois–Michigan Canal, many of them having worked on the Erie Canal. The "canal" Irish tended to settle along the river in the area known originally as Hardscrabble or Lee's Farm; the building of the canal brought a change in name to Bridgeport. This working-class community anchored the northern end of Archer Avenue. St. Bridget's Church at Archer Avenue and Arch Street stands as a reminder of the canal workers who flocked to Chicago before the Civil War. The present structure of 1906 resembles a cathedral built by Irish monks in Novara, Italy, in 1170; its survival in the face of the construction of the Stevenson Expressway in 1964 is a tribute to the efforts of its pastor and to Bridgeport's political clout. (Planners swung the expressway directly behind St. Bridget's and its Shrine of Our Lady of the Highway.)

The river and the canal soon attracted Chicago's most famous industry: Meat packing plants opened along the South Branch and fouled the river with pollution. The packinghouses in turn attracted skilled German and Bohemian butchers and brought more Irish to Bridgeport. On Christmas Day, 1865, the Union Stock Yard opened west of Halsted Street, between Pershing Road (39th Street) and 47th Street, just to the south of Bridgeport. The huge livestock market became the center of the nation's meat packing industry. In time, an immigrant city grew up around the more than 400 acres of livestock pens, chutes, and railroad yards. Bridgeport's Irish, Germans, and Bohemians found themselves surrounded by Poles, Lithuanians, Slovaks, Italians, French Canadians, black Americans, and others; this was the beginning of the ethnic mélange of the South Side.

In 1905 the Chicago stockyards were rocked by the publication of Upton Sinclair's muckraking novel *The Jungle*. Sinclair portrayed the life of a Lithuanian immigrant family that lived in Back of the Yards, just to the southwest of the stockyards and Bridgeport. The Chicago stockyards soon had an international reputation for unwholesome practices, and it was not the last time the area was looked upon unfavorably in literature or in the press.

In fact the area contains four of the most written about, most famous neighborhoods in the history of urban America. Bridgeport, McKinley Park, Back of the Yards, and Canaryville surround the old Union Stock Yard. Bridgeport, the oldest settlement, predates the founding of the stockyards; much of its fame rests on its working-class ethnicity and its peculiar brand of politics. Richard J. Daley, its best-known political son, was only one of four Chicago mayors born and raised in Bridgeport, who together ran the city from the death of Anton Cermak in 1933 until the election of Jane Byrne in 1979. For many people, the name Bridgeport still means politics, especially Irish machine politics.

Bridgeport today has more than a dozen resident ethnic groups, some of them the overflow from neighboring communities. Pilsen, to the north, across the Chicago River, was once the center of Chicago's lumber industry; by 1900 it had become the largest Bohemian community outside Chicago; today it is the home of the city's principal concentration of Mexicans. Chinatown, to the northeast, its heart at the intersection of Cermak Road and Wentworth Avenue, was once occupied by Germans and Irish; Italians followed them before the Chinese arrived after 1900. The Chinatown community today is a growing and prosperous one, with a good deal of cohesion, and new immigrants have helped to solidify the Asian presence in the inner city.

Canaryville, to the south of Bridgeport, between Pershing Road and 49th Street, Halsted and the old New York Central Railroad yards, is a largely Irish-American neighborhood with many Mexicans and Appalachian whites. Here, at the corner of 45th Street and Lowe Avenue, is St. Gabriel's, perhaps the most famous church in the Stock Yard District. One of John Root's finest designs, the Romanesque structure was built in 1887–1888 with financial help from the packinghouse owners who were close friends of Fr. Maurice Dorney, the founder of the parish in 1880.

The neighborhoods that once surrounded the stockyards have more than 30 Roman Catholic churches and many Protestant houses of worship. Each is a monument to the faith and community-building spirit of an ethnic group that settled in the area. Polish packinghouse workers, who came to the area in large numbers between 1880 and 1920, alone built six of the structures. Today many of the old national parishes are of mixed ethnicity; many have services in the language of their founders, as well as in English and Spanish. Worshipers entering the magnificent church of St. John of God at 52nd Street and Throop, across the street from Sherman Park, are greeted by the flags of Poland, Mexico, the United States, and the Vatican.

The Stock Yard District, once known as Town of Lake, a suburb of Chicago until it was annexed in 1889, behaved in some ways like a city in itself. As its residents moved to the south and west after World War I, out of the core neighborhoods of wooden two-flats and cottages in close proximity to the stockyards and the packinghouses, they created suburbs in the new neighborhoods of the Southwest Side, principally along Archer Avenue. These areas are part of Chicago's "bungalow belt."

During the 1920s bungalows appeared throughout the Southwest, Northwest, and Southeast sides. The single-family dwellings, with their small front- and backyards, were the pre-Depression equivalent of suburban sprawl. Today they comprise much of Chicago's second tier of ethnic neighborhoods: Brighton Park, Gage Park, and Marquette Park all owe their existence to the movement away from the stockyard communities of Bridgeport, McKinley Park, Back of the Yards, and Canaryville. And the movements of ethnic groups can be traced across the Southwest Side in the churches and other institutions they left behind.

The Lithuanian community, for example, organized its first church, St. George's, in 1892 in Bridgeport. (The present structure was dedicated in 1902.) A second Lithuanian parish, Providence of God, was founded in 1900, north of St. George's in the Pilsen community. Three more Lithuanian parishes opened in 1904, including Holy Cross in Back of the Yards. Ten years later the Lithuanian community was supporting 10 Roman Catholic parishes, a consequence of the large East European emigration to America that took place before 1914. These arrivals became part of Chicago's first tier of ethnic neighborhoods.

As Lithuanians settled into better jobs following World War I, many of them decided to move away from the old industrial districts, and they looked to the bungalow belt for newer, more spacious housing. In the 1920s the Marquette Park area near the intersection of Marquette Road and California Avenue attracted Lithuanian Americans. A Lithuanian order of religious sisters had laid the foundation for the community in 1911 by opening the Academy of St. Casimir (later Maria High School). In 1928 ground was broken for a Lithuanian parish, Nativity B.V.M., at 68th Street and Washtenaw, and the parish quickly became a central institution in the Lithuanian community. In the same year the Sisters of St. Casimir opened Holy Cross Hospital near the church and the high school.

The large institutional base drew more Lithuanians to the neighborhood throughout the interwar period. After World War II, another major emigration from Eastern Europe rejuvenated the Lithuanian community, and Marquette Park became its new center. The present Nativity Church, designed by John Mulokas and dedicated on May 12, 1957, is a striking example of Lithuanian architecture. Its dedication to Our Lady of Siluva celebrates the site of a famous Shrine to the Blessed Virgin in Lithuania.

The movement of Lithuanians away from the inner city has been typical of that of ethnic groups that originally settled in the area. By 1988 many of the Marquette Park Lithuanians were relocating in the southwest suburbs near Lemont. Yet the neighborhood they left behind continues to nourish the community; many people and cultural institutions choose to stay in Chicago, and Marquette Park remains the Lithuanian "gold coast."

The Union Stock Yard closed its gates on August 1, 1971, after 105 years of active livestock trading. In reality the meat packing business had begun to leave the city nearly 20 years earlier, when Wilson and Company announced the closing of its huge Chicago plant. By the early 1960s the big packers had left the city, and Chicago was facing its first post-industrial crisis. The area west of the Union Stock Yard, formerly the center of one of the nation's great industries, now resembled a ghost town.

Recent years have seen a partially successful attempt to redevelop some of the land the stockyards and packinghouses had occupied. A visit to the Old Stone Gate at Exchange and Peoria, which marks the entrance to the area, will show you industrial buildings mixed with open prairie and abandoned packinghouse buildings. Yet the new industries, important as they are to the city's economic base, employ only a fraction of the number of workers formerly employed by Chicago's most infamous industry. Meanwhile, new immigrants from Poland, Mexico, and elsewhere continue to come to the district in search of employment.

The economic future of Chicago's Southwest Side looked bleak just a few years ago. Now a resurgent Midway Airport at 55th Street and Cicero and a new rapid transit line that is scheduled to open by 1993 have infused the local economy with optimism. Bridgeport, in part because of its proximity to downtown and an excellent public transportation system that will improve when the Southwest Rapid Transit opens, is already witnessing economic rebirth. Areas a little farther down Archer Avenue should see new development as Midway Airport increases its capacity and the rapid transit line reaches them. The entire area along

the canal and the river is now part of the Illinois–Michigan
Canal National Heritage Corridor, and there are plans for
riverfront parks and other amenities. In the shadow of
great economic, cultural, and social change, Chicago's ethnic communities continue to maintain their heritage in the
old and the new neighborhoods.

The Southwest Side is easily accessible by public or private
transportation. The Archer Avenue (No. 62) bus, which can
be boarded on State Street, makes its way southwest
through the corridor. The Dan Ryan Rapid Transit Line
will take you to Chinatown (Cermak Avenue) or to
Comiskey Park (35th Street), the home of the Chicago
White Sox. By automobile, you can take Archer and turn
down Halsted Street (800 W), Ashland Avenue (1600 W),
Western Avenue (2400 W), or another major street and follow it until you find an interesting side street or attraction
to explore. If you continue west on Archer past Kedzie Avenue, stop at the Dom Podhalan or Polish Highlanders Hall
at 4808 South Archer Avenue; it is as authentic a Polish
mountain chalet as you are likely to see this side of the Odra
River. A visit to the Balzekas Museum of Lithuanian Culture at 6500 South Pulaski Road would be worthwhile (*see*
Sightseeing Checklists in Chapter 3). Wonderful and inexpensive Lithuanian restaurants line 71st Street from Western to California avenues (2600 W). Some of the best Middle
Eastern restaurants in Chicago are located along 63rd
Street between Western and Central Park avenues (3600
W). While the Northwest Side, along Milwaukee Avenue,
is famous for Polish cuisine, the South Side holds its own:
Tatra Inn serves a satisfying smorgasboard at 6038 South
Pulaski. Mexican restaurants abound in Back of the Yards
near the intersection of Ashland Avenue and 47th Street
and in Pilsen along 18th Street and on Blue Island Avenue.
Mi Pueblo, at 2908 West 59th Street, resembles a Mexican
hacienda. The Southwest Side Italian community is well
represented with restaurants along Oakley Avenue (2300
W), Western just north of 26th Street, and on 63rd Street,
where Palermo's at 3715 West 63rd Street and Little Joe's
at 63rd Street and Richmond are noteworthy. Many of the
churches hereabouts have beautiful interiors, and Sunday
is the best time to visit them, when services are scheduled.
At other times of the week, you may find the church you
want to see closed unless you call in advance of your visit.

# The Builders of Chicago

By Barbara
Shortt

A practicing
architect and an
architectural
historian,
Barbara Shortt
writes frequently
on architecture
and travel.

**W**hen Mrs. O'Leary's cow kicked over the lantern and started the Great Chicago Fire of 1871, she set the scene for the birth of a Modern Architecture that would influence the entire globe. If Chicago today is a world capital of modern architecture landmarks—a city whose buildings embody contemporary architectural history from its beginnings in the 1880s—it is thanks to this cataclysmic fire and a unique set of cultural circumstances that were fueled by the new wealth of the thriving port city. In 1871 Chicago was isolated from European and East Coast opinion. At the same time, it was not uncivilized frontier, nor had it been traumatized by the Civil War. And it was strongly conscious of being the metropolis of the American heartland. Yet it had absolutely no existing architectural tradition; physically and aesthetically, it was wide open.

Because Chicago had been built mainly of wood, it was wiped out by the fire. Virtually the only building left standing downtown, where it still dominates the intersection of North Michigan and Chicago avenues, was the bizarre yellow stone Water Tower of 1869. Oscar Wilde, that infamous aesthete, called it a "monstrosity" when he visited Chicago in 1882. Today, with its fake battlements, crenellations, and turrets, it looks like a transplant from Disneyland rather than a real part of a vibrant and serious city. It serves now as a tourist information center, and even amid the amazingly varied architecture of central Chicago it appears to be an anachronism.

In the years following the fire, many remarkable people flocked to the building opportunity in the city that sprawled for miles along the western shore of Lake Michigan and inland along the branches of the Chicago River. A brilliant engineer named William LeBaron Jenney and a young Bostonian trained at MIT and Paris named Louis Sullivan, who would become a great architect, philosopher, writer, and teacher, were joined by a group of ingenious architects and engineers from diverse parts of America and Europe: Dankmar Adler (from Denmark), William Holabird (from New York), John Wellborn Root, Frank Lloyd Wright (from Wisconsin), Henry Hobson Richardson (from Louisiana via Boston and Paris), Daniel H. Burnham, and Martin Roche, among others. During the 1880s and 1890s in Chicago, these men did nothing less than create the foundations of modern architecture and construction.

The skyscraper was born here. The "curtain-wall," a largely glass exterior surface that does not act as a "wall" supporting the building but is supported on the floors from within, originated here. Modern metal-frame, multi-story construction was created here. The Chicago Window—a popular window design used in buildings all over America (until air-conditioning made it obsolete), consisting of a large fixed glass panel in the center, with a narrow operable sash on each side—was developed here. Chicago builders also discovered how to fireproof the metal structures that supported their buildings, which would otherwise melt in fires and bring total collapse: They covered the iron columns and beams with terra-cotta tiles that insulated the structural metal from heat.

Philosophically, the Chicago architects believed they were creating a democratic architecture to express the soul of American civilization, an architecture pragmatic, honest, healthy, and unashamed of wealth and commerce. Louis Sullivan, a philosopher, a romantic, and a prolific writer (his most famous book on architecture, *Kindergarten Chats*, is a Socratic dialogue), originated and propagated the ideas that "form follows function" and "a building is an act." For Sullivan, social purpose and structure had to be integrated to create an architecture of human satisfaction.

Technologically, the Chicago School, as they became known, were aware of the latest developments in European iron structures, such as the great railroad stations. Jenney had his engineering degree from Paris in 1856—he was older than the others, many of whom worked for him—yet he, Richardson, and John Root were the only conventionally well educated men of the group. At the same time, they had in Chicago a daring and innovative local engineering tradition. Jenney, a strict rationalist, incarnated this nononsense tradition and gave romantics like Sullivan and, later on, Sullivan's disciple Wright the tools with which to express their architectural philosophy.

The term *Chicago School of Architecture* refers to the work of these men, whose offices served as their true school: Jenney and Mundie, Root and Burgee, Adler and Sullivan, Holabird and Roche, Burnham and Root, H. H. Richardson, and Frank Lloyd Wright. In many instances it requires a scholarly effort to figure out precisely who did what, as they worked for and with one another, living in each other's pockets, shifting partnerships, arguing the meaning of what they did as well as how best to do it. Jenney and Adler were essentially engineers uninterested in decoration; with the exception of Richardson's Romanesque motifs, Sullivan's amazing ornament, and Wright's spatial and ornamental forms, these builders did not have distinct, easily discernible "styles." It becomes an academic exercise to try to identify their individual efforts.

The Chicago School's greatest clients were wealthy businessmen and their wives. The same lack of inhibition that led Mrs. Potter Palmer and Mrs. Havemeyer to snap up Impressionist paintings that had been rejected by French academic opinion (and today are the core of the Art Institute collection) led sausage magnates to hire young, inventive, local talent to build their mansions and counting-houses. Chicagoans may have been naive, but history has vindicated their taste.

Although they started building in the 1870s, nothing of note remains from before 1885. The oldest important structure is H. H. Richardson's massive granite Italian Romanesque-inspired Glessner House, with its decorative interiors derived from the innovative English Arts and Crafts movement. The only Richardson building left in Chicago, the Glessner House is considered by some his highest creation; Wright was influenced by its flowing interior space. At the corner of 18th Street and the Prairie Avenue Historic District, it now houses the offices of the Chicago Architecture Foundation.

Downtown, Richardson designed a Wholesale Building for Marshall Field that was later demolished. An addition to the Field store in the same architectural vocabulary, done by Burnham in 1893 and now part of the Marshall Field block, stands at the corner of Wabash and Washington streets. Burnham completed the block in 1902–1907, but in the airy, open, metal-frame, Chicago Window style.

In 1883 William LeBaron Jenney invented the first "skyscraper construction" building, in which a metal structural skeleton supports an exterior wall on metal shelves. (The metal frame or skeleton, a sort of three-dimensional boxlike grid, is still used today.) His earliest surviving metal-skeleton structure, the Second Leiter Building of 1891, is now Sears, Roebuck and Company, at the southeast corner of State and Van Buren streets in the Loop. The granite-face facade is extremely light and open, suggesting the metal frame behind. The building looks so modern that it comes as a shock to realize it is nearly a century old.

At 209 South La Salle Street, the Rookery Building of 1886, a highly decorated, structurally transitional building by Burnham and Root, employs masonry bearing walls (brick, terra-cotta, and stone) on the two major street facades and lots of iron structure (both cast-iron columns and wrought-iron beams) elsewhere. Here the decoration emphasizes the structural elements—pointing out, for example, the floor lines. Note also how specially shaped bricks are used at the edges of the window openings and to make pilasters. The plan, a freestanding square "donut," was unusual at the time. A magnificent iron and glass skylight covers the lower two stories of the interior courtyard, which was renovated in 1905 by Frank Lloyd Wright, who designed light fixtures and other decorative additions.

The nearby Marquette Building of 1894 at 140 South Dearborn Street, by Holabird and Roche, is almost a prototype for the modern office building, with its skeleton metal frame covered by decorative terra-cotta and its open, cellular facade with Chicago Windows. The marble lobby rotunda has Tiffany mosaic portraits of Indian chieftains and Père Marquette, a hymn to local history.

The most advanced structure from this period, one in which the exterior wall surface is freed of all performance of support, is Burnham's Reliance Building of 1895 at 36 North State Street. Here the proportion of glass to solid is very high, and the solid members are immensely slender for the era. Today the white terra-cotta cladding needs cleaning, and the building's seedy condition mars its beauty; the casual observer would be surprised to learn that most critics consider it the masterpiece of the Chicago School's office buildings.

To appreciate fully the giant leap taken by the architects of the Reliance, look at Burnham and Root's Monadnock Building of 1889–1892, at 53 West Jackson Boulevard. Its 16 stories are supported by conventional load-bearing walls, which grow to six feet thick at the base! While elegant in its stark simplicity (the result of a cheap-minded entrepreneur who had all the decoration removed from the plans while Root was traveling), its ponderousness contrasts sharply with the delicate structure and appearance of the Reliance Building. The Monadnock Building may have been the swan song of conventional building structure in Chicago, yet its verticality expressed the aspirations of the city.

Jenney's Manhattan Building of 1890, at 431 South Dearborn Street, with its variously shaped bay windows, was the first tall building (16 stories) to use metal-skeleton structure throughout; it is admired more for its structure than for its appearance. Both it and the equally tall Monadnock would never have come into being without Elisha Otis's elevator invention, which was already in use in New York City in buildings of 9 or 10 stories at most.

**T**he impetus toward verticality was an essential feature of Chicago commercial architecture. Verticality seemed to embody commercial possibility, as in "the sky's the limit!" Even the essential horizontality of the 12-story, block-long Carson Pirie Scott store is offset by the rounded corner tower at the main entrance.

The Chicago School created new decorative forms to apply to their powerful structures, and they derived them largely from American vegetation rather than from classical motifs. The apogee of this lush ornament was probably reached by Sullivan in his Carson Pirie Scott and Company store of 1899–1904 at State and Madison streets. The cast-iron swirls of rich vegetation and geometry surround the ground-floor show windows and the entrance, and they grow to the second story as well, with the architect's initials, LHS, worked into the design. (A decorative cornice that was originally at the top was removed.) The facade of the intermediate floors is extremely simple, with wide Chicago Windows surrounded by a thin line of delicate ornament; narrow vertical and horizontal bands, all of white terra-cotta, cover the iron structure behind.

Terra-cotta plaques of complex and original decoration cover the horizontal spandrel beams (the beams that cover the outer edges of the floors, between the vertical columns of the facades) of many buildings of this era, including the Reliance and the Marquette. Even modest residential and commercial structures in Chicago began to use decorative terra-cotta, which became a typical local construction motif through the 1930s.

Adler and Sullivan's Auditorium Building of 1887–1889 was a daring megastructure sheathed in massive granite, the same material Richardson used, and its style derives from his Romanesque forms. Here the shades of stone color and the rough and polished finishes provide contrasts. Built for profit as a civic center at South Michigan Avenue and Congress Street, facing Lake Michigan, the Auditorium Building incorporated a theater, a hotel, and an office building; complex engineering solutions allowed it to carry heavy and widely varying loads. Adler, the engineer, devised a hydraulic stage lift and an early air-conditioning system for the magnificent theater. Sullivan freely decorated the interiors with his distinctive flowing ornamental shapes.

In the spirit of democracy and populism, Adler wanted the Auditorium to be a "people's theater," one with lots of cheap seats and few boxes. It is still in use today as the Auditorium Theater, Adler's belief in the common man having been upheld when thousands of ordinary Chicagoans subscribed to the restoration fund in 1968. The rest of the building is now Roosevelt University.

Frank Lloyd Wright, who had worked for a year on the Auditorium Building in Adler and Sullivan's office, remained in their employ and in 1892 designed a house for them in a wealthy area of the Near North Side of town. The Charnley House, 1365 North Astor Street, built of long, thin, yellowish Roman brick and stone, has a projecting central balcony and shows a glimmer of Wright's extraordinary later freedom with volumes and spaces. The Charnley House, with its exquisite interior woodwork and the exterior frieze under the roof, has now been completely restored. Soon after the Charnley House project, Wright left Adler and Sullivan to work on his own.

Wright's ability to break apart and recompose space and volume, even asymmetrically, was given full range in the many houses he built in and around Chicago. What became typical of American domestic "open plan" interiors (as opposed to an arrangement of closed, boxlike rooms) derived from Wright's creation, but they could never have been practical without the American development of central heating, which eliminated the need for a fire in each room.

Wright was the founder of what became known as the Prairie School, whose work consisted largely of residences rather than buildings intended for commerce. Its principal characteristic was a horizontality evocative of the breadth of the prairies that contrasted with the lofty vertical shafts of the business towers. Like his teacher Sullivan, Wright also delighted in original decorative motifs of geometric and vegetable design.

The opening of the Lake Street el railway west to the new suburb of Oak Park gave Wright an enormous opportunity to build. In 1889 he went to live there at 951 Chicago Avenue, where he created a studio and a home over the next 22 years. Dozens of houses in Oak Park, of wood, stucco, brick, and stone, with beautiful leaded- and stained-glass windows and carved woodwork, were designed or renovated by him. He was almost obsessional in his involvement with his houses, wanting to design and control the placement of furniture and returning even after his clients had moved in. For Wright a house was a living thing, both in its relationship to the land and in its evolution through use.

Yet Wright's masterpiece in Oak Park is not a house but the Unitarian Unity Temple of 1906, at Kenilworth Avenue and Lake Street, a short walk from the Oak Park Avenue el stop. Because of intense budget limitations, he built it of the daring and generally abhorred material, poured concrete, and with only the simplest details of applied wood stripping. Nevertheless, Wright's serene creation of volume and light endures to this day. It is lit by high windows from above and has operable colored-glass skylights inserted into the "coffers" of the Roman-style "egg-crate" ceiling, intended for ventilation as well as light. The design of the windows and skylights echoes the designs applied to the walls, the door grilles, the hinges, the light fixtures; everything is integrated visually, no detail having been too small to consider.

Unity Temple was built on what became known as an H plan, which consisted of two functionally separate blocks connected by an entry hall. The Unity Temple plan has influenced the planning of public buildings to the present day. Recently restored to its original interior greens and ochers, Unity Temple is definitely worth a pilgrimage.

On the South Side of Chicago is the most famous of all Wright's houses, the Robie House of 1909, now on the University of Chicago campus, at 5757 South Woodlawn Avenue. Its great horizontal overhanging roof lines are echoed by the long limestone sills that cap its low brick walls. Wright designed everything for the house, including the furniture. Wright's stock has soared of late: A single lamp from the Robie House sold at auction recently for three-quarters of a million dollars!

The World's Columbian Exposition of 1893 was held at Midway Park in South Chicago. For complex political reasons, the planning was turned over mainly to eastern architects, who brought the influence of the international Beaux-Arts style to Chicago. A furious Louis Sullivan prophesied that "the damage wrought to this country by the Chicago World's Fair will last half a century." He wasn't entirely wrong in his prediction; the classicist style vied sharply over the next decades with the native creations of the Chicago and Prairie schools, all the while incorporating their technical advances. But the city fathers succumbed to the "culture versus commerce" point of view; thus most of the museums and public buildings constructed before World War II in Chicago were built in classical Greek or Renaissance styles.

Many of these public buildings are fine works in their own right, but they do not contribute to the development of 20th-century architecture. The most notable of them, the Public Library of 1897, at 78 East Washington Street, by Shepley, Rutan and Coolidge, has gorgeous interiors of white and green marble and glass.

Many of Chicago's museums are situated in Grant Park and along Lake Shore Drive, magnificent points from which to view the city skyline. The park and the drive were built on landfill in the 1910s and 1920s after the tracks of the Illinois Central Railroad along the old lakefront had been bridged over. Lake Shore Drive, with its parks and beaches, seems such an integral part of today's city that it is hard to imagine a Chicago without it. Daniel Burnham called for this development in his "Chicago Plan" of 1909.

In 1922 an important international competition offered a prize of $100,000 for the design of a Tribune Building that would dominate the Chicago River just north of the Loop. Numerous modernist plans were submitted, including one by Walter Gropius, of the Bauhaus. Raymond Hood's Gothic design—some called it Woolworth Gothic—was chosen. The graceful and picturesque silhouette of the Tribune Tower was for many years the symbol of Chicago, not to be overshadowed until general construction resumed, following World War II. More important, the Tribune Building moved the center of gravity of downtown Chicago north and east, causing the Michigan Avenue bridge to be built and opening the Near North Side to commercial development along Michigan Avenue.

The postwar Chicago School was dominated by a single personality who influenced modern architecture around the world: Ludwig Mies van der Rohe. The son of a stonemason, Mies was director of the Bauhaus in Dessau, Germany, the world's leading modern design center, from 1930 until Nazi pressure made him leave in 1937. On a trip to the United States he met John Holabird, son of William, who invited him to head the School of Architecture at the Armour Institute, later the Illinois Institute of Technology. Mies accepted—and redesigned the entire campus as part of the deal. Over the next 20 years he created a School of Architecture that disseminated his thinking into architecture offices everywhere.

Whatever Mies owed to Frank Lloyd Wright, such as Mies's own open-plan houses, his philosophy was very much in the tradition of Chicago, and the roots of Bauhaus architecture can be traced to the Chicago School. Mies's attitudes were profoundly pragmatic, based on solid building techniques, technology, and an appreciation of the nature of the materials used. He created a philosophy, a set of ethical values based on a purist approach; his great aphorisms were "Less is more" and "God is in the details." He eschewed applied ornament, however, and in that sense he was nothing like Wright. All Mies's "decoration" is generated by fine-tuned structural detail. His buildings are sober, sometimes somber, highly orderly, and serene; their aesthetic is based on the almost religious expression of structure.

The campus of IIT was built in 1942–1958 along South State Street, between 31st and 35th streets. Mies used few materials in the two dozen buildings he planned here: light cream colored brick, black steel, and glass. Quadrangles are only suggested, space is never rigidly defined. There is a direct line of descent from Crown Hall (1956), made of black steel and clear glass, with its long-span roof trusses exposed above the level of the roof, to the great convention center of 1970 on South Lake Shore Drive at 23rd Street, McCormick Center by C. F. Murphy, with its great exposed black steel space-frame roof and its glass walls.

Age requirements forced Mies to retire from IIT in 1958, but his office went on to do major projects in downtown Chicago, along Lake Shore Drive, and elsewhere. He had impressed the world in 1952 with his black steel and clear glass twin apartment towers, set at right angles to one another, almost kissing at the corner, at 860–880 North Lake Shore Drive. Later he added another, darker pair just to the north, 900–910.

In 1968 Heinrich and Schipporeit, inspired by "860" and by Mies's Berlin drawings of 1921 for a free-form glass skyscraper, built Lake Point Tower. This dark bronze metal and glass trefoil shaft, near the Navy Pier at East Grand Avenue, is a graceful and dramatic joy of the Chicago skyline. It is one of the few Chicago buildings, along with Bertram Goldberg's Marina City of 1964—twin round concrete towers on the river between State and Dearborn streets—to break with strict rectilinear geometry.

Downtown, Mies's Federal Center is a group of black buildings around a plaza, set off by a bright red steel Alexander Calder stabile sculpture, on Dearborn Street between Jackson Boulevard and Adams Street. The Dirksen Building, with its courthouse, on the east side of Dearborn, was built in 1964; the Kluczynski office building at the south side of the plaza and the single-story Post Office to the west were added through 1975. The north side of the large Federal Plaza is enclosed by the Marquette Building of 1894, thereby integrating the past with the present.

The IBM Building of 1971, the last office building designed by Mies, is a dark presence north of the river, between Wabash and State streets.

**P**erhaps the most important spinoff of Miesian thinking was the young firm of Skidmore, Owings & Merrill, which bloomed after the war. Their gem of the postwar period was the Inland Steel Building of 1957, at 30 West Monroe Street, in the Loop. The bright stainless-steel and pale green glass structure, only 18 stories high, with exposed columns on the long facade and a clear span in the short dimension, has uninterrupted interior floor space. It is considered a classic.

SOM became the largest architecture firm in America, with offices in all major cities. In Chicago the firm built, among other works, the immensely tall, tapering brown Hancock Tower of 1965–1970, with its innovative exterior criss-cross wind-bracing, and the even taller Sears Tower (1970–1975), with two of its nine shafts reaching to 1,450 feet, now the tallest structure in the world. SOM may have achieved the epitome of the vertical commercial thrust of the Chicago School.

Meanwhile, Mies's Federal Plaza started a Chicago tradition, that of the outdoor plaza with a focus of monumental art. These plazas are real, usable, and used; they are large-scale city gathering places, not the mingy setbacks of New York office megaliths, and they shape the architectural and spatial character of downtown Chicago.

A string of plazas, featuring sculptures by Picasso and Dubuffet and mosaic murals by Chagall, leads one up Dearborn and Clark streets, to the Chicago River. At the river one finds more outdoor space. The south bank quays, one level down from the street, are a series of imaginatively landscaped gardens. Here one can contemplate the ever-changing light on the river and the 19th-century riveted-iron drawbridges, which prefigure Calder's work. Other monumental outdoor sculpture downtown includes Joan Miró's *Chicago* and Claes Oldenburg's *Batcolumn*.

The Jean Dubuffet sculpture stands before the State of Illinois Building of 1985 at the corner of Randolph and Clark streets. Here there are really two plazas: one outdoors, the other inside the stepped-back, mirrored-glass and pink-paneled irregular donut of a building. This wild fantasy is the work of Helmut Jahn, a German who came to Chicago in the 1960s to study at IIT. His colorful, lighthearted, mirrored Chicago buildings provide a definite counterpoint to the somber Mies buildings of the 1950s and 1960s, and they appear everywhere, influencing the design and choice of materials of the architecture of the 1980s.

Jahn's first important contribution to the Chicago scene was a sensitive addition to the Board of Trade in 1980. The Board of Trade was housed in an architectural landmark at 141 West Jackson Boulevard, at the foot of La Salle Street, a jewel of Art Deco design by the old Chicago firm of Holabird and Root in 1930. Murphy/Jahn's glittering addition echoed numerous features of the original structure. Both parts of the building have sumptuous interior atrium spaces. Marble, nickel, and glass motifs from the earlier edifice are evoked and reinterpreted—but not copied—in the high-tech addition. Within the new atrium, framed by highly polished chromium-plated trusses and turquoise panels, hangs a large Art Deco painting that was found in the older building during renovation. This complex captures the spirit of Chicago architecture: Devoted to commerce, it embraces the present without denying the past.

Next came Jahn's sleek, curving Xerox Center of white metal and reflective glass, at Monroe and Dearborn streets (1980). Mirrored glass, introduced by Jahn, has become one of the favorite materials in new Chicago commerical buildings. It is successful as a foil to the dark Miesian buildings, especially along the river, where it seems to take on a watery quality on an overcast day. His latest accomplishment is the elegant but playful high-tech United Airlines Terminal 1 at O'Hare (1987). The terminal has been praised as a soaring technological celebration of travel, in the same splendid tradition as the 19th-century European iron and glass railroad stations that Jenney had studied.

Two disparate threads of architectural creation are weaving the modern tissue of Chicago, providing aesthetic tension and dynamism, much as in the period following the World's Columbian Exposition of 1893. The solid, muscular past provides an armature that can support diversity and even fantasy without cracking apart. Yet Chicago is a down-to-earth place whose greatest creations have been products of a no-nonsense approach. "The business of Chicago is business"; when Chicago becomes self-consciously "cultural," it fares less well.

Chicago is a city with a sense of continuity, where the traditions of design are strong. Money and technology have long provided a firm support for free and original intellectual thought, with a strong populist local bias. Chicagoans talk of having a "second city" mentality, yet at the same time they have a strong sense of self; perhaps being "second" has indeed freed them to be themselves.

# 3 Exploring Chicago

Chicago's variety is dazzling. The canyons of the Loop bustle with bankers, lawyers, traders, brokers, politicians, and wheeler-dealers of all kinds, transacting their business in buildings that make architecture buffs swoon. Equally busy but sunnier is the Near North (near the Loop, that is), where the smart shops of Michigan Avenue give way on either side to the headquarters of myriad trade associations, advertising agencies, one of the nation's leading teaching hospitals, and cathedrals of the Roman Catholic and Episcopal churches.

Cultural life flourishes. The Schubert, Blackstone, and Goodman theaters, the Chicago bases for Broadway-scale shows, have been joined by more than 40 little theaters based in the neighborhoods, where young actors polish their skills. The art galleries of Ontario and Superior streets are alive and well, augmented by a large new neighborhood of galleries in resurgent River North. The Lyric Opera has extended its season into January, offering nine productions annually that play to houses averaging 95% full; Chicago Opera Theatre augments the Lyric's offerings with a spring season of smaller works. Chicago Symphony subscriptions are a sellout; the Ravinia Festival and the Grant Park Concerts pack people in. Music lovers hungry for more turn to smaller performing groups: the Orchestra of Illinois, Music of the Baroque, the Chicago Brass Ensemble, Concertante di Chicago, and dozens more.

The city's skyline is one of the most exciting in the world. In the last two decades the Sears tower, the Amoco Building, the John Hancock Building, The Associates Center, the NBC Building, Illinois Center, 333 West Wacker, the CNA Building, Lake Point Towers, and other structures have joined such legendary structures as the Fisher Building, the Robie House, and the Rookery.

Leave downtown and the lakefront, however, and you soon encounter a city of neighborhoods: bungalows, two-flats, three-flats, and six-flats, churches and shopping strips with signs in Polish, Spanish, Chinese, Arabic, Hebrew, or Korean, and an ethnic community life that remains vibrant.

The neighborhoods are the part of Chicago that a visitor rarely sees. Yet it is in the neighborhoods that one can encounter the life of ordinary people, enjoy a great ethnic feast for a pittance, and visit the museums and churches that house cultural artifacts reflecting the soul and spirit of the community. The Chicago of the neighborhoods is the underpinning of the world-class city, and both must be experienced to understand the real Chicago.

In the tours that follow, we explore in depth the many faces of Chicago. We'll begin **Downtown,** in the heart of the world-class city, visiting handsome old landmark buildings and shimmering new ones, the centers of business and trade and the mainstays of culture, new residential areas and renewed older districts. Our visit to **Downtown South** shows how old forms take on new functions that merge with the life of the central city.

Then we'll head south to **Hyde Park and Kenwood,** home of the University of Chicago. We'll see turn-of-the-century mansions and workingmen's cottages, we'll look at the process of urban renewal and the changes it has wrought in the neighborhood,

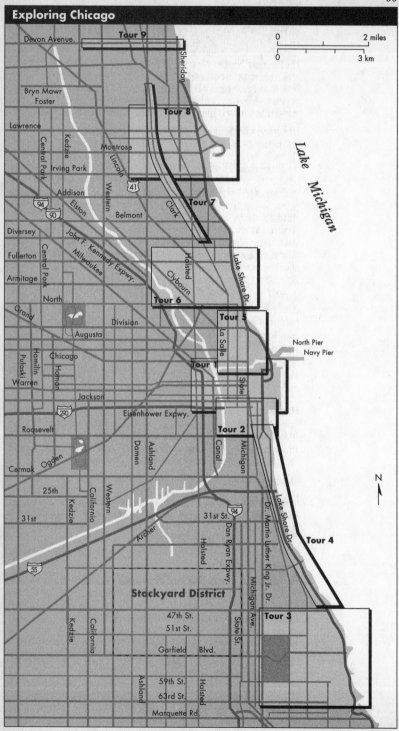

# Exploring Chicago

Tour 9

Tour 8

Tour 7

Tour 6

Tour 5

Tour 1

Tour 2

Tour 3

Tour 4

0    2 miles

0    3 km

Lake Michigan

Devon Avenue

Sheridan

Bryn Mawr
Foster

Lawrence

Central Park

Kedzie

Montrose

Lincoln

Western

Irving Park

Addison

Elston

Belmont

Clark

Diversey

Fullerton

Central Park

Milwaukee

Armitage

John F. Kennedy Expwy.

North

Halsted

Clybourn

Grand

Division

Lake Shore Dr.

Augusta

La Salle

Hamlin

Chicago

Homan

State

Pulaski

Warren

Jackson

North Pier

Navy Pier

Eisenhower Expwy.

Roosevelt

Michigan

Canal

Cermak    Ogden

25th

Damen

Ashland

Western

California

Kedzie

31st

Archer

31st St.

Dan Ryan Expwy.

Lake Shore Dr.

Dr. Martin Luther King Jr. Dr.

Halsted

Stockyard District

47th St.

51st St.

Michigan Ave.

State St.

Kedzie

California

Garfield    Blvd.

Ashland

59th St.

63rd St.

Halsted

Marquette Rd.

N

and we'll ramble through museums, churches, and bookstores. We'll head north again via **South Lake Shore Drive,** viewing Chicago's splendid skyline along the way.

In the **Near North,** we'll explore the riches of **Michigan Avenue** and the side streets of **Streeterville,** then proceed to **River North,** to see how the rehabilitation process has transformed an area of factories and warehouses into a neighborhood of up-scale shopping strips and more than 50 art galleries.

In **Lincoln Park,** we'll visit the campuses of the old McCormick Seminary and De Paul University. Then we'll head up North Lincoln Avenue for a stop at the historic Biograph Theatre and a look at the shops. We'll explore the Old Town Triangle, visiting one of the oldest streets in Chicago and one of the most expensive and contrasting the religious expressions found in St. Michael's Church with those at the Midwest Buddhist Temple. Finally, we'll look at the oldest park in Chicago's "emerald necklace."

We'll take a bus or a car the length of **North Clark Street** to see how the continuing waves of immigration leave their mark on the face of the city.

Further north, we'll visit **Argyle Street and Uptown** for a brief look at how the immigrant Vietnamese have created a very American economic miracle in one of Chicago's most depressed neighborhoods.

Finally, we'll visit **Devon Avenue** on the city's far north side to see how immigrants from the Indian subcontinent live virtually side by side with Orthodox Jews newly arrived from Russia. Here we'll find different customs and cultures in juxtaposition, and we'll sample their ethnic cuisines.

## Highlights for First-time Visitors

**Art Institute** (Tour 1: Downtown)

**Field Museum of Natural History**
(Tour 4: South Lake Shore Drive)

**Shedd Aquarium** (Tour 4: South Lake Shore Drive)

**Chicago Historical Society** (Tour 6: Lincoln Park)

**Water Tower** (Tour 5: Near North)

**Museum of Science and Industry**
(Tour 3: Hyde Park and Kenwood)

**Grant Park** (Tour 2: Downtown South)

**Picasso sculpture in Daley Center** (Tour 1: Downtown)

**Door of Carson Pirie Scott building** (Tour 1: Downtown)

**Lobbies of The Rookery and the Board of Trade**
(Tour 1: Downtown)

**The Robie House** (Tour 3: Hyde Park and Kenwood)

## Tour 1: Downtown

*Numbers in the margin correspond to points of interest on the Tour 1: Downtown map.*

Downtown Chicago is a city lover's delight. It comprises the area south of the Chicago River, west of Lake Michigan, and north of the Congress Parkway/Eisenhower Expressway. Downtown Chicago's western boundary used to be the Chicago River, but the boundary continues to push westward even as this book is written. Handsome new skyscrapers line every foot of South Wacker Drive east and west of the river, and investors have sent construction crews across the bridges in search of more land to fuel the expansion.

We begin our tour on North Michigan Avenue at South Water Street. You can reach it from the north via the No. 2, 3, 11, 145, 146, 147, 151, or 157 bus; get off before the bridge, cross it, and walk the short block to South Water Street. Coming from the south, you can take the No. 3, 6, 56, 141, 145, 146, 147, 151, or 157 bus; get off at Lake Street and walk one block north to South Water Street. If you arrive by car, you'll want to park it, for this tour is best done on foot. If possible, take this tour on a weekday; the lobbies of many of the office buildings discussed here are closed on weekends, and these interiors are some of the most interesting sights in the Loop.

On the southwest corner of the intersection stands the elegant **1** Art Deco **Carbide and Carbon Building** (233 N. Michigan Ave.). Designed by the Burnham Brothers in 1929, its sleek gold and black exterior is accented by curving, almost lacy brasswork at the entrance. Inside, the lobby is splendid, with more burnished brass, glass ornamentation, and marble.

Walk south on Michigan Avenue, turn right on Lake Street, **2** and continue to State Street and the north end of the **State Street Mall.** Built a decade ago with federal funds, the mall was intended to revive the faltering State Street shopping strip by providing trees, sculptures, and outdoor cafés to encourage shoppers to visit the area and patronize the stores. Because of restrictions on the federal grant, however, the street could not be made a true pedestrian mall; closed to private vehicles, it remained open to police cars, emergency vehicles, and buses. The mall has been a spectacular failure. The improvements and amenities were minimal: The new hexagonal gray concrete bricks are no more appealing than the original sidewalk, the few pieces of sculpture are undistinguished, and the outdoor cafés fail to thrive amid the exhaust fumes of the buses. The exodus of better stores to North Michigan Avenue and elsewhere has continued.

Turn left onto this urban paradise and walk half a block to the **Chicago Theatre** (175 N. State St.). Threatened with demolition a few years ago, the 70-year-old theater was saved through the efforts of a civic-minded consortium that bought the building and oversaw a multimillion-dollar restoration. It has had several different managers who have been unable to make the theater a financial success. National tours of singers, musicals, **3** and variety acts are booked sporadically. Next door, the **Page Brothers Building** is one of only two buildings in Chicago known to have a cast-iron front wall. Notice the delicate detail work on the horizontal and vertical bands between the windows. The building behind the facade, now being renovated, will become part of a new Chicago Theatre complex. Notice also the very handsome building, directly across State Street, that houses WLS-TV.

**❹** Continue south, turn left on Randolph Street, and walk to Michigan Avenue. On the northwest corner, the **Associates Center** (150 N. Michigan Ave.), the office building with the distinctive diamond-shape, angled face visible for miles, is the first building in Chicago to be wired for computer use (outlets in every office eliminate the need for costly cabling). An amusing sculpture sits in its small plaza.

**❺** Two blocks east, the **Amoco Building** (200 E. Randolph St.), formerly the Standard Oil Building, was for a short time the largest marble-clad building in the world. Unfortunately, the thin slabs of marble, unable to withstand Chicago's harsh climate, began to warp and fall off soon after the building was completed. A two-year, $60-million project to replace the marble with light-colored granite was scheduled to be completed in 1992. The building looks as striking as it did before, but its massive presence is best viewed from a distance. The building sits on a handsome but rather sterile plaza, and Harry Bertoia's wind chime sculpture in the reflecting pool makes interesting sounds when the wind blows. Next door is the **Prudential Building**, replaced as Chicago's tallest building in the late '60s by the John Hancock. Behind it rises a postmodern spire added in 1990.

**❻** Return west on Randolph Street to Michigan Avenue, walk south a block, and turn right on East Washington Street, to the **Chicago Public Library Cultural Center** (78 E. Washington St., tel. 312/269–2900). When you've stepped inside the Romanesque-style entrance, notice the marble and the mosaic work before you climb the curving stairway to the third floor. There you will see a splendid back-lit Tiffany dome, restored during the 1977 renovation of the building. This is Preston Bradley Hall, used for public events. Other parts of the building were modeled on Venetian and ancient Greek elements. If you love Tiffany domes, you will find another one on the second floor. More than an architectural marvel, the Cultural Center offers concerts, permanent collections, and changing exhibitions. A foreign-language reading room stocks newspapers and periodicals from around the world. Civil War buffs will enjoy the artifacts on display in the Grand Army of the Republic room.

**❼** Turn right on leaving the Cultural Center from the Washington Street side, walk to Wabash Avenue, and enter **Marshall Field & Co.** (111 N. State St.). This mammoth store, now undergoing a massive renovation, boasts some 500 departments, and it's a great place for a snack (the Crystal Palace ice cream parlor) or a meal (the grand Walnut Room or Hinky Dink Kenna's in the basement). Another spectacular Tiffany dome can be found on Field's southwest corner, near State and Washington streets. The renovation, close to completion at press time, suffered a setback when the store's sub-basements were damaged in last year's flood. But the project, which includes rearranged departments and cleaned and refreshed interiors, should be finished by the time you read this.

**❽** Further west on Washington Street, we come to the **Chicago Temple** (77 W. Washington St.), whose beautiful spire can be seen only at some distance (the bridge across the river at Dearborn Street is a good spot for viewing it). In the plaza is Joan Miró's sculpture *Chicago* (1982).

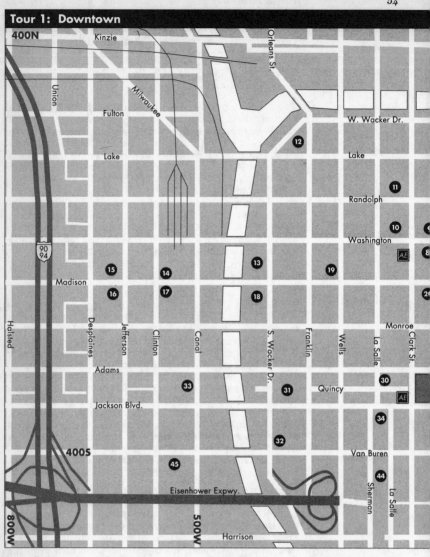

## Tour 1: Downtown

Amoco Building, **5**
Art Institute of Chicago, **23**
Associates Center, **4**
AT&T Building, **17**
Auditorium Theatre, **41**
Berghoff Restaurant, **28**

Buckingham Fountain, **42**
Carbide and Carbon Building, **1**
Carson Pirie Scott, **22**
Chicago Board of Trade, **34**
Chicago City Hall-Cook County Building, **10**
Chicago Mercantile Exchange, **18**

Chicago Public Library Cultural Center, **6**
Chicago Temple, **8**
Civic Opera House, **13**
CNA Building, **38**
Daley Center, **9**
*Dawn Shadows*, **19**
Federal Center and Plaza, **29**

Fine Arts Building, **40**
First National Bank Plaza, **20**
Fisher Building, **36**
Harold Washington Library Center, **37**
Main Post Office, **45**
Marquette Building, **27**
Marshall Field & Co., **7**

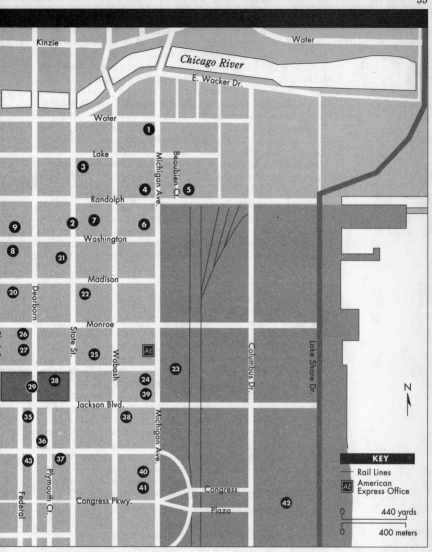

Kinzie

Water

*Chicago River*

E. Wacker Dr.

Water

❶

Lake

❸

Michigan Ave.

Beaubien Ct.

❹ ❺

Randolph

❾ ❷ ❼ ❻

Washington

❽ ㉑

Madison

⑳ ㉒

Dearborn

Monroe

㉖ ㉗ ㉕ State St. Wabash [AE] ㉓

Columbus Dr.

Lake Shore Dr.

㉔ ㊴ ㉙ ㉘

Jackson Blvd.

㉟ ㊳ ㊱ ㊲ ㊳ ㊴ ㊵ ㊶

Michigan Ave.

Plymouth Ct.

Federal

Congress

Congress Pkwy. Plaza ㊷

N

**KEY**

— Rail Lines

[AE] American Express Office

0 ——— 440 yards

0 ——— 400 meters

**⑨** Directly opposite is the **Daley Center,** named for the late Mayor Richard J. Daley, where the Cook County court system is head-quartered. The building is constructed of a steel known as Corten, which was developed as a medium that would weather naturally and attractively (and weathering has certainly im-proved its appearance). In the plaza is a sculpture by Picasso that is made of the same material. Known simply as "the Picas-so," it provoked an outcry when it was installed in 1967. Specu-lation about what it is meant to represent (knowledgeable observers say it is the head of a woman; others have suggested it is a pregnant cow) has diminished but not ended. In the plaza, as well, is an eternal flame dedicated to the memory of the American soldiers who died in Korea and Vietnam. In summer-time the plaza hosts concerts, dance presentations, and a week-ly farmer's market.

Directly across Clark Street from the Daley Center is the **⑩ Chicago City Hall–Cook County Building,** a handsome neo-classical structure designed by Holabird and Roche in 1911 whose appearance is generally ignored by the citizens who rush in and out to do business with the City. Inside are spacious halls, high ceilings, plenty of marble, and lots of hot air, for this is where the Chicago City Council holds its infamous meetings.

Head north on Clark for a block and you'll reach the much-**⑪** discussed **State of Illinois Center** (100 W. Randolph St.). Gover-nor James Thompson, who personally selected the Helmut Jahn design for the building, hailed it in his dedication speech in 1985 as "the first building of the twenty-first century." Those who work there, and many ordinary Chicagoans as well, have groaned in response, "I hope not." It is difficult to say more about the design of the building than to point out that it presents multiple shapes and faces. Narrow alternating verti-cal strips of mirrored and plain glass give the impression of taf-feta streamers flying from a giant maypole. Some people love it and some do not; the structure's sky blue, white, and red exte-rior colors have elicited such adjectives as "garish" and "tacky" from viewers. Its enormous interior atrium embraces a volume of 8 million cubic feet. The dramatically patterned circular floor at its base and the soaring vistas, with handsome exposed ele-vators and a sky-lit glass dome, are impressive.

On the northwest corner of Randolph and Clark streets stands *Monument to a Standing Beast,* a sculpture by Jean Dubuffet. Its curved shapes, in white with black traceries, set against the curving red, white, and blue of the center, merely add to the visual cacophony. In another setting it might be a pleasing and enjoyable work.

Now let's look at a building roughly contemporary to the State of Illinois Center that has had a very different public reception. Head west on Randolph Street, turn right on La Salle Street, left on Lake Street, and walk two blocks to Franklin Street. **⑫** The building at **333 West Wacker Drive,** designed by Kohn, Pe-dersen, Fox in 1983 and constructed on a triangular plot, is a softly curving building with forest green marble columns, a spacious plaza, and a shimmering green glass skin. Its unprom-isingly irregular shape, dictated by the parcel on which it sits, is particularly lovely seen at sunset from the bridge over the Chicago River at Orleans Street, when the river and surround-ing buildings are mirrored in the glass.

A two-block walk south on Wacker Drive will take you to the
⑬ **Civic Theatre** and, a bit farther on, the **Civic Opera House** (20 N.
Wacker Dr., tel. 312/346–0270), where Chicago's Lyric Opera
gives its performances. Built by the utilities magnate and ma-
nipulator Samuel Insull, the handsome Art Deco building is
also an elegant older office building. The Civic Opera House is
very grand indeed, with marble floors and pillars in the main
hall, crystal chandeliers, and a marvelous sweeping staircase to
the second floor. Lyric Opera performances are oversubscribed
(subscriptions are willed to succeeding generations), so you
can't expect simply to drop in on one of the productions during
the season that runs from late-September through January.
Nevertheless, if you stop by the corner of Madison Street and
Wacker Drive early on the evening of a performance, you may
find ticket holders with the extra ticket to sell.

We'll turn right onto Madison Street and continue west to Clin-
⑭ ton Street and the eastern end of the smashing **Northwestern
Atrium Center** (500 W. Madison St.), which replaced the old
Northwestern Station and serves as one of several stations
throughout the city for commuter trains to outlying suburban
areas. The building combines a boxlike office tower with glass
half-cylinders piled one atop the other at the lower levels.
Broad contrasting horizontal bands of mirrored and smoked
glass alternate up the building for a ribbon effect that is reminiscent of a similar theme—by the same architects—at the
State of Illinois Center. Inside, the marble floors and exposed
girders, painted a soft grayish blue, remind you of the appearance of the grand old railroad stations in this country and in Europe. The girders seen against the rippling exterior glass make
beautiful geometric patterns. The area over the entrance simu-
lates a rose window in steel and clear glass. The gates to the
tracks, elevated above street level to allow street traffic to proceed east and west via underpasses, are reached by going up
one level and heading to the north end of the building. Go up
another flight for a grand view northward looking out over the
tracks; this level is the entrance to the office spaces of the building.

⑮ One block west is the **Social Security Building** (600 W. Madison
St.), once a distant outpost in a dangerous neighborhood that
was selected by the federal government because it was a low-
rent district. Today the structure is one of several good-looking
contemporary and renovated buildings in the area. Of interest
here is the Claes Oldenburg sculpture *Batcolumn*, a gigantic
baseball bat that failed to get critical acclaim when it was un-
veiled in 1977. Yet a 100-foot-high baseball bat is an amusing
sight, and the current development west of the river will allow
even more people the opportunity for a twice-daily smile at this
whimsical construction.

Directly across from the *Batcolumn* are the buildings that
⑯ make up the **Presidential Towers** residences. The easternmost
and main building of the four is at 555 West Madison Street.
Best seen from a distance, these attractive, if not architectural-
ly distinguished, structures have lured some suburbanites
back to the city and persuaded other young adults not to move
away. The amenities are good: an upscale supermarket, several
fast food restaurants, a drug store, and other shops catering to
the daily needs of the residents. The complex extends west to
Desplaines Street and south to Monroe Street, with the build-

ings aligned on a southwesterly diagonal. At press time, the developers were threatened with foreclosure on some government loans because of their failure to provide low-income housing as was stipulated in their loan agreements.

To the east of Presidential Towers, just opposite the Northwestern Atrium Center, is the ugly, windowless, poured-concrete **AT&T Building.** All that can be said in its defense is that when it was built, it must have seemed unlikely that visitors would stray so far from the heart of downtown.

As you recross the river on Madison Street, regard the pale grape colored buildings to your right; they are the twin towers of the **Chicago Mercantile Exchange** (10 and 30 S. Wacker Dr.). The visitor's gallery of the Merc, open weekdays from 7:30 AM to 3:15 PM, looks down on the frenetic activity on the trading floor. Here is where hog belly futures (they have to do with the supermarket price of bacon), soybeans, and dollars are traded on national and international markets.

Stop at the northwest corner of Madison and Wells streets for a look at a Louise Nevelson sculpture of 1983—a vigorous, forceful construction of darkened steel incongruously titled *Dawn Shadows.*

Farther along Madison Street, the **First National Bank of Chicago,** designed by Perkins and Will in 1973, was a sensation when it was built because this structure slopes upward from its base in a shape that looks like an ornate letter A. Today it's just another good-looking downtown office building. On your left is the very different recent addition to the First National complex, 3 **First National Plaza.**

Now turn right onto Dearborn Street. Halfway down the block is the famous **First National Bank Plaza,** which runs the length of the block from Dearborn to Clark streets. In the summer the plaza is the site of outdoor performances by musicians and dancers and a hangout for picnickers and tanners. In any season you can visit the Chagall mosaic known as *The Four Seasons* (1974) at the northeast end of the plaza, between Madison and Monroe streets on Dearborn Street. It is said that when Chagall arrived in Chicago to install the mosaic, he found it a more vigorous city than he had remembered, and he began immediately to modify the work to reflect the stronger and more vital elements he found around him. Not one of Chagall's greatest works, it is nevertheless a pretty, pleasing, sometimes lyrical piece.

If you continue east on Madison Street and turn left on State Street, you'll come to the **Reliance Building** (32 N. State St.). Designed by Daniel Burnham in 1890, it was innovative for its time in its use of glass as well as terra-cotta for its exterior, and once it was quite beautiful. Today, the building is not much to look at; the street level houses the kind of sleazy shop that is typical of State Street, and the whole building needs a good cleaning.

Return to Madison Street to find **Carson Pirie Scott** (1 S. State St.), known to architecture students as one of Louis Sullivan's outstanding works. The building illustrates the Chicago Window, a large fixed central window with smaller movable windows on each side. Notice also the fine exterior ornamentation at street level, particularly the exquisite work over the entrance on the southeast corner of Madison and State streets. Dedicated shoppers may be less interested in the architecture of the building than in its contents; Chicago's "second" department store (always mentioned after Marshall Field & Co.) would be a standout anywhere else. Its Corporate Level offers tasteful clothing for male and female executives, while its main-floor InPulse store lures the teenage set.

From the south end of Carson's, head east on Monroe Street and south on Michigan Avenue to Adams Street and the imposing entrance to the marvelous **Art Institute of Chicago.** You'll recognize the Art Institute by its guardian lions on each side of the entrance. (The lions have a special place in the hearts of Chicagoans, who outfitted them with Chicago Bears helmets when the Bears won the Superbowl.) A map of the museum, available at the Information Desk, will help you find your way to the works or periods you want to visit. The Art Institute has outstanding collections of Medieval and Renaissance paintings as well as Impressionist and Postimpressionist works. Less well-known are its fine holdings in Asian art and its photography collection. Be sure to visit the Rubloff paperweight collection; a Chicago real estate magnate donated these shimmering, multicolored functional objects. The Thorne Miniature Rooms show interior decoration in every historical style; they'll entrance anyone who's ever furnished a dollhouse or built a model. And don't miss the Stock Exchange room, a splendid reconstruction of a part of the old Chicago Stock Exchange, which was demolished in 1972. The Daniel F. and Ada L. Rice Building, opened in September 1988, has three floors of exhibition galleries, a large space for temporary exhibitions, and a skylit central court dotted with sculpture and plantings.

If you have a youngster with you, make an early stop at the Children's Museum downstairs. Your child will be given a set of Gallery Games, including "I Spy" (which challenges small folk to locate particular works in the museum's collections), "Scrutinize" (which includes a set of postcards to be taken home), and "Bits and Pieces." The delightful and informative games will keep your youngster from becoming hopelessly bored as you tramp through the galleries. The museum store has an outstanding collection of art books, calendars, merchandise related to current exhibits, and an attractive selection of gift items. When you're ready for refreshments, the Institute provides a cafeteria, a dining room serving Continental cuisine, and a terrace café (in warm weather). *S. Michigan Ave. at Adams St., tel. 312/443-3600. Admission: $6 adults, $3 children and senior citizens, free Tues. Open weekdays 10:30-4:30 (Tues. until 8), Sat. 10-5, Sun. noon-5. Closed Christmas Day.*

**Time Out** From Memorial Day to mid-September, an outdoor **café** in the **Art Institute's courtyard** is a charming spot for lunch. In more inclement weather, there's a **cafeteria** offering snacks and family fare; a more upscale **restaurant** was scheduled to open in early 1993.

**Orchestra Hall** (220 S. Michigan Ave., tel. 312/435-6666), opposite the Art Institute, is the home of the internationally acclaimed Chicago Symphony Orchestra. Don't expect to find symphony tickets at the box office; subscription sales exhaust virtually all the available tickets. (You'll have better luck at

hearing the symphony during the summer if you make the trek
to Ravinia Park in the suburb of Highland Park.) Sometimes it
pays to stop by Orchestra Hall about an hour before a concert;
there may be last-minute ticket returns at the box office, or
there may be street-corner vendors. If you'd like to see the inside of Orchestra Hall, regardless of who's performing, buy a
ticket to one of the recitals that are scheduled frequently, particularly on Sunday afternoons. For an incredible view, get a
balcony ticket. The balconies are layered one atop the other in
dramatic fashion, and because the seats are steeply banked,
the view is splendid and the acoustics are excellent.

**②⑤** The **Palmer House** (17 E. Monroe St., tel. 312/726–7500), one of
Chicago's grand old hotels, is reached by returning to Adams
Street and proceeding west one block. Cross Wabash Avenue,
turn right, and enter about halfway down the block. The
ground-floor level is an arcade with patterned marble floors
and antique lighting fixtures where you'll find upscale shops,
restaurants, and service establishments. But it's the lobby—
up one flight of stairs—that you must see: Richly carpeted,
outfitted with fine furniture, and lavishly decorated (look at
the ceiling murals), this room is one of the few remaining examples of the opulent elegance that was once de rigueur in
Chicago's fine hotels.

Exit the Palmer House on the State Street side, walk north to
**②⑥** Monroe Street, and turn left. The **Xerox Building** (55 W. Monroe St.) was designed in 1982 by the same firm (Murphy/Jahn)
that would be responsible three years later for the State of Illinois Center. The building's wraparound aluminum and glass
wall extends from the Monroe Street entrance around the corner onto Dearborn Street, communicating both vitality and
beauty.

Now head south half a block on Dearborn Street. The
**②⑦** **Marquette Building** (140 S. Dearborn St.) of 1894, by Holabird
and Roche, features an exterior terra-cotta bas relief and interior reliefs and mosaics depicting scenes from early Chicago
history.

Continue south to Adams Street and then jog a bit eastward to
**②⑧** have a look at the westernmost building of the **Berghoff Restaurant** (17 W. Adams St.). Although at first glance it appears as
though the front is masonry, it is in fact ornamental cast iron.
The practice of using iron panels cast to imitate stone was common in the latter part of the 19th century (this building was
constructed in 1872), but this building and the **Page Brothers
Building** on State Street, built in the same year, are the only
examples known to have survived. The iron front on the
Berghoff building was discovered only a few years ago, and other such buildings may yet be extant, waiting to be found.

**②⑨** Return now to Dearborn Street and the **Federal Center and Plaza.** The twin Federal Buildings, the Kluczyinski (219 S. Dearborn St.) and the Dirksen (230 S. Dearborn St.), built in 1964,
are classic examples of the trademark Mies van der Rohe glass
and steel box. In the plaza, on the southwest side of Dearborn
and Adams streets, is the wonderful Calder stabile *Flamingo*,
dedicated on the same day in 1974 as Calder's *Universe* at the
Sears Tower. It is said that Calder had a grand day, riding
through Chicago in a brightly colored circus bandwagon accompanied by calliopes, heading from one dedication to the other.

㉚ Continue west on Adams Street. At La Salle Street is **The Rookery** (209 S. La Salle St.), an imposing redstone building designed in 1886 by Burnham and Root. The Rookery was built partly of masonry and partly of the more modern steel frame construction. The magnificent lobby was remodeled in 1905 by Frank Lloyd Wright. The building has recently reopened following a $2.5 million renovation that restored the Rookery's airy marble and gold-leaf lobby to its 1905 appearance. The result is a marvelous and lighthearted space that should not be missed.

Cross La Salle Street and head west on the little two-block lane called Quincy Street. At its terminus on Franklin you will be ㉛ directly opposite the entrance to the **Sears Tower** (233 S. Wacker Dr.). A Skidmore, Owings & Merrill design of 1974, Sears Tower has 110 stories and is almost 1,500 feet tall. Although this is the world's tallest building, it certainly isn't the world's most livable one. Despite costly improvements to the Wacker Drive entrance (most of the street traffic is on the Franklin Street side) and the main floor arcade area, the building doesn't really attract the passerby.

Once inside, you'll probably be baffled by the escalators and elevators that stop on alternate floors (the elevators have double cars, one atop the other, so that when one car has stopped, say, at 22, the other is at 21). If you need to go to the upper reaches of the building (other than to go via direct express elevator to the 103rd-floor Skydeck), you'll find that you have to leave one elevator bank, walk down the hall and around a corner, and find another to complete your trip. Stories have been told about new employees on the upper stories spending their entire lunch hour trying to find a way out. In high winds the building sways noticeably at the upper levels and, most alarming, in 1988 there were two occasions on which windows were blown out. According to the architects and engineers, the odds against this happening even once were astronomical; imagine how red their faces must have been the second time it happened. When it did happen, the streets surrounding the building were littered with shards of glass, and papers were sucked out of offices that had lost their windows. On a clear day, however, the view from the Skydeck is unbeatable. (Check the visibility ratings at the security desk before you decide to ride up and take it in.) And don't miss the Calder mobile sculpture *Universe* in the lobby on the Wacker Drive side.

㉜ A block south on Wacker Drive is **311 South Wacker Drive,** designed by Kohn Pedersen Fox and completed in 1990. This tower is the first of three intended for the site; the other two are on hold until the economy picks up. The building's most distinctive feature is the "white castle" crown, which is blindingly lighted at night. (During migration season so many birds killed themselves crashing into the illuminated tower that the building management was forced to tone down the lighting, though it wasn't turned off.) The interior has a spectacular winter garden atrium entry with palm trees: a perfect spot for lunch in the colder months.

From the south end of the Sears Tower we'll head west on Jackson Boulevard and across the river to Canal Street. The wonderful old (1917) **Union Station** (210 S. Canal St.) is everything a ㉝ train station should be, with a 10-story dome over the main waiting room, a skylight, columns, and gilded statues. Amtrak trains arrive and depart here.

**34** We return east on Jackson to the **Chicago Board of Trade** (141 W. Jackson), one of the few important Art Deco buildings in Chicago (the Civic Opera House and the Carbide and Carbon building are the others). It was designed in 1930 by the firm of Holabird and Roche; at the top is a gilded statue of Ceres, the Greek goddess of grain, an apt overseer of the frenetic commodities trading that goes on within. The observation deck that overlooks the trading floor is open to the public weekdays, 9 AM–2 PM. The lobby is well worth your attention.

Farther east, taking up a good portion of the block from Jackson Boulevard to Van Buren Street, is the massive, darkly handsome
**35** **Monadnock Building** (53 W. Jackson Blvd.). The north half was built by Burnham and Root in 1891, the south half by Holabird and Roche in 1893. This is the tallest building ever constructed entirely of masonry. The problem with all-masonry buildings is that the higher they go, the thicker the walls at the base must be to support the upper stories, and the Monadnock's walls at the base are six feet thick. Thus you can see why the introduction of the steel frame began a new era in construction. The building was recently and tastefully renovated inside (the original wrought-iron banisters, for example, have been retained) and cleaned outside, restoring it to its former magnificence from the rather dilapidated and slightly creepy hulk it had become. This is a popular office building for lawyers because of its proximity to the federal courts in the Kluczynski Building.

**36** Across the street is the **Fisher Building** (343 S. Dearborn St.), designed by D. H. Burnham & Co. in 1896. This Gothic-style building, exquisitely ornamented in terra-cotta, is for some reason (perhaps because of favorable rents) the headquarters of dozens of arts and other not-for-profit organizations. Turn left onto Van Buren Street for a view of the beautifully carved cherubs frolicking over what was once a side entrance to the building, now glassed in.

Taking up the entire block between Van Buren and Congress
**37** streets, the new **Harold Washington Library Center** is a postmodern homage to classical-style public buildings. Chosen from six proposals submitted to a design competition, the granite and brick structure has some of the most spectacular terracotta work seen in Chicago since the 19th century: ears of corn, faces with puffed cheeks (representing the Windy City), and the logo of the Chicago Public Library are a few of the building's embellishments. In its final stages of construction, the building looked so much like the vintage skyscrapers around it that visitors mistook it for a renovation project. The Center's holdings include more than 2 million books and special collections on Chicago Theater, Chicago Blues, and the Civil War. For a special treat, check out the children's library on the second floor, an 18,000-square-foot haven for the city's youngsters that includes a charming storytelling alcove. The primary architect was Thomas Beeby, of the Chicago firm Hammond Beeby Babka, who now heads the School of Architecture at Yale University. *400 S. State St., tel. 312/747–4300. Admission free. Open Mon.–Thurs. 9–7, Fri.–Sat. 9–5. 45-minute tours given daily at 10 and 2.*

Proceed east again on Jackson Boulevard to Wabash Avenue for
**38** a look at the rust-color **CNA Building.** On no one's list of landmarks, the structure is interesting principally because it
leaves such a noticeable mark on the skyline. Chicagoans who
thought the color was an undercoat of rustproofing paint that
would be covered over by something more conventional were
wrong.

Farther along Jackson Boulevard, at Michigan Avenue, is the
**39** **Railway Exchange Building** (80 E. Jackson Blvd.; enter on
Michigan Ave.), better known as the Santa Fe building, because of the large "Santa Fe" sign atop it that is part of the
nighttime skyline. Designed in 1904 by Daniel Burnham, who
later had his office there, it underwent an extensive and very
successful renovation a few years ago. The interior atrium is
spectacular. The ArchiCenter, where Chicago Architecture
Foundation tours originate, is located here.

**40** One block south is the **Fine Arts Building** (410 S. Michigan
Ave.). Notice first the handsome detailing on the exterior of
the building; then step inside to see the marble and the woodwork in the lobby. The motto engraved in the marble as you enter says, "All passes—art alone endures." The building once
housed artists and sculptors in its studios; today its principal
tenants are professional musicians and those who cater to musicians' needs. A fine little music shop is hidden away on the
ninth floor, and violin makers and other instrument repair
shops are sprinkled about. The building has an interior courtyard, across which strains of piano music and soprano voices
compete with tenors as they run through exercises and arias.
The ground floor of the building, originally the Studebaker
Theatre (the building was constructed to house the showrooms
of the Studebaker Co., then makers of carriages), was converted into four cinemas in 1982, and the individual theaters
have preserved much of the beautiful ornamentation of the
original. The Fine Arts Theatres are an asset to the city for
their exceptional selection of foreign films, art films, and movies by independent directors.

Continue on Michigan Avenue to the Congress Parkway and
**Roosevelt University,** a massive building that houses the re-
**41** markable **Auditorium Theatre** (430 S. Michigan Ave.). Built in
1889 by Dankmar Adler and Louis Sullivan, the hall seats 4,000
people and has unobstructed sightlines and near-perfect acoustics. The interior ornamentation, including arched rows of
lights along the ceiling, is breathtaking. Though it's normally
closed to the public unless there's a show or concert, ask for a
tour of this elegant hall that was allowed to fall into disrepair
and even faced demolition in the 1950s and early 1960s. (Deter-
mined supporters raised $3 million to provide for the restora-
tion, which was undertaken by Harry Weese in 1967.) Another
beautiful, though less well-known, space is the library on the
10th floor of the building.

Head east on Congress Parkway to Columbus Drive and, set in
**42** its own plaza, **Buckingham Fountain.** Between Memorial Day
and Labor Day you can see it in all its glory, when it's elaborately illuminated at night.

Return west on Congress Parkway to Dearborn Street and look
ahead and to your right. The odd, triangular, poured-concrete
building looming up on the right-hand side of Clark Street is

④③ the **Metropolitan Detention Center** (71 W. Van Buren St.). A jail
(rather than a penitentiary, where convicted criminals are
sent), it holds people awaiting trial as well as those convicted
and awaiting transfer. When erected in 1975, it brought an outcry from citizens who feared large-scale escapes by dangerous
criminals. (Their fears have not been realized.) The building
was designed by the same Harry Weese who saved the Auditorium Theatre; with its long, slit windows (5 inches wide, so no
bars are required), it looks like a modern reconstruction of a
medieval fort, where slits in the walls permitted archers to
shoot at approaching invaders.

Continue west on Congress to the striking building of 1985 by
④④ Skidmore, Owings & Merrill known as **One Financial Place**
(440 S. La Salle St.), which has an exterior and interior of Italian red granite and marble. Among its striking features is the
arched section that straddles the rushing traffic on the Congress Parkway/Eisenhower Expressway below. The building's
tenants include the Midwest Stock Exchange, whose visitor's
gallery is open weekdays, 8:30–4, and the La Salle St. Club,
which offers limited but elegant hotel accommodations and is
the home of the superb Everest restaurant (*see* Chapter 6).

Another walk west across the river will take you to Chicago's
④⑤ **Main Post Office** (433 W. Van Buren St.), the world's largest.
Tours of this mammoth, highly automated facility are given
weekdays at 10:30 AM.

---

## Tour 2: Downtown South

*Numbers in the margin correspond to points of interest on the
Tour 2: Downtown South map.*

The Downtown South area, bounded by Congress Parkway/Ei-
senhower Expressway on the north, Michigan Avenue on the
east, Roosevelt Road on the south, and the Chicago River on
the west, presents a striking and often fascinating contrast to
the downtown area we have just visited. Once a thriving commercial area and the center of the printing trades in Chicago, it
fell into disrepair as the printing industry moved south in
search of lower costs. Sleazy bars, pawnbrokers, and porno-
graphic shops filled the area behind what was then the Conrad
Hilton Hotel, crowding each other on Wabash Avenue and
State Street and on the side streets between. Homeless winos
found a place to sleep at the Pacific Garden Mission (646 S.
State St.). Declining business at the mammoth Hilton meant
decreasing revenues; floors were closed off, too expensive to
maintain, and the owners considered demolishing the building.

Then, about a decade ago, investors became interested in renovating the run-down yet sturdy loft and office buildings in the
old printing district. With the first neighborhood rehab efforts
just beginning, Michael Foley, a young Chicago restaurateur
from an old Chicago restaurant family, opened a restaurant on
the edge of the redevelopment area. The innovative cuisine at
Printer's Row (*see* Chapter 6) attracted favorable notice, and
the restaurant became a success; soon other restaurants,
shops, and businesses moved in, and today the Printer's Row
district is a thriving urban neighborhood enclave.

At about the time that the first renovations were being undertaken in Printer's Row, a consortium of investors, aided by

preferential interest rates from downtown banks, obtained a
large parcel of land in the old railroad yards to the south and
put up an expansive new development. This was Dearborn
Park, affordable housing targeted at young middle-class families. Although its beginnings were rocky—the housing was attractive but there was no supermarket, no dry cleaner, and no
public school nearby—Dearborn Park, too, became successful.

To the west, the architect and developer Bertrand Goldberg (of
Marina City fame) acquired a sizable tract of land between
Wells Street and the Chicago River. Driven by a vision of an innovative, self-contained city within a city, Goldberg erected
the futuristic River City, the massed, almost cloudlike complex
that seems to rise from the river at Polk Street. This development has been less commercially successful than Dearborn
Park, yet the willingness of a developer to make an investment
of this size in the area was an indication that the neighborhood
south of downtown was here to stay.

Spurred by signs of revitalization all around, the owners of the
Conrad Hilton scrapped their plans to abandon the hotel and
instead mounted a renovation of tremendous proportion. Now
one of the most beautifully appointed hotels in the city, the Chicago Hilton and Towers once again attracts the business it
needs to fill its thousands of rooms.

We'll begin our tour of Downtown South at the corner of Balbo
Drive and Michigan Avenue. You can drive here—traffic and
parking conditions are far less congested in the Downtown
South area than they are in Downtown—or you can take the
Jeffery Express (No. 6) bus from the north (catch it at State
and Lake streets) or from Hyde Park.

❶ East of the intersection of Balbo Drive and Michigan Avenue is
the heart of beautiful **Grant Park.** On a hot summer night during the last week of August 1968, the park was filled with young
people protesting the Vietnam War and events at the Democratic presidential nominating convention that was taking
place at the Conrad Hilton Hotel down the street. Rioting
broke out; heads were cracked, protesters were dragged away
screaming, and Mayor Daley gave police the order to "shoot to
kill." Later investigations into the events of that evening deter-
mined that a "police riot"—not the misbehavior of the protesters, who had been noisy but not physically abusive—was
responsible for the violence that erupted. Those who remember those rage-filled days cannot visit this idyllic spot without
recalling that time.

Today Grant Park is a lovely mix of gardens (especially above
Monroe Street and around the fountain), tennis courts, softball
diamonds, and a field surrounding the Petrillo bandshell, at Columbus Drive and Monroe Street, where outdoor concerts are
held. While it's not as heavily used as Lincoln or Jackson parks,
Grant Park is home to several blockbuster events: the Grant
Park Society Concerts held four times a week in the summer;
notable blues, jazz, and gospel festivals; and the annual Taste
of Chicago, a vast picnic featuring foods from more than 70 restaurants that precedes a fireworks show on July 3 (*see* Festivals
and Seasonal Event in Chapter 1).

❷ The **Blackstone Hotel** (636 S. Michigan Ave.), on the northwest
corner of the intersection, is rich with history. Presidential
candidates have been selected here, and presidents have

# Tour 2: Downtown South

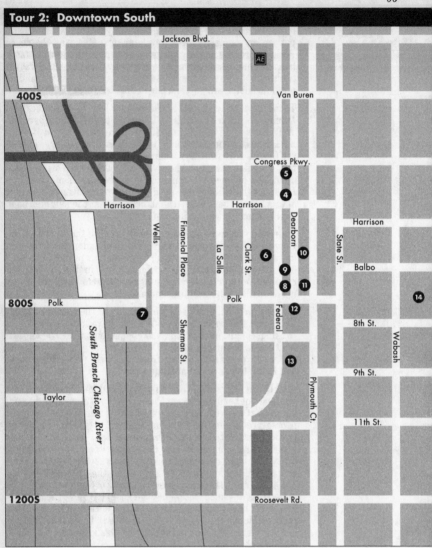

Jackson Blvd.

AE

400S

Van Buren

Congress Pkwy.

⑤

④

Harrison Harrison Harrison

Wells

Financial Place

La Salle

Clark St.

Dearborn

⑩

State St.

Balbo

⑥

⑨

⑧ ⑪

800S Polk Polk

Federal

⑦

⑫

⑭

Sherman St.

South Branch Chicago River

⑬

8th St.

Plymouth Ct.

9th St.

Wabash

Taylor

11th St.

1200S

Roosevelt Rd.

Blackstone Hotel, **2**
Chicago Hilton and Towers, **14**
Dearborn Park, **13**
Dearborn Station, **12**
Donohue Building, **11**
Franklin Building, **8**
Grace Place, **10**

Grant Park, **1**
Hyatt on Printer's Row, **5**
Printer's Row Restaurant, **4**
Printer's Square, **6**
River City, **7**
Sandmeyer's Bookstore, **9**
Spertus Museum of Judaica, **3**

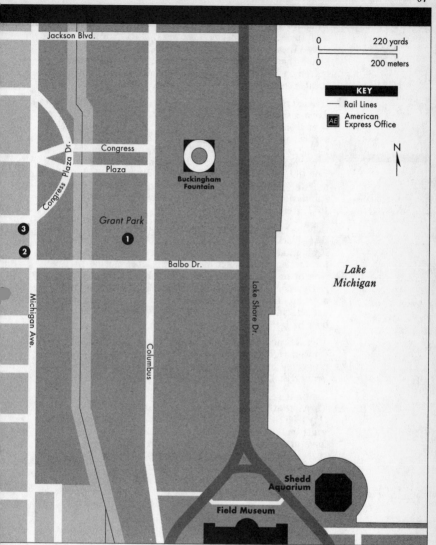

Jackson Blvd.

Congress Plaza Dr.

Congress
Plaza

Buckingham
Fountain

Grant Park

❶

❸
❷

Michigan Ave.

Balbo Dr.

Columbus

Lake Shore Dr.

Lake
Michigan

Shedd
Aquarium

Field Museum

0        220 yards

0        200 meters

KEY
— Rail Lines
Aᴇ American
Express Office

N

stayed here. Note the ornate little roofs that cap the first-floor windows. Inside, the elegant lobby has impressive chandeliers, sculptures, and handsome woodwork. Next door is the **Blackstone Theatre,** another vintage building, where Broadway-bound shows were once booked; the theater was recently acquired by De Paul University for its own use and that of local theater companies.

❸ Head north on Michigan Avenue to the **Spertus Museum of Judaica,** a small museum housed in Spertus College. The permanent collections include Medieval Jewish art, which is surprisingly like the better-known Christian art of the same period, without the central Christian themes and imagery. The museum regularly mounts exhibitions on topics broadly relevant to Judaism; a recent one displayed photographs by late author Jerzy Kosinski. *618 S. Michigan Ave., tel. 312/922–9012. Admission: $3.50 adults, $2 children. Open Sun.–Thurs. 10–5, Fri. 10–3.*

Continue to the corner of Harrison Street, turn left, and walk
❹ three blocks to Dearborn Street. The pioneering **Printer's Row Restaurant** (550 S. Dearborn St.) is a wonderful place to stop for an elegant (but not inexpensive) lunch during the week.
❺ Nearby on Dearborn Street is the **Hyatt on Printer's Row** (538 S. Dearborn St.). Beautifully appointed, the hotel is located in a group of renovated old buildings that have been interconnected. On the corner is the **Prairie Restaurant** (500 S. Dearborn St.).

Turn left and walk west to Federal Street and turn left again. On your right as you head south is a massive beige-gray brick
❻ renovated apartment complex, **Printer's Square** (640–780 S. Federal St.).

Continue south, turn west on Polk, and walk to Wells Street.
❼ Turn left at Wells Street and continue to the entrance to **River City** (800 S. Wells St.). Apartments, all with curving exterior walls (making it a bit difficult to place square or rectangular furniture), ring the circumference of the building. Interior spaces are used for shops, walkways, and tenant storage closets. The building boasts a state-of-the-art health club. The west side of River City fronts on the river, providing a splendid view for apartment dwellers on that side, and 70 spaces for mooring boats are available. If you'd like to take a tour, speak to the guard.

Taylor Street, south of the River City entrance, will take you east to Sherman Street; turn left on Sherman Street, right on Polk Street, and left on Dearborn Street. If you're driving, this is a good place to park. We'll walk up the west side of Dearborn Street to the end of the block and return on the east side.

❽ The first building on your left is the grand old **Franklin Building** (720 S. Dearborn St.), originally "The Franklin Co.: Designing, Engraving, Electrotyping" and now condominium apartments. The decorative tilework on the facade leads up to the scene over the front door, *The First Impression;* representing a medieval event, it illustrates the first application of the printer's craft. Above the entryway is the motto "The Excellence of Every Art Must Consist in the Complete Accomplishment of Its Purpose."

**⑨** Next door, **Sandmeyer's Bookstore** (714 S. Dearborn St.) has an iron stairway set with glass bricks and a fine selection of books about Chicago.

In June this street is the locale of the Printer's Row Book Fair, a weekend event where dealers offer a wide variety of books and prints and where demonstrations of the papermaking and bookbinding crafts are given. Street performers and food vendors add to the festivity.

**⑩** Across the street a rehabbed brick building is hung with banners announcing **Grace Place** (637 S. Dearborn St.). This is not the newest condo on the block but a consortium of two churches: Grace Episcopal Church and Christ the King Lutheran Church. Each of the congregations is too small to support its own church building, so the two have joined together to share facilities.

Another renovated building (705 S. Dearborn St.) houses **Paper Row,** a card and gift shop, and **Wine Plus,** a wine merchant. The distinguished **Prairie Ave. Bookshop** (707 S. Dearborn St.) concentrates on new and out-of-print books about architecture, planning, and design. These shops are part of the grand **⑪ Donohue Building,** whose main entrance is at 711 South Dearborn Street. The entrance is flanked by marble columns topped by ornately carved capitals, with tile work over the entrance set into a splendid granite arch. Note also the beautiful ironwork and woodwork in the doors and frames of the shops as you proceed south.

**Time Out**   For a quick pick-me-up, stop at the **Deli on Dearborn** (723 S. Dearborn St.) or at the **Moonraker Restaurant and Tavern** (733 S. Dearborn St.). In summer, you can sit outside at either establishment, although the cool interior of the Moonraker may be more welcome after a tramp through the city streets.

**⑫** The recently restored **Dearborn Station** (47 W. Polk St.) at the foot of Dearborn Street, designed in Romanesque-Revival style in 1885 by the New York architect Cyrus L. W. Eidlitz, has a red sandstone and red brick facade ornamented with terra-cotta. The striking features inside the station are the brass fixtures set against the cream and white walls and woodwork and the white, rust, and jade marble floor. Since its opening in 1985, Dearborn Station has been successful in attracting office tenants, less so in attracting retail tenants. At press time, the inside of the station was closed on weekends, and the future of the project is unclear.

**⑬** Walk east, turn right on Plymouth Court, and look south, where you can see **Dearborn Park.** A planned mix of high-rise, low-rise, and single-family units, some in red brick and some in white, the development has a tidy look. The residents are enthusiastic about Dearborn Park, and they have developed a warm and supportive community life.

Walk down Plymouth Court to 9th Street and turn left. Walk one block to State Street and turn left again. Look at the attractive high rise on the northeast corner. Built recently on a site that would have been unthinkable only a few years earlier, this building has reinforced the resurgent residential community of the area. If you look to the south from here, you can see that redevelopment is under way now in many of the nearby

buildings. The Cineplex Odeon (826 S. Wabash Ave.) opened in
1988 and shows first-run movies on five screens.

**14** Walk east on 8th Street, across Wabash Avenue, to the **Chicago
Hilton and Towers** (720 S. Michigan Ave.). Enter by the revolv-
ing doors, head a bit to your right and then straight, and stroll
through the opulent lobby, tastefully done in shades of mauve
and soft sea green. Notice the gilded horses that flank the main
entrance on the inner wall and the sweeping stairway to your
right off the main entrance that leads to the Grand Ballroom.
Sneak a peek at the Grand Ballroom if possible; there isn't a
more spectacular room in the city. On opening night at the Opera, when a midnight supper and dance is held here, a brass
quintet stationed at the top of this stairway plays fanfares as
the guests arrive. Be sure not to miss the exquisite Thai hanging on the north wall of the lobby (directly behind and above the
concierge's desk).

**Time Out**   The **Lobby Cafe** at the Hilton has an attractive light lunch and
dinner menu. The food is good, and the setting is wonderful for
those who enjoy people-watching. Should you prefer a cocktail
in the lobby lounge, choose a table by the windows looking out
on Michigan Avenue, sit back, relax, and listen to the music of
the string ensemble that plays here afternoons until 5 PM.

When you're ready to leave, the Jeffery Express (No. 6) bus to
Hyde Park stops on Balbo Drive, directly across Michigan Avenue from the Hilton. Or you can catch any bus that stops on the
northeast corner and then transfer to a Michigan Avenue bus at
Randolph Street.

### Tour 3: Hyde Park and Kenwood

*Numbers in the margin correspond to points of interest on the
Tour 3: Hyde Park and Kenwood map.*

Site of the World's Columbian Exposition of 1893, residence at
the turn of the century of the meat-packing barons Swift
and Armour, home of the University of Chicago, locale of five
houses designed by Frank Lloyd Wright, and the nation's oldest stable racially integrated neighborhood, Hyde Park and the
adjoining Kenwood are important historically, intellectually,
and culturally.

Although farmers and other settlers lived in Hyde Park in the
early 1800s and Chicago's oldest Jewish congregation was
founded here in 1847, the growth and development of the area
really got under way as a result of two events: the World's Columbian Exposition of 1893 and the opening of the University of
Chicago in 1892. The Columbian Exposition, whose influence
on American public architecture was to prove far-reaching,
brought about the creation of the Midway Plaisance and the
construction of numerous buildings, of which the Museum of
Science and Industry is the most famous survivor. The Midway
Plaisance, surrounding the heart of the 1893 fair, still runs
along the southern edge of the University of Chicago's original
campus. Another legacy from the exposition was the civic mon-
iker "The Windy City," used by *New York Sun* editor Charles
Dana to ridicule Chicago's bid for hosting the exposition.

The University of Chicago was built through the largesse of
John D. Rockefeller. Coeducational from the beginning, it was

known for progressive education. The campus covers 184 acres, dominating the life of Hyde Park and South Kenwood. Much of the original campus was designed by Henry Ives Cobb, also responsible for the Newberry Library at the corner of Dearborn and Walton streets on the Near North Side. The university's stately gothic quadrangles recall the residential colleges in Cambridge, England, and the Ivy League schools of the East Coast. But the material is Indiana limestone, and the U. of C. retains a uniquely Midwestern quality.

The university boasts 61 Nobel laureates as graduates, resident researchers, or faculty members. Its schools of economics, law, business, and medicine are world famous. The University of Chicago Hospitals are leading teaching institutions. It was at U. of C. in 1990 that a baby received a successful transplant of a section of her mother's liver—the first operation of its kind. Perhaps the most world-altering event to take place at U. of C. (or anywhere else, for that matter) was the first self-sustaining nuclear chain reaction in 1942, created by Enrico Fermi and his team of physicists under an unused football stadium. Although the stadium is gone, there's a plaque on the spot now, near the Crerar Science Library.

In the 1890s the university embarked on a program to build housing for its faculty members, and the mansions that line Woodlawn Avenue are the result. Then the neighborhood began to attract well-to-do private individuals who commissioned noted architects to construct homes suitable to persons of great wealth. Many of their houses still stand in Kenwood.

With the coming of the Depression, followed by World War II, the neighborhood entered a period of decline. Grand homes fell into disrepair as the numbers of those with the resources to maintain them dwindled. Wartime housing shortages led to the conversion of stately houses into multifamily dwellings.

Alarmed by the decline of the neighborhood, concerned citizens formed the Hyde Park-Kenwood Community Conference. Aided by $29 million from the University of Chicago, which was anxious that it might not be able to retain—never mind recruit—faculty members, this group set about restoring the neighborhood. Prizes were offered to those who would buy and "deconvert" rooming houses, and the city was pressured to enforce the zoning laws.

The effort that was to have the most lasting effect on the neighborhood was urban renewal, one of the first such undertakings in the nation. Again with the backing and support of the University of Chicago, 55th Street from Lake Park Avenue to Cottage Grove Avenue was razed. Most of the buildings on Lake Park Avenue and on many streets abutting 55th Street and Lake Park Avenue were torn down as well. With them went the workshops of painters and artisans, the quarters of "little magazines" (some 20 chapters of James Joyce's *Ulysses* were first published at one of them), the Compass Theatre—where Mike Nichols and Elaine May got their start—and Second City (since relocated to Lincoln Park), and more than 40 bars where jazz and blues could be heard nightly. In their place came town houses designed by I. M. Pei and Harry Weese and a shopping mall designed by Keck and Keck. Cynics have described the process as one of "blacks and whites together, shoulder to shoulder—against the poor."

In the end, these efforts were successful beyond the wildest imaginings of their sponsors, but more than 20 years elapsed before the neighborhood regained its luster. The 18-room houses on Woodlawn Avenue that sell today for $600,000 could still be had for $35,000 in the early 1960s.

To reach the start of our Hyde Park tour if you're arriving by car, take Lake Shore Drive south to the 57th Street exit and turn left into the parking lot of the Museum of Science and Industry. Or you can take the Illinois Central Gulf (ICG) RR train from Randolph Street and Michigan Avenue; get off at the 55th Street stop and walk east through the underpass two blocks, then south two blocks.

Our exploration of Hyde Park and Kenwood begins at the ➊ **Museum of Science and Industry,** built for the Columbian Exposition as a Palace of Fine Arts. Plan on at least half a day to explore this hands-on museum, where you can visit a U–505 submarine, descend into a coal mine, experience an auditory miracle in the whispering gallery, learn how telephones work, trace the history of computing and the development of computer hardware, explore spacecraft and the history of space exploration, visit "Main Street of Yesterday," learn how the body works, and much more. The Omnimax Theater shows science and space-related films on a giant screen. *5700 S. Lake Shore Dr., tel. 312/684–1414. Admission: $5 adults, $2 children. Open Memorial Day–Labor Day, daily 9:30–5:30; Labor Day–Memorial Day, weekdays 9:30–4, weekends and holidays 9:30–5:30.*

Exiting the museum, cross 56th Street, and head west. Turn right under the viaduct and go north on Lake Park Avenue. ➋ You'll pass the **Hyde Park Historical Society** (5529 S. Lake Park Ave., tel. 312/493–1893), a research library halfway down the block.

➌ Just north stands the **Chevrolet building** (5508 S. Lake Park Ave.), named for the car dealership that formerly occupied it. The beautiful terra-cotta border decorates an otherwise functional building, one of only two buildings in the area left standing after urban renewal.

Head west on 55th Street to one of the happy results of urban ➍ renewal, **1400–1451 East 55th Street,** an apartment building designed by I. M. Pei. He also designed the town houses that border it on the north, between Blackstone and Dorchester avenues. Turn right and head up Blackstone Avenue, passing a variety of housing between 55th and 51st streets. Although these houses command prices in the hundreds of thousands of dollars today, they were originally cottages for workingmen, conveniently located near the cable-car line that ran west on 55th Street.

Continue north on Blackstone Avenue to 53rd Street, Hyde Park's main shopping strip. Across the street and ½ block east ➎ is **Harper Court.** Another product of urban renewal, Harper Court was built to house craftspeople who were displaced from their workshops on Lake Park Avenue. Despite subsidized rents, it never caught on with the craftspeople, who moved elsewhere, while Harper Court evolved into a successful shopping center and community gathering place.

**Time Out**  **Cafe Coffee** (5211 S. Harper) serves an invigorating selection of
coffees, pastries, and snacks. Those who are very hungry
might prefer the **Valois Cafeteria** (1518 E. 53rd St.) ½ block
away, where inexpensive meals are served all day.

Leaving the north exit of Harper Court, go west to Woodlawn
**6** Avenue and turn right. The **Heller House** (5132 S. Woodlawn
Ave.) was built by Frank Lloyd Wright in 1897; note the plaster
naiads cavorting at the top. Now proceed south on Woodlawn
**7** Avenue to 55th Street. On the east side of the street is **St.
Thomas the Apostle Church and School** (5467 S. Woodlawn
Ave.), built in 1922 and now a national landmark. Note its terra-cotta ornamentation.

Now we come to the northern edge of the University of Chicago
campus. A walking tour of the campus is offered daily (tel. 312/
702–8374), but if you'd like to see things on your own, continue
**8** west to University Avenue and the **Lutheran School of Theology** (1100 E. 55th St.). Built in 1968 by the firm of Perkins and
Will, the massive structure seems almost to float from its foundation, lightened by the transparency of its smoked-glass ex-
teriors. Across the street is **Pierce Hall** (5514 S. University
Ave.), a student dormitory designed by Harry Weese.

One block west on Greenwood Avenue, between 55th and 56th
**9** streets, is the **David and Alfred Smart Museum of Art.** Founded
in 1974 with a gift from the Smart Family Foundation, whose
members David and Alfred founded *Esquire* magaine, the museum and an adjacent sculpture garden display the fine-arts
holdings of the university. The 5,000-piece permanent collection is diverse and includes works by Old Masters; photographs
by Walker Evans; furniture by Frank Lloyd Wright; sculptures
by Degas, Matisse, Rodin, and Henry Moore; ancient Chinese
bronzes; and modern Japanese ceramics. *5550 S. Greenwood
Ave., tel. 312/702–0200. Admission free. Open weekdays 10–4,
weekends noon–6.*

**10** Walk west on 55th Street to Ellis Avenue and the **Court Theatre**
(5535 S. Ellis Ave., tel. 312/753–4472), a professional repertory
company that specializes in revivals of the classics. An intimate
theater, the Court offers unobstructed sight from every seat in
the house. A flag flies atop the theater when a show is on.

Continue south on Ellis Avenue about ½ block beyond 56th
**11** Street; on your left is the Henry Moore sculpture *Nuclear Energy,* commemorating the first controlled nuclear chain reaction, which took place below ground roughly where the
sculpture stands, in the locker room under the bleachers of
what was then Stagg Field. Across 57th Street, set into the
**12** small quadrangle on your right, is the **John Crerar Science Library** (5730 S. Ellis Ave., tel. 312/702–7715). Inside the library
is John David Mooney's splendid sculpture *Crystara*, composed
of enormous Waterford crystal pieces made to order for this
work, which was commissioned for the site.

**13** Farther down the block is the **University of Chicago Bookstore,**
which has, in addition to scholarly books, a large selection of
general-interest books, an outstanding collection of cookbooks,
and clothing, mugs, and other souvenirs. *5750 S. Ellis Ave.,
tel. 312/702–8729. Open weekdays 9–5.*

**14** On the east side of Ellis Avenue at 58th Street is **Cobb Hall,**
home of the Renaissance Society. The society was founded in

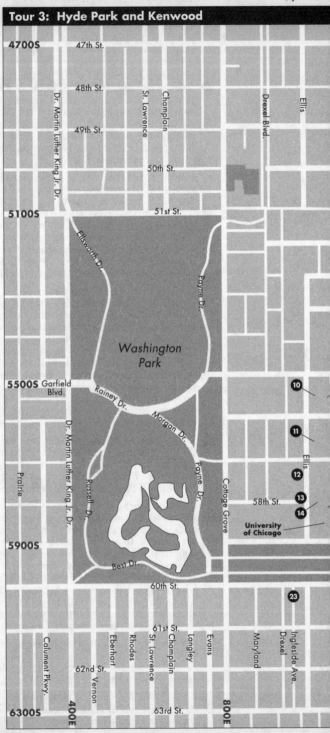

Tour 3: Hyde Park and Kenwood

0       440 yards

0       400 meters

**KEY**

— Rail Lines

N

*Lake Michigan*

Greenwood

49th St.

*Kenwood Park*

50th St.

Hyde Park Blvd.

6

52nd St.

5

53rd St.

Blackstone

54th St.

Greenwood

University

Woodlawn

Kimbark

Kenwood

Hyde Park Blvd.

Cornell

8

7

55th St.

4

3

9

2

56th St.

16

18

57th St.

Dorchester

26 27

25

17

20

19

15

Stony Island

21

22

24

59th St.

*Midway Plaisance*

60th St.

1

Lake Shore Dr.

*Jackson Park*

Cornell

62nd St.

Kimbark

Kenwood

Hayes Dr.

1200E

1600E

1915 to identify living artists whose work would be of lasting significance and influence. It was among the first hosts of works by Matisse, Picasso, Braque, Brancusi, and Miró. Come here to see what the next generation of great art may look like. *Cobb Hall 418, 5811 S. Ellis Ave., tel. 312/702–8670. Admission free. Open weekdays 10–4, weekends noon–4.*

North of Cobb Hall is the **University of Chicago Administration Building.** Between the two is a small passageway to the **quadrangle** of the university. Here is a typical college campus, green and grassy, with imposing neo-Gothic buildings all around. Tucked into the southwest corner between two other buildings ⑮ is **Bond Chapel** (1025 E. 58th St., tel. 312/702–8200), a lovely Gothic-style chapel. The fanciful gargoyles outside belie the simple interior of dark wood, stained glass, and delicate ornamentation. The effect is one of intimacy and warmth.

Cross the quadrangle and head east to the circular drive. Bear left, then turn left at the intersecting road. Follow this path north, and you will pass a reflecting pool (Botany Pond) before you exit through the wrought-iron gate. Directly ahead is the ⑯ **Joseph Regenstein Library,** framed in the gate. The "Reg," the main library of the university, was designed by Skidmore, Owings, and Merrill and built in 1970.

Turn right on 57th Street and continue east. The massive build-⑰ ing on the corner, **Mandel Hall** (5706 S. University Ave., tel. 312/702–8511; enter on 57th St.), is a gem of a concert hall that has been tastefully restored. Peek in, if you can, for a glimpse of gold leaf and soft greens against the dark wood of the theater. Professional musical organizations, including ensembles from the Chicago Symphony and such groups as Les Arts Florissants from France, perform in the 900-seat hall throughout the year. The building also houses the student union.

Continue east on 57th Street one block to Woodlawn Avenue. ⑱ On the northwest corner is the **First Unitarian Church** (5750 S. Woodlawn Ave., tel. 312/324–4100), whose graceful spire is visible throughout the area. Turn right on Woodlawn Avenue and head south, noting the stately brick mansions that line both sides of the street. To the north the building at 5605 is on the National Register of Historic Places. Many of the buildings were built by the University of Chicago in the 1890s to provide housing for professors. Professors continue to live in several of them; others have been repurchased by the university for institutional use.

Continue south on Woodlawn Avenue to Frank Lloyd Wright's ⑲ **Robie House.** Built in 1909, Robie House exemplifies the Prairie style. Its cantilevered roof offers privacy while allowing in light. The house sits on a pedestal; Wright abhorred basements, thinking them unhealthful. You can tour Robie House and examine the interiors, including the built-in cupboards, the leaded-glass windows, and the spacious kitchen. Rescued by the university from the threat of demolition, the building now houses the university alumni office and is used for small official dinners and receptions. *5757 S. Woodlawn Ave., tel. 312/ 702–8374. Free tours daily at noon.*

Cross Woodlawn Avenue and continue west one block to the ⑳ **Chicago Theological Seminary** (5757 S. University Ave.). Its basement accommodates the **Seminary Cooperative Bookstore** (tel. 312/752–4381), which includes an extensive selection of

books in the humanities among its wide offerings. Defying the rules of marketing, this store—which does not advertise, is not visible from the street, and has no parking—has more sales per square foot than any other bookstore in Chicago. Upstairs in the chapel is the Reneker organ, donated by the widow of a university trustee. Free concerts are given Tuesday at noon on this exquisitely handcrafted replica of an 18th-century organ.

**㉑** Across 58th Street is the **Oriental Institute,** which focuses on the history, art, and archaeology of the ancient Near East, including Assyria, Mesopotamia, Persia, Egypt, and Syro-Palestine. Permanent displays include statuary, small-scale amulets, mummies, limestone reliefs, gold jewelry, ivories, pottery, and bronzes from the 2nd millennium BC through the 13th century AD. *1155 E. 58th St., tel. 312/702–1062 or 312/702–9521 for recorded information. Admission free. Open Tues. and Thurs.–Sat. 10–4, Wed. 10–8:30, Sun. noon–4.*

Go down University Avenue one block to 59th Street. To your **㉒** left, set back on a grassy expanse, is the neo-Gothic **Rockefeller Memorial Chapel** (5850 S. Woodlawn Ave., designed by Bertram Goodhue and named in honor of the founder of the university. The interior, which recently underwent extensive structural and cosmetic renovation, has a stunning vaulted ceiling; hand-sewn banners decorate the walls. A university carillonneur gives regular performances on the carillon atop the chapel. Tours of the chapel are given by appointment (tel. 312/702–8374).

Continue south again, crossing 59th Street and entering the **Midway Plaisance.** Created for the World's Columbian Exposition, this green, hollowed-out strip of land was intended to replicate a Venetian canal. When the "canal" was filled with water, houses throughout the area were flooded as well, and the idea had to be abandoned. At the eastern end of the Plaisance, by Cottage Grove Avenue, you can see Lorado Taft's masterpiece *The Fountain of Time,* completed in 1922. Taft (1830–1926) was one of the most distinguished sculptors and teachers of his time. Like many, he got his start by creating pieces for the Columbian Exposition. One of these, the *Fountain of the Great Lakes,* is now at the Art Institute. Other works adorn Chicago's parks and public places, as well as those of other cities.

Heading west on 60th Street, you'll pass the **School of Social Service Administration** (969 E. 60th St.), an undistinguished example of the work of Mies van der Rohe. One block farther, at **㉓** 60th Street and Ingleside Avenue, is **Midway Studios,** the home and workplace of Lorado Taft. A National Historic Landmark since 1966, the building now houses the university's studio-art program and serves as an exhibit space for student works. *6016 S. Ingleside Ave., tel. 312/753–4821. Admission free. Open weekdays 9–5.*

On 60th Street between Ellis and University avenues is the **Laird Bell Law Quadrangle** (1111 E. 60th St.). This attractive building, with fountains playing in front, is the work of Finnish architect Eero Saarinen. Two blocks farther east, between Kimbark Street and Kenwood Avenue, is the **New Graduate Residence Hall** (1307 E. 60th St.). This poured-concrete structure, elaborately ornamented, is reminiscent of the American embassy in New Delhi, India—unsurprisingly, architect Edward Durrell Stone designed both.

Cross the Midway again to 59th Street and continue east. The neo-Gothic structure just past Dorchester Avenue is **International House** (1414 E. 59th St., tel. 312/753–2270), where many foreign students live during their tenure at the university. It was designed in 1932 by the firm of Holabird and Roche. Continue east to Blackstone and turn left. **5806 South Blackstone Avenue**, a house designed in 1951 by Bertrand Goldberg of Marina City and River City fame, is an early example of the use of solar heating and natural cooling.

Continue north on Blackstone Avenue to 57th Street and turn right. **Powell's Bookstore** (1501 E. 57th St., tel. 312/955–7780) generally has a box of free books out front, and inside you'll find a tremendous selection of used and remaindered books, especially art books, cookbooks, and mysteries. Walk west on 57th Street to Dorchester Avenue; on your left, at **5704 South Dorchester Avenue**, is an Italian-style villa constructed before the Chicago Fire. The two houses at **5642** and **5607 South Dorchester Avenue** also predate the fire.

On 57th Street, spanning the block between Kenwood Avenue and Kimbark Street, is the **Ray School** complex. One of the best public elementary schools in the city, Ray hosts the annual Hyde Park Art Fair, one of the oldest (1947) annual outdoor art-fairs in the country.

Farther west is **O'Gara & Wilson Book Shop Ltd.** (1311 E. 57th St., tel. 312/363–0993), which has another outstanding selection of used books. Nearby is **57th Street Books** (1301 E. 57th St., tel. 312/684–1300), a cooperatively owned bookstore that is sister to the Seminary Cooperative Bookstore on University Avenue and that specializes in current books of general interest. Copies of the *New York Times Book Review* and the *New York Review of Books* are always on a table toward the rear, next to the coffeepot. An extensive children's section has its own room, where reading aloud to youngsters is encouraged.

**Time Out** This street has several spots where you can get a quick bite and rest your feet. **Medici Pan Pizza** (1327 E. 57th St.) has sandwiches and snacks as well as pizza, as does **Edwardo's** (1321 E. 57th St.). For a caffeine jolt, try **Caffe Florian** (1450 E. 57th St.). Breakfast fare is your best bet at **Ann Sather** (1329 E. 57th St.).

To get back to the museum and our starting point, backtrack east on 57th Street, go under the viaduct, and cross Stony Island Avenue. The museum will be in front of you, and to the right are the lagoons of Jackson Park.

## Tour 4: South Lake Shore Drive

The South Lake Shore Drive tour offers spectacular views of the downtown skyline; it serves as a bonus for those who have visited Hyde Park and Kenwood and are returning north via car or the Jeffery Express (No. 6) bus or (during the afternoon rush hour) the Hyde Park Express (No. 2). If you followed Tour 1 (*see above*) or Tour 5 (*see below*), you will have visited some of the skyscrapers described here. This driving tour allows you to see these buildings from a distance, and in relation to the surrounding skyline.

Enter Lake Shore Drive at 57th Street northbound, with the lake to your right. At 35th Street you will pass, on your left, the **Stephen Douglas Memorial.** Douglas was the U.S. Senator who debated the merits of slavery with Abraham Lincoln; you can see the monument, Douglas at the top, from the drive, but you'd have to go inland to Lake Park Avenue to visit the lovely park and gardens there.

Directly ahead, the **Sears Tower** (233 S. Wacker Dr.) is the world's tallest building. In case the perspective makes it appear unfamiliar, you can recognize it by the angular setbacks that narrow the building as it rises higher. To its left is the "white castle" top of **311 S. Wacker,** which is blindingly lighted at night (*see* Tour 1). Ahead and to your right is the low-rise, dark **McCormick Place Convention Hall** (2300 S. Lake Shore Dr.); opposite it, to your left, is the **McCormick Hotel.** Immediately north of the hotel, the low-rise **McCormick Place North** is the latest addition to the complex, its completion having been delayed by almost a year because of political machinations and scandals, in true Chicago style.

The rust-color building to the east is the **CNA Building** (55 E. Jackson Blvd.). When it was newly constructed, Chicagoans believed that the color was that of a first coat of rustproofing paint. They were wrong. The **Associates Center** (150 N. Michigan Ave.), is the building with the more or less diamond-shape, angled face at the top (*see* Tour 1).

The tall white building to the right of the Associates Center is the **Amoco Building** (200 E. Randolph St.), with its new granite exterior (*see* Tour 1). Next to the Amoco Building is the severe gray **Prudential Building,** with its postmodern annex rising behind it.

The building with the twin antennae, to the right of the Amoco Building, is the **John Hancock Center** (875 N. Michigan Ave.), the world's third-tallest building, at 98 stories (*see* Tour 5). Off to the right, seemingly out in the lake, are the sinuous curves of **Lake Point Towers** condominium apartments (505 N. Lake Shore Dr.).

Coming up on the left, the building with the massive columns on an ancient Grecian model is **Soldier Field** (425 E. McFetridge Dr.), the home of the Chicago Bears. A new stadium on the near west side is in the planning stages, and many Chicagoans look forward to having Lake Shore Drive to themselves again on fall and winter Sunday afternoons. To visit the three museums on Chicago's museum campus, turn right into the drive that's just past Meigs Field, drive to the end, and park. Or follow the signs to the left that lead to the Field Museum parking lot.

On your left as you turn onto the peninsula is the **John G. Shedd Aquarium.** The dazzling new **Oceanarium,** with two beluga whales and several Pacific dolphins, is the big draw here. But don't miss the sharks, tarpon, turtles, and myriad smaller fish and other aquatic forms in the coral-reef exhibit. Hundreds of other watery "cages" display fish from around the world, some bizarre and many fantastically beautiful. *1200 S. Lake Shore Dr., tel. 312/939–2426. Admission: $3 adults, $2 children and senior citizens. Open daily 9–5.*

At the far end of the peninsula is the **Adler Planetarium,** featuring exhibits about the stars and planets and a popular program of Sky Shows. Past shows have included "The Space Telescope Story" and "Planetary Puzzles." *1300 S. Lake Shore Dr., tel. 312/322–0304 (general information), 312/322–0300 (Sky Show information), or 312/322–0334 (information on current month's skies). Admission to planetarium free. Sky Show admission: $3 adults, $1.50 children 6–17. Open Mon.–Thurs. and weekends 9:30–4:30, Fri. 9:30–9.*

The **Field Museum of Natural History,** located across Lake Shore Drive from the aquarium and accessible through a pedestrian underpass, is one of the country's great natural-history museums. From the reconstructed Pawnee earth-lodge (completed with the assistance of the Pawnee tribe of Oklahoma) to the Mastaba tomb-complex from ancient Egypt, the size and breadth of the museum's collections are staggering. The Mastaba complex alone includes a working canal, a living marsh where papyrus is grown, a shrine to the cat goddess Bastet, burial-ceremony artifacts, and 23 mummies. The museum's gem room contains more than 500 gemstones and jewels. Place for Wonder, a three-room exhibit for children, lets youngsters handle everything on display, including a ½-ton stuffed polar bear, shells, animal skins, clothing and toys from China, aromatic scent jars, and gourds. Music, dance, theater, and film performances are also scheduled. *Lake Shore Dr. at E. Roosevelt Rd., tel. 312/922–9410. Admission: $10 families, $3 adults, $2 students and senior citizens; free Thurs. Open daily 9–5.*

After you've had your fill of museums, retrieve your car and continue north. As you round the curve past the Shedd Aquarium, look to your right for a view of the harbor. Off to the left looms the handsome, massive complex of the **Chicago Hilton and Towers** (720 S. Michigan Ave.), and soon thereafter the **Buckingham Fountain** will appear immediately to your left. To the far right, at the north and east, you can just see the ornate towers of **Navy Pier** (*see* Tour 5).

Having reached the Loop, we've come to the end of the South Lake Shore Drive tour.

## Tour 5: Near North

*Numbers in the margin correspond to points of interest on the Tour 5: Near North map.*

Some of the most beautiful and interesting sights in Chicago are within a short walk of the multitude of hotels on the Near North Side. If business has brought you here, and you have a few hours to kill between meetings, you can wander over to the lakefront and Navy and North piers, browse the shops and museums of Michigan Avenue, or take a turn around the galleries of River North. If you have a whole day to spend, you can do all three comfortably. For more information on shopping Michigan Avenue, *see* Chapter 4.

**Magnificent Mile/Streeterville** The **Magnificent Mile,** a stretch of Michigan Avenue between the Chicago River and Oak Street, got its name from the swanky shops that line both sides of the street (*see* Chapter 4) and from its once-elegant low-rise profile, which used to contrast sharply with the canyons of the Loop. Unfortunately, a parade of new high-rises is making the Mag Mile more canyonlike each year, but you can still see patches of what the entire street used to look like.

To the east of the Magnificent Mile is swanky **Streeterville**, which began as a disreputable landfill presided over by notorious lowlife "Cap" Streeter and his wife Maria. The couple set out from Milwaukee in the 1880s on a small steamboat bound for Honduras. When their boat was stranded on a sandbar between Chicago Avenue and Oak Street, Streeter claimed the "land" as his own, seceding from both the city of Chicago and the state of Illinois. After building contractors were invited to dump their debris on his "property," the landfill soon mushroomed into 186 acres of saloons and shanties. Today this once-infamous area is filled with high-rise apartment buildings and a smattering of older structures, and has attracted young professionals who work nearby. Where Cap Streeter's own shanty once sat is the John Hancock Center.

West of Streeterville, from Michigan Avenue to Dearborn Street, is a peculiar stretch that mixes a few skyscrapers, lots of parking lots and garages, a sprinkling of shops and restaurants, and some isolated examples of the stone town houses that once filled the neighborhood. Despite its lack of cohesion the area is the seat of various types of power, containing as it does two cathedrals and the headquarters of the American Medical Association, housed in a sterile new high rise at Wabash and Grand avenues.

**❶** Our tour starts at the north side of the **Michigan Avenue Bridge,** which spans the Chicago River. The sculptures on the four pylons of the bridge represent major Chicago events: its discovery by Marquette and Jolliet, its settlement by du Sable, the Fort Dearborn Massacre of 1812, and the rebuilding of the city after the fire. The site of the fort is just across the river, where 360 North Michigan Avenue now stands.

**❷** Around the bridge are several notable skyscrapers, old and new. On the west side of Michigan Avenue is the **Wrigley Building** (400 N. Michigan Ave., tel. 312/923–8080), corporate home of the Wrigley chewing-gum empire. It was built in the early 1920s by the architectural firm of Graham Anderson Probst and White, the same firm that designed the Merchandise Mart (*see below*) and Union Station. The building is sheathed in terra cotta that's remained remarkably white, considering the pollution around it. Its wedding-cake embellishments and clock tower make it an impossible structure to overlook. The building is brightly illuminated at night.

**❸** Looking west you'll see the twin "corncobs" of Bertrand Goldberg's **Marina City,** built in the early 1960s. Many architects love the complex, but engineers aren't so sure. If you get up close you can see patches in the concrete of the balconies. When it was first built Marina City was popular with young professionals who worked in the area; today it's less sought-after, although it does have the dubious distinction of housing the only bowling alley in downtown Chicago. Just east of it is Mies van der Rohe's boxlike **IBM Building.** Next to that is the headquarters of the *Chicago Sun-Times*.

**❹** Across Michigan Avenue is the crenellated **Tribune Tower** (435 N. Michigan Ave., tel. 312/222–3232). In 1922 *Tribune* publisher Colonel Robert McCormick chose this Gothic design for the building that would house his paper, after rejecting a slew of

# Tour 5: Near North

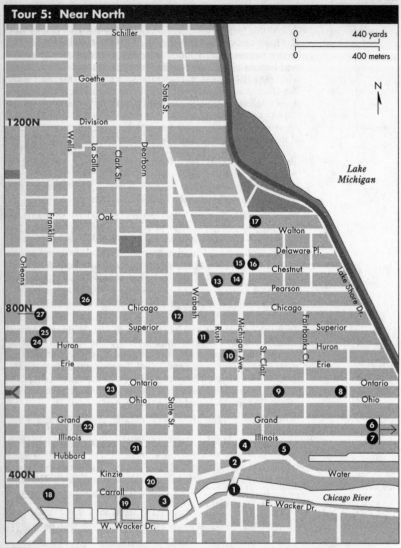

Anti-Cruelty Society
building, **22**
Aquariums by
Design, **25**
Courthouse Place, **21**
Drake Hotel, **17**
Fourth Presbyterian
Church, **15**
Holy Name
Cathedral, **12**

John Hancock
Center, **16**
Marina City, **3**
May Weber Museum
of Cultural Arts, **8**
Merchandise Mart, **18**
Michigan Avenue
Bridge, **1**
Moody Bible
Institute, **26**
Museum of
Contemporary Art, **9**

Navy Pier, **6**
NBC Tower, **5**
North Pier, **7**
Quaker Oats
building, **19**
Quigley Seminary, **13**
River North
Concourse, **27**
Rock and Roll
McDonald's, **23**
St. James
Cathedral, **11**

SuHu, **24**
Terra Museum of
American Art, **10**
33 West Kinzie
Street, **20**
Tribune Tower, **4**
Water Tower, **14**
Wrigley Building, **2**

functional modern designs. Look for chunks of material taken
from other famous buildings, such as Westminster Abbey and
St. Peter's Basilica, embedded in the exterior wall of the tower.
On the ground floor, behind plate-glass windows, are the studi-
os of WGN radio, part of the *Tribune* empire that also includes
WGN-TV, cable-television stations, and the Chicago Cubs.
(Modesty was not one of Colonel McCormick's prime traits:
WGN stands for the *Trib*'s self-bestowed nickname, World's
Greatest Newspaper.)

**⑤** Behind the Tribune Tower is the new **NBC Tower** (200 E. Illinois St.). This 1989 limestone-and-granite edifice by Skidmore
Owings and Merrill looks suspiciously like the 1930s-vintage
Rockefeller Center complex in New York, another of NBC's
75homes. The gift shop on the ground floor stocks NBC memorabilia.

As you look east you'll see that the riverbanks have been turned
into a landscaped promenade. The arc of water that occasionally shoots across the river from the south side is Centennial
Fountain.

For a lakefront detour, go down the steps beside the Tribune
Tower at Grand Avenue and walk east, under Lake Shore Drive
**⑥** and across a large parking lot, to **Navy Pier.** Constructed in
1916 as a commercial-shipping pier, it was renamed in honor of
the Navy in 1927 (the Army got Soldier Field). Currently under construction to become a European-style garden, with
plantings and fountains, it's a wonderful place to enjoy the lake
breezes and take in the skyline. The boats that dock there offer
brunch, lunch, and dinner cruises at premium prices. The
food's better on land, but the voyage can be pleasant on a hot
summer night. Operators include *Spirit of Chicago* (tel. 312/
836–7899) and *Odyssey* (tel. 708/639–7739).

**Time Out** Just south of Navy Pier is **Rocky and Sons Fish House,** which
offers various forms of fried fish in a ramshackle building that
looks like something from Maine or Cape Cod. Eat your fish on
the waterfront and watch the ducks converge for a handout.
Sodas (Rocky's sells only coffee) and nonfish items can be had at
the adjacent snack wagon.

For more conventional fare, head west on Illinois Street to
**⑦** **North Pier.** This fairly recent shopping complex in an old building offers interesting stores, a food court, waterside dining in
several restaurants, a miniature golf course, and the **Chicago
Children's Museum.** The museum contains exhibits on African
art, architecture, and a recycling center, but the big draws are
the three hands-on exhibits for children 2–12 and a "touch and
feel" exhibit for preschoolers. *435 E. Illinois St. (N. Pier building), tel. 312/527–1000. Admission: $3 adults, $2 children.
Open Tues.–Fri. 12:30–4:30 and Thurs. 5 PM–8 PM, weekends
10–4:30.*

As you leave North Pier, walk north on McClurg Court to On-
**⑧** tario Street. Turn left and you'll find the tiny **May Weber Museum of Cultural Arts,** which changes exhibits every three
months; recent shows have explored the textiles and household
arts of Japan and the crafts of the Yoruba tribe. *299 E. Ontario
St., tel. 312/787–4477. Admission: $1. Open Wed.–Sun.
noon–5.*

**⑨** Farther west on Ontario is the **Museum of Contemporary Art.** Started by a group of art patrons who found the great Art Institute unresponsive to modern work, this museum concentrates on 20th-century art, principally works created after 1940. Limited display space means that the collection of more than 4,000 works can be shown only in rotation; about six major exhibitions and 12 smaller ones are mounted each year. Because the museum closes in preparation for major exhibitions, be sure to call before planning a visit. The museum may move in 1994 to larger quarters on the site of the old armory on Chicago Avenue. *237 E. Ontario St., tel. 312/280–5161. Admission: $4 adults; $2 students, senior citizens, and children under 16; free Tues. Open Tues.–Sat. 10–5, Sun. noon–5.*

If you see lots of people in white coats in the neighborhood, don't be surprised. Stretching east of Michigan Avenue from Ontario to Chicago avenues are the buildings of one of the city's most prominent medical centers, **Northwestern Memorial Hospital.** The complex includes a veteran's hospital, a rehabilitation hospital, and a women's hospital, plus outpatient buildings. The downtown campus of Evanston's **Northwestern University,** including the law school and business school, is also here.

**⑩** Continue west to Michigan Avenue, cross it and turn right for the third museum in the Near North, the **Terra Museum of American Art.** Daniel Terra, Ambassador-at-Large for Cultural Affairs under Ronald Reagan, made his collection of American art available to Chicago in 1980; in 1987, the collection was moved here from Evanston. Subsequent acquisitions by the museum have added to the superb collection here, which includes works by Whistler, Winslow Homer, three generations of Wyeths, Sargent, and Mary Cassatt. *664 N. Michigan Ave., tel. 312/664–3939. Admission: $4 adults, $2.50 senior citizens and children 12–18. Open Wed.–Sun. 10–5, Tues. 10–8.*

**⑪** Two blocks west of Michigan Avenue at Huron Street is the **St. James Cathedral** (65 E. Huron St., tel. 312/787–7360). First built in 1856, the original St. James was largely destroyed by the Chicago Fire in 1871. The second structure from 1875 is still Chicago's oldest Episcopal church.

**Time Out** In sunny weather the plaza just east of St. James is a great place to eat a sandwich while you people-watch. For great fixings, try **L'Appetito** (Wabash Ave. and Huron St.), a take-out deli that has some of the best Italian subs in Chicago.

**⑫** Another block west and one block north is the Catholic stronghold, **Holy Name Cathedral** (735 N. State St., tel. 312/787–8040). This yellow-stone Victorian cathedral built between 1874 and 1875 is the principal church of the archdiocese of Chicago. Although the church is grand inside, the exterior is somewhat disappointing.

**⑬** Go east on Chicago Avenue to Rush Street and turn left (north). At Pearson and Rush streets is **Quigley Seminary,** a 1918 Gothic-style structure. Its chapel is a little jewel, with perfect acoustics and a splendid rose window.

**⑭** Continue east on Pearson Street to **Water Tower Park,** one of Chicago's icons. One of the few buildings to survive the fire of 1871, the **Water Tower** houses a 37-foot pipe once used to equalize water pressure for the matching **pumping station** across the street. Today the water tower and pumping station house the **Chicago Office of Tourism** and the **visitors center,** respectively.

**⑮** A block north on the west side of Michigan Avenue is the **Fourth Presbyterian Church** (126 E. Chestnut Street). The courtyard of the church, a grassy spot adorned with simple statuary and bounded by a covered walkway, is an oasis amid Michigan Avenue's commercial bustle; many a weary shopper has found respite here. The courtyard is situated between the church and the rectory. The granite church itself is a prime example of the Gothic Revival style popular at the turn of the century. Noontime organ concerts are given occasionally in the sanctuary.

**⑯** Across Michigan Avenue towers the 98-story **John Hancock Center,** which briefly held the title of world's tallest building when it was completed in 1969. The crisscross braces help keep the building from swaying in the high winds that come off the lake, although people who live in the apartments on the upper floors have learned not to keep anything fragile on a high shelf. There's an observation deck on the 96th floor that charges admission, although you can see the same view in a more festive setting by having an exorbitantly priced drink in the bar that adjoins **The 95th** restaurant (*see* Chapter 6). *Tel. 312/751–3681. Observation deck admission: $3.65 adults, $2.35 students 5–17 and senior citizens. Open daily 10–midnight.*

**⑰** At the head of the Magnificent Mile is the **Drake Hotel** (140 E. Walton Pl.), one of the city's oldest and grandest; take a look in the marble-and-oak lobby, complete with cherub-laden fountain, even if you're not staying here. The lobby is one of the city's most popular spots for afternoon tea. In nice weather you can cross Oak Street in front of the Drake's main entrance and take the underground passage that leads to Oak Street Beach and the lakefront promenade. (Watch out for speeding bicyclists, skateboarders, and Roller bladers.)

**River North**  Bounded on the south and west by branches of the Chicago River, River North has eastern and northern boundaries that are harder to define than those of Streeterville and the Magnificent Mile. As in many neighborhoods, the limits have expanded as the area has grown more attractive; today they extend roughly to Oak Street on the north and Clark Street on the east. Richly served by waterways and by railroad tracks that run along its western edge, the neighborhood was settled by Irish immigrants in the mid-19th century. As the 20th century approached and streetcar lines came to Clark, La Salle, and Wells streets, the area developed into a vigorous commerical, industrial, and warehouse district.

But as economic conditions changed and factories moved away, the neighborhood fell into disuse and disrepair. Despite its location less than a mile from Michigan Avenue and the bustling downtown, River North became just another deteriorated urban area, the deterioration underscored by the depressed quality of life in the massive Cabrini-Green public-housing project at the neighborhood's northern and western fringe.

As commerce moved away, artists and craftspeople moved into River North, attracted by the spacious abandoned storage areas and shop floors and the low rents. Developers began buying up properties with an eye toward renovation. Today, although some buildings remain unrestored, and patches of the neighborhood retain their earlier character, the area has gone through a renaissance. Scores of art galleries, dozens of restaurants, and numerous trendy shops have opened here, bringing life and excitement to a newly beautiful neighborhood. Walking through River North, one is aware of the almost complete absence of contemporary construction; the handsome buildings are virtually all renovations of properties nearly a century old. However, rising rents have combined with the recession to drive out some small retailers, and at press time many renovated spaces stood empty.

The typical River North building, made of the famed Chicago red brick, is a large, rectangular, solidly built structure with high ceilings and hardwood floors. Even those buildings of the period that were intended to be strictly functional were planned with an often loving attention to detail in the fine woodwork in doors and door frames, in the decorative patterns set in the brickwork, in the stone carvings and bas reliefs, and in the wrought-iron and handsome brass ornamentation.

**18** Our tour begins on the plaza of the massive **Merchandise Mart,** on the river between Orleans and Wells streets. The mart contains more square feet of space than any other building in the country except the Pentagon. Built by the architectural firm of Graham Anderson Probst and White in 1930, it's now owned by the Kennedys, of political fame. Inside are wholesale showrooms for all sorts of merchandise, much of it related to interior decoration. You can view the showrooms either accompanied by an interior designer or on one of the Mart's tours. The first two floors of the mart were converted into a retail shopping mall in late 1991. Most of the shops here are representatives of national chains. The anchor is a branch of the downtown department store Carson Pirie Scott. The somewhat macabre row of heads on the plaza is the Merchandise Mart Hall of Fame, installed at Joseph P. Kennedy's behest in 1953. The titans of retail portrayed here include Marshall Field, F. W. Woolworth, and Edward A. Filene. *13-156 The Merchandise Mart, tel. 312/644-4664, fax 312/644-4668. Showrooms open for tours only. Admission to tours: $7 adults, $5.50 seniors and students. Children under 16 not admitted on tours. Tours given Mon., Wed., Fri. 10 and 1:30; closed major holidays.*

The nondescript building to the west is the **Apparel Center,** the mart's equivalent for clothing.

From the plaza, walk north on Wells Street to Kinzie Street. Turn east on Kinzie Street, cross Clark Street, and look to your right to see two recent additions to Chicago's architectural **19** scene. At the river's edge is the **Quaker Oats building,** a massive, glass-skin box designed by Skidmore, Owings & Merrill that was built to house the company's world headquarters after decades in the nearby Merchandise Mart. In the lobby there's an immense replica of the famous Quaker Oats box. This handsome office building dwarfs the Japanese **Hotel Nikko** (320 N. Dearborn St.) to the east. The hotel was built by a consortium headed by Japan Air Lines to provide both top-quality Japanese-style accommodations to Japanese businessmen and luxury Western-style facilities to traveling Americans (*see* Chapter 7).

Before you turn left on Dearborn Street, notice the splendid or- **20** namental brickwork of **33 West Kinzie Street,** a Dutch Renaissance–style building. Once a commercial building, it was twice renovated and is now the home of Harry Caray's restaurant, owned by the famed sportscaster (*see* Chapter 6).

Proceed north to Hubbard Street, turn left, and pause at (21) **Courthouse Place** (54 W. Hubbard St.), a splendid granite building that has been beautifully renovated; notice the bas reliefs over the arched, pillared doorway. Inside, the restored lobby has black-and-white pictures of the original site. Continuing west you come to **Rowbottoms & Willoughby** (72 W. Hubbard St., tel. 312/329–0999), an upscale casual-clothing store. Around the corner on Clark Street, you can see a remnant of the neighborhood's former condition, a sleazy porno peep-show shop, two doors down from **Quadrant** (406 N. Clark Ave.), a trendy snack shop featuring a large selection of homemade muffins.

Go north on Clark Street to Grand Avenue. Turn left and continue one block west to La Salle Street. The funny, charming (22) edifice on the southwest corner is the **Anti-Cruelty Society building** (153 W. Grand Ave., tel. 312/644–8338), designed by whimsical Chicago architect Stanley Tigerman.

Walk north on La Salle to Ontario Street and turn right. The (23) **Rock and Roll McDonald's** at Clark Avenue and Ontario Street has a standard McD's menu (with slightly higher prices), 24-hour service, and a profusion of rock-and-roll artifacts, '50s and '60s kitsch, and just plain bizarre items to entertain you while you eat. Jukeboxes blast at all hours, and vintage '50s cars often crowd the parking lot on Saturday night. It's one of the highest-grossing McDonald's franchises in the world, so the company lets the operator decorate as he pleases. Even if you don't like the food, it's worth sticking your head in the door just to admire the Howdy Doody puppets, the '59 Corvette, and the rest of the collection.

One more block east, at Ontario and Dearborn streets, is the Romanesque pile that used to house the Chicago Historical Society before it moved to its Lincoln Park location. After several incarnations, it has become **Excalibur,** a dance club popular with young professionals and visiting suburbanites.

Now double back and head west on Ontario Street. At Wells Street, turn right, and walk to Huron Street. Huron, Superior (one block north), and Hudson (a north–south street west of (24) Orleans) streets form an area known as **SuHu**—a word play on New York's SoHo, for this, too, is an arts district, home of more than 50 art galleries, showing every kind of work imaginable. Don't be shy about walking in and browsing; a gallery's business is to sell the works it displays, so most galleries welcome interested visitors and, time permitting, the staff will discuss the art they are showing. On Friday evening many galleries schedule openings of new shows and serve refreshments; you can sip jug wine as you stroll through the newly hung exhibit. Consider a gallery tour an informal, admission free alternative to a museum visit. Although each gallery sets its own hours, most are open weekdays and Saturday 10–5 or 11–5 and are closed Sunday. For announcements of openings and other news of the art scene, write for the *Chicago Gallery News*, 107 West Delaware Place, Chicago, IL 60610, or stop by and pick up a copy at the Pumping Station (*see above*).

Virtually every building on Superior Street between Orleans and Franklin streets houses at least one gallery. At 301 West Superior is **Eva Cohon** (tel. 312/664–3669), with contemporary American and Canadian painting, sculpture, and works on paper. At 311 West Superior Street is **East West Contemporary Art** (tel. 312/664–8003) with works by Chinese artists. Equally

㉕ pleasing—although not a gallery—is **Aquariums by Design** (730 N. Franklin St., tel. 312/944–5566). Custom-made aquariums may not sound exciting, but the works here are as aesthetically pleasing as they are functional; the beautiful shapes, objects, and lighting make them a visual pleasure with or without fish. Notice, too (as in many other River North shops), the extensive and creative use of neon lights and signage. Like the area itself, neon has made a comeback in new and often lovely forms.

Nestled under the El tracks at Superior and Franklin streets is **Brett's Kitchen,** an excellent spot for a sandwich or an omelet during the week. On weekends Brett closes up shop and moves to a concession in Lincoln Park by the Waveland Avenue Golf Course.

Go north on Franklin Street to Chicago Avenue. Two blocks

㉖ east on Chicago Avenue is the **Moody Bible Institute** (820 N. La Salle St., tel. 312/329–4000), a massive contemporary brick structure. Other campus buildings spread out behind it to the north. Here students of various conservative Christian denominations study and prepare for religious careers.

Backtrack to Orleans Street. The bleak high rises you see to the northwest are the southeastern edge of the infamous **Cabrini Green** public-housing project—so close to the affluence of River North but a world away. Cabrini Green is one of many war zones created in Chicago by public housing. Although some believe it's only a matter of time before the project is razed to accommodate developers of luxury properties who are eyeing the land, relocating the hundreds of people who live there is a political hot potato few want to face. Meanwhile the residents struggle to raise families amid squalor and disrepair, and gang violence claims several lives every year.

㉗ The **River North Concourse** (750 N. Orleans St. at Chicago Ave.) houses many galleries along with a collection of stores and businesses. The striking lobby is done in exposed brick and glass block, and a bank of television monitors decorates the Orleans Street entrance. On the ground floor is **Chiaroscuro,** a gallery/shop with jewelry, clothing, furniture, and paper goods that could all be classified as objets d'art.

**Time Out** If you're weary from gallery hopping, **Cafe Tête-à-Tête,** on the second floor of 750 North Orleans Street, is a good spot for a croissant and espresso, sandwich, or more substantial entrée. Finish off with gelati or a Viennese-style pastry. The room is pleasantly airy, and the art on the walls (from the building's various galleries) is for sale.

To return by public transportation to Michigan Avenue in the Near North, take the eastbound Lincoln (No. 11) bus at the intersection of Chicago Avenue and La Salle Street. The bus travels Chicago Avenue to Michigan Avenue and turns south on Michigan Avenue. Or you can take the Chicago (No. 66) bus from the same stop, eastbound to Michigan Avenue and trans-

fer to the Water Tower Express (No. 125) for points north between Chicago Avenue and Walton Street.

## Tour 6: Lincoln Park

*Numbers in the margin correspond to points of interest on the
Tour 6: Lincoln Park map.*

In the early years of the 19th century the area bounded by
North Avenue (1600 N.) on the south, Diversey Parkway (2800
N.) on the north, the lake on the east, and the Chicago River on
the west was a sparsely settled community of truck farms and
orchards that grew produce for the city of Chicago, 3 miles to
the south. The original city burial ground was located on the
lakefront at North Avenue. The park that today extends from
North Avenue to Hollywood Avenue (5700 N.) was established
in 1864, after the city transferred about 20,000 bodies to
Graceland and Rosehill cemeteries, then far north of the city
limits (*see* Tour 7). Many of the dead were Confederate soldiers
who perished at Camp Douglas, the Union's infamous prison
camp on the lakefront several miles south. Called Lincoln Park
after the then-recently assassinated president, this swath of
green became the city's first public playground. The neighborhood adjacent to the original park also became known as Lincoln Park (to the confusion of some visitors).

By the mid-1860s the area had become more populated. Germans predominated, and there were Irish and Scotch immigrants. The construction in 1860 of the Presbyterian
Theological Seminary (later the McCormick Seminary, which
moved to Hyde Park in 1977) brought modest residential construction. By the end of the century, immigrants from Eastern
Europe—Poles, Slovaks, Serbians, Hungarians, Romanians,
and some Italians as well—had swelled the population, and
much of the housing stock in the western part of the neighborhood dates from this period.

Between the world wars, expensive new construction, particularly along the lakefront and the park, was undertaken in Lincoln Park. At the same time, the once elegant houses to the
west that had begun to deteriorate were being subdivided into
rooming houses—a process that was occurring at roughly the
same period in Hyde Park, 10 miles to the south. By 1930 a
group of blacks had moved to the southwestern corner of Lincoln Park. Italians were feared because the "black hand" was
active here. The St. Valentine's Day Massacre and the FBI
shooting of John Dillinger at the Biograph Theatre took place
on North Lincoln Avenue.

Following World War II, the ethnic groups that had been first
to arrive in Lincoln Park, having achieved some affluence, began to leave for the suburbs and the northern parts of the city.
Poor Appalachians, Hispanics, and blacks, who did not have the
resources to maintain their homes, moved in. By 1960 nearly a
quarter of the housing stock in Lincoln Park had been classified
as substandard.

As housing prices fell, artists and others who appreciated the
aesthetic value of the decaying buildings and were willing to
work to restore them moved to the southeastern part of the
area. The newcomers joined established residents in forming
the Old Town Triangle Association; residents to the north, who

had successfully resisted subdivision, formed the Mid-North Association. Neighborhood institutions, including De Paul University, the McCormick Seminary, four hospitals, a bank, and others dismayed by the decline of the area, formed the Lincoln Park Conservation Association in 1954. As the University of Chicago had done in Hyde Park, this association began exploring the possibilities of urban renewal as a means of rejuvenating the area.

As renewal plans progressed, blacks and Hispanics became incensed by what appeared to be minority removal, but the sit-ins and demonstrations that followed were ultimately unsuccessful. The original buildings along North Avenue were bulldozed and replaced with anonymous modern town-house developments, and many north–south streets were blocked off at North Avenue to create an enclosed community to the north.

Since the 1960s the gentrification of Lincoln Park has moved steadily westward, spreading as far as Clybourn Avenue, formerly a light industrial strip.

Our tour is divided into three parts. First we'll explore North Lincoln Avenue, the "main drag" of Lincoln Park, which is full of shops, restaurants, and theaters. The Biograph Theatre, where John Dillinger met his end, still stands here. DePaul University rules the center of the neighborhood. Then we'll see the Old Town Triangle, which has some of the oldest streets in Chicago and some of the most expensive, and accommodates a diverse population. Here you'll see some prime examples of gentrification. Finally we'll visit the lakefront and see several attractions in the city's oldest and most popular park.

**DePaul and North Lincoln Avenue** Our tour starts at the DePaul University campus. The CTA is the best way to get here from the Loop and the Near North Side. Take the Howard A or B train or the Ravenswood A or B train to Fullerton Avenue. Sheffield Avenue will be the nearest north–south street. If you're driving, take Lake Shore Drive to Fullerton Avenue and drive west on Fullerton Avenue to Sheffield Avenue. Parking is scarce, especially evenings and weekends, so public transit or a cab is recommended.

The massive brick complex extending halfway down the block on the southwest corner of Fullerton and Sheffield avenues, ❶ now known as the **Sanctuary** (2358 N. Sheffield Ave.), was built in 1895 as the St. Augustine Home for the Aged.

Walk south on Sheffield Avenue and turn left onto Belden Avenue. ❷ nue. Continue east to the entrance to the **DePaul University** campus. Begun in 1898, the university today enrolls about 12,000 students, many of whom commute from neighboring suburbs. DePaul has a large continuing-education program, and thousands of Chicago adults attend the many evening and weekend classes. This portion of the campus is the former ❸ **McCormick Seminary** grounds, where antislavery groups met during the Civil War and Chicagoans sought refuge from the Great Fire in 1871. Note the elegant New England–style church on your right as you enter. The small street inside the U on your left is Chalmers Place. The massive Queen Anne building on the north side has decorative shingles aligned in rows of different shapes; at the west end of the building is a great turret. Now enter the cul-de-sac, whose brick houses, more than 100 years old and once faculty residences at McCormick Seminary, are now privately owned. Note the semicircular brickwork around the windows. At the west end of the street is the Gothic seminary building. Continue south past the seminary, east on Chalmers Place, and south again to exit the university grounds where you entered on Belden Avenue.

Continue east on Belden Avenue and turn left onto Halsted Street. Walk north to the intersection of Fullerton Avenue, Halsted Street, and Lincoln Avenue.

**4** Lincoln Avenue is a diagonal that creates a three-way intersection with Fullerton Avenue and Halsted Street. To the southeast, where Halsted Street and Lincoln Avenue come together at a point is the huge **Children's Memorial Resale Shop** (2374 N. Lincoln Ave., tel. 312/281–3747), which carries every kind of used merchandise imaginable: furniture, clothing, kitchenware, china, books, and more.

We'll head up the east side of Lincoln Avenue and return on the west side. This shopping strip tells a good deal about the neighborhood. Upscale and trendy without being avant-garde, the strip caters to well-educated young and middle-age professionals, emphasizing recreation and leisure-time needs over more mundane requirements. You'll be hard pressed to find a drugstore or a shoemaker's shop on this strip: those conveniences have moved to Clark Street, several blocks east, or to Sheffield Avenue.

**5** The **Biograph Theater** (2433 N. Lincoln Ave., tel. 312/348–1350), where gangster John Dillinger met his end at the hands of the FBI, is now on the National Register of Historic Places. The Biograph shows first-run movies with an emphasis, as you might expect from the neighborhood, on foreign and art films.

**6** Several doors north is **Bookseller's Row** (2445 N. Lincoln Ave., tel. 312/348–1170), one of several bookstores on the strip, where you'll find used, out of print, and fine books, together with a few new ones as well. **Wax Trax Records** (2449 N. Lincoln Ave., tel. 312/929–0221), the place for everything in popular music, including oldies and imports, is a must stop if you have teenagers with you. **Fiber Works** (2457 N. Lincoln Ave., tel. 312/327–0444) has an attractive selection of clothing and yarns in natural fibers. The **Children's Bookstore** (2465 N. Lincoln Ave., tel. 312/248–2665) is probably the best of its kind in the city. **Finders Keepers** (2469 N. Lincoln Ave., tel. 312/525–1510), a resale shop for the Latin School of Chicago, has the kind of used merchandise also found at the Children's Memorial Resale Shop.

**7** Across Lincoln is the **Apollo Theatre Center** (2540 N. Lincoln Ave., tel. 312/935–6100), which offers local productions of Broadway and off-Broadway hit shows.

**Time Out** If you're hungry for a light snack, pop in at **Periwinkle** (2511 N. Lincoln Ave.), an attractive small café that expands to its adjacent garden in summer. The coffee is outstanding, and the desserts are sinfully rich, although dinner offerings are uneven.

**8** **Omiyage** (2482 N. Lincoln Ave., tel. 312/477–1428) is a Japanese shop that has a little of lots of different things: jewelry, plates, cookware, miscellany. The items are attractive and tasteful, the prices reasonable.

# Tour 6: Lincoln Park

Apollo Theatre Center, **7**

Biograph Theater, **5**

Bookseller's Row, **6**

Chess pavilion, **28**

Chicago Academy of Sciences, **12**

Chicago Historical Society, **23**

Children's Memorial Resale Shop, **4**

Crilly Court, **20**

De Paul University, **2**

Green, Inc., **21**

Lincoln Park Conservatory, **26**

Lincoln Park Zoo, **24**

Marge's Pub, **14**

McCormick Seminary, **3**

Midwest Buddhist Temple, **17**

Moody Memorial Church, **22**

North Avenue Beach, **27**

Omiyage, **8**

1800 North Hudson Avenue, **18**

1800 North Sedgwick, **15**

1838 and 1836 North Lincoln Park West, **13**

Potbelly Sandwich Works, **11**

St. Michael's Church, **19**

Sanctuary, **1**

Shakespeare Garden, **25**

Threepenny Theatre, **9**

2312-2310 North Lincoln Avenue, **10**

Wisconsin Street, **16**

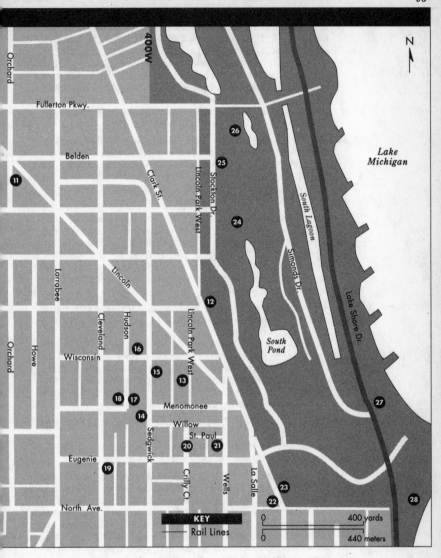

Orchard

400W

N

Fullerton Pkwy.

Belden

Lincoln Park West

Stockton Dr.

Clark St.

11

26

25

24

Lake
Michigan

South Lagoon

Larrabee

Lincoln

Simonds Dr.

Lake Shore Dr.

12

Cleveland

Hudson

Orchard

Howe

Wisconsin

16

South
Pond

15

Lincoln Park West

13

18  17

Menomonee

14

Willow

St. Paul

20      21

27

Sedgwick

Eugenie

19

Crilly Ct.

Wells

La Salle

23

22

28

North Ave.

**KEY**

Rail Lines

0                    400 yards

0                    440 meters

On the corner of Montana Street is **Guild Books** (2456 N. Lincoln Ave., tel. 312/525–3667). Unlike the two bookstores mentioned above, this one has new and remaindered titles; like the other two stores, it's a good spot for bargain hunting. Next to the Guild Bookstore is **Blake** (2448 N. Lincoln Ave., tel. 312/477–3364), a trendy clothing store. If your tastes run to more practical items you might prefer **Uncle Dan's Army Navy Store** (2440 N. Lincoln Ave., tel. 312/477–1918), a treasure trove of camouflage outfits, hats, camp cookware, tents, sleeping bags, duffel bags, foot lockers, and badges.

**❾** The **Threepenny Theatre** (2424 N. Lincoln Ave., tel. 312/935–5744) used to be a revival house where golden oldies lived again, but that business died when VCRs became ascendant. The Threepenny now shows new films in competition with the Biograph across the street.

**❿** The buildings at **2312–2310 North Lincoln Avenue** were designed by Adler & Sullivan in the 1880s. **Wise Fools Pub** (2270 N. Lincoln Ave., tel. 312/929–1510) is one of the few remaining places on Lincoln Avenue to hear folk and blues. The **John Barleycorn Memorial Pub** (636 W. Belden Ave., tel. 312/348–8899) is one of Chicago's better-known pubs; it's filled with ship models, and classical music accompanies a continuous show of art slides.

**⓫** Some of the best submarine sandwiches in town are available at the **Potbelly Sandwich Works** (2264 N. Lincoln Ave., tel. 312/528–1405), which is worth a visit even if you're not hungry. The walls are decorated with old-fashioned signs, the tables are covered in tile. Vintage malted-milk machines whir behind the counter. A massive old Toledo scale sits against the wall. In the oaken loft is a player piano and a small potbelly stove. The centerpiece of the restaurant is a huge potbelly stove that you'll have to walk around to get to the service counter.

Across the street are **The Body Politic** and the **Victory Gardens Theatre** (2261 N. Lincoln Ave., tel. 312/871–3000), two long-established and respected small theater groups; like many others, they share space and facilities to reduce expenses.

**⓬** This ends our tour of Lincoln Avenue. At this point you'll want to either retrieve your car or jump on the Lincoln Avenue bus (No. 11) and go south to Lincoln and Armitage avenues (2000 N.). At Armitage Avenue turn left and continue to Clark Street to reach the imposing classical-style building that houses the **Chicago Academy of Sciences**. Despite its scholarly name, this is not an institution of higher learning but a museum specializing in the natural history of the Midwest. The permanent exhibits include dioramas showing the ecology of Chicago millions of years ago, before it was settled by man, and back-lit ceiling images of the night sky seen from Chicago. Special exhibits are mounted regularly. *2001 N. Clark St., tel. 312/549–0343. Admission: $1 adults, 50¢ children and senior citizens, free Mon. Open daily 10–5.*

**Old Town Triangle** Old Town Triangle is filled with courts and lanes that run for only a block or so; to complicate matters, many of the streets have been made one-way in a pattern that can make it difficult to get from one place to another. (Urban planners commonly use this device in redeveloped areas to discourage the inflow of unwanted traffic.) Therefore, if you're driving, you may find it easier to park your car near the start of the tour and explore on foot. If you came by public transportation, you are now rewarded by not having to find a place to park.

To reach Old Town Triangle, take Clark Street or Lincoln Avenue south to Wisconsin Street, turn west, and proceed to Lincoln Park West. Be sure to have a look at the elegant row of gracious old painted-brick buildings at **1850–1858 North Lincoln Avenue.**

⑬ A left turn onto Lincoln Park West will lead you to two marvelous frame houses at **1838 and 1836 North Lincoln Park West.** Frame houses are relatively uncommon in Lincoln Park, in part because of the restrictions on wood construction that went into effect following the Chicago Fire in 1871. (Some poorer areas in the southwest of Lincoln Park do have extensive frame construction; the regulations were not always strictly enforced.)

The smaller of the two buildings, 1836, was built just after the fire; it has narrow clapboards, bay windows, leaded glass, and decorative iron grillwork around the miniature widow's walk above the front entrance. Note also the decorative cutouts in the wood over the front door. The exterior painting has been done in contrasting brown, beige, and white to reveal the details of the woodwork.

The larger house, 1838, is a grand structure built of wider clapboards and painted—in true Victorian style—in vividly contrasting gray, green, and salmon. Ornaments and traceries are outlined. (The painter, James F. Jereb, has signed his work at the south end of the house, a foot or so above the ground.) Notice, too, the overhanging veranda, the twin attic windows, and the ornately carved supports under the veranda and eaves. The style of the wrought-iron fence is of the appropriate period.

⑭ Continue south, turn west on Memomonee and go one block to Sedgwick Street. On the southwest corner of the intersection is **Marge's Pub** (1750 N. Sedgwick St., tel. 312/944–9775), the oldest commercial property in Lincoln Park and a good place to stop for a beer. The building, with its redbrick construction, decorated in stone around the windows, is a familiar style in older Lincoln Park buildings.

⑮ Turn right onto the **1800 North Sedgwick Street** block and proceed about halfway up the block. On the right you will notice a change from the traditional brick architecture. The materials used to build these houses begin with handsome contemporary red brick and move on to poured concrete, oddly colored brick, and gray wood. This strip may be the most expensive in Chicago. Each of the houses was custom-designed for its owner at an astronomical price by a different world-renowned architect. Such were the egos involved that the architects could agree on nothing—not style, not materials, not lot size, not even the height of the buildings. Although some of the structures might look good on another site, particularly if surrounded by some land, here they look like transplanted misfits, jammed in together, out of character with the neighborhood and with each other. Despite their monetary value, little about them is aesthetically pleasing.

⑯ Continue on Sedgwick Street to the intersection with Wisconsin Street. On the north side of **Wisconsin Street,** extending west to Hudson Avenue, is another example of new construction, a massive condominium complex that fails aesthetically for just the opposite reason that the Sedgwick Street custom-designed buildings fail. Here the architect has augmented basic redbrick construction with virtually every design element one might see in turn-of-the-century buildings of the neighborhood, including bays and huge arched windows. The mammoth scale of the building is an anachronism; worse, the overuse of traditional stylistic elements makes the building look like a parody of, rather than a complement to, the buildings it seeks to imitate. Look at the period brick building on the northeast corner of Sedgwick and Wisconsin streets for a reminder of how satisfying elegant simplicity can be.

Walk west on Wisconsin Street, turn south on Hudson Avenue, and proceed one block to Menomonee Street. The Oriental-looking building where the street curves is the **Midwest Buddhist Temple** (435 W. Menomonee St., tel. 312/943–7801). In mid-June, Old Town Triangle hosts the Old Town Art Fair, which claims to be the oldest juried art fair in the country, and the Midwest Buddhist Temple is one of the most popular food vendors at the fair.

Before you turn on Menomonee Street, regard the half-timber house at the corner, **1800 North Hudson Avenue,** a particularly handsome example of a style that's unusual for Lincoln Park.

Go west one block on Menomonee then south on Cleveland Avenue to Eugenie Street and **St. Michael's Church** (458 W. Eugenie St., tel. 312/664–1511). This massive, ornate Romanesque building was constructed on land donated in the 1850s by Michael Diversey (the early beer baron after whom Diversey Parkway was named) to provide a church where the area's German community could worship. The structure partially withstood the fire of 1871, and the interior of the church was restored after the fire by the German residents of the neighborhood. Their work is a legacy of exquisite craftsmanship. Outside, notice the classical columns of different heights, the elaborate capitals, the many roofs with stonework at the top, and the elegant spire.

Walk east on Eugenie Street about five blocks and turn left onto **Crilly Court,** one of the oldest streets in Chicago. For nearly half a century this little enclave was also one of Chicago's stablest neighborhoods, with residents who had lived here for more than 40 years. A few years ago, the buildings were acquired by developers, who converted them into condominiums. The existing tenants were given the option to buy, but most of them—some quite elderly—could not afford to and were forced to move.

When you come to St. Paul Avenue, turn east, proceed to Wells Street, and turn right. **Green, Inc.** (1716 N. Wells St., tel. 312/266–2806) is a plant-lover's delight, with shrubs and trees set out on the sidewalk in good weather and a marvelous selection of cacti, many of which are displayed in the window. The building that houses the stores on this block has designs stamped in tin between the upper and lower bay windows. The building to the south has several more shops.

**Time Out**   For a pick-me-up, stop at **Savories** (1700 N. Wells St.), a coffee, tea, and spice shop that also sells pots, mugs, and other accessories. The coffee is fresh and delicious (try the daily special), and so are the iced coffees and teas. Sample one of the rich scones or the sour-cherry cobbler; the muffins, buns, and pastries, too, are delectable.

**Lincoln Park** With Old Town Triangle behind us, we re-enter Lincoln Park, where we ended our tour of North Lincoln Avenue with a visit to the Academy of Sciences (*see above*). For those who've followed the tour to this point, go south on Wells Street, turn left on North Avenue, and walk east to Clark Street. If you're just picking up the tour at this point, you can reach Lincoln Park by taking the No. 151 Sheridan Road bus north from North Michigan Avenue. Get off at North Avenue. If you're driving, take Lake Shore Drive to the La Salle Street/North Avenue exit. Make a right turn onto Stockton Drive and look for metered parking. The area can be extremely congested, especially on weekends, so driving is not recommended.

The massive Romanesque structure on the west side of Clark
**㉒** Street is **Moody Memorial Church** (1630 N. Clark St., tel. 312/943–0466), one of the largest Protestant churches in the nation. The nondenominational church, named after 19th-century evangelist Dwight L. Moody, is associated with the Moody Bible Institute (*see* Tour 5).

Across Clark is the southwestern entrance to the park. First
**㉓** pay a visit to the **Chicago Historical Society,** which stands at the northeast corner of North Avenue and Clark Street. The original stately brick Georgian structure was built in 1932, and if you walk around to the eastern side (facing the lake) you can see what it looked like at the time. On the Clark Street side the original facade has been covered by a sparkling all-glass addition, which contains a café at its south end (the curved portion). In the café's north wall is a terra-cotta arch designed by Daniel Burnham more than 100 years ago. The historical society's permanent exhibits include the much-loved diorama room that portrays scenes from Chicago's history and has been a part of the lives of generations of Chicago children. Other highlights include collections of costumes and the famous statue of Abraham Lincoln, whose nose gleams from having been rubbed by countless children. In addition the society mounts temporary exhibitions; its Civil War installation, "A House Divided," will run for the next several years and shouldn't be missed by Civil War buffs. *1601 N. Clark St., tel. 312/642–4600. Admission: $3 adults, $2 senior citizens, $1 children, free Mon. Open Mon.–Sat. 9:30–4:30, Sun. noon–5.*

All of Chicago's parks, and **Lincoln Park** in particular, are dotted with sculptures—historical, literary or just plain fanciful. East of the historical society is one of the most famous, a standing figure of Abraham Lincoln, completed in 1887 by the noted American sculptor Augustus Saint-Gaudens, whose portrayals of military heroes and presidents adorn almost every major city east of the Mississippi River. The sculptor used a life mask of Lincoln's face and casts of his hands that were made before he became president.

Wandering north through the park along Stockton Drive will
**㉔** bring you to **Lincoln Park Zoo,** one of the finest small urban zoos in the country. (Look for the red barn, home of "Farm in the Zoo": The main entrance is just north of it.) Begun in 1868 with a pair of swans donated by New York's Central Park, the 35-acre zoo grew through donations of animals from wealthy Chicago residents and the purchase of a collection from the

Barnum and Bailey Circus. Many of the big houses, such as the lion house and the elephant house, are built in the classical brick typical of 19th-century zoos. The older buildings are surrounded by newer outdoor habitats that try to recreate the animals' natural, wild surroundings. Outside the lion house there's a window that lets zoo visitors stand almost face to face with the tigers (if the giant cats are in the mood).

Lincoln Park Zoo is noted for its Great Ape House; the 23 gorillas are considered the finest collection in the world. Since most of them have been bred in captivity, there are always several babies about. It's fascinating to spend an hour watching the members of each community interact. In addition to the reptile house, the large mammal house (elephants, giraffes, black rhinos), the monkey house, the bird house, the small-mammal house, and a huge polar-bear pool with two bears, the zoo has several rare and endangered species. The Spectacle Bear (named for the eyeglasslike markings around its eyes) from Peru is one; another, China's Père David's deer, has been extinct in the wild for centuries. The latter is unlike any deer you've seen before, with backward antlers, big feet, and a horselike face. Several koalas live in a "koala condo" in the same building as the main gift shop. Youngsters will enjoy the children's zoo, the Farm in the Zoo (farm animals and a learning center with films and demonstrations), and the Kids' Corner Discovery Place, with hands-on activities. *2200 N. Cannon Dr., tel. 312/294–4660. Admission free. Open daily 9–5.*

The homely bronze figure at Stockton Drive opposite Dickens Street is Hans Christian Andersen, seated there since 1896. Beside him is the beautiful swan from his most famous story, "The Ugly Duckling."

㉕ Also near the zoo, at the western edge of the park, opposite Belden Avenue, is the **Shakespeare Garden,** featuring flowers and plants mentioned in the bard's works. The bronze statue of the author was sculpted by William Ordway Partridge in 1894, after he had exhibited a plaster model of the work at the Columbian Exposition.

㉖ North of the zoo is the **Lincoln Park Conservatory,** which has a palm house, a fernery, a cactus house, and a show house in which displays are mounted: the azalea show in February, the Easter show in March or April, the chrysanthemum show in November, and the Christmas show in December. **Grandmother's Garden,** between Stockton Drive and Lincoln Park West, is a collection dating from 1893 of informal beds of perennials, including hibiscus and chrysanthemums. A large outdoor garden has flowering plants. *2400 N. Stockton Dr., tel. 312/294–4770. Admission free. Open Sun.–Thurs. 10–6, Fri. 10–9. Hours vary during shows.*

In the conservatory garden is an uncommonly joyful fountain where bronze storks, fish, and small mer-boys cavort in the spraying water. The 1887 **Bates Fountain** was the collaborative effort of Saint-Gaudens and his assistant, Frederick Mac-Monnies.

㉗ At Fullerton turn right and walk under Lake Shore Drive to the lakefront. From here you can stroll in either direction for several miles. **North Avenue Beach** is likely to be thronged on summer weekends but sparsely populated at other times. To get back to the Near North Side, about 2 miles from here, walk south past North Avenue Beach and follow the lakefront promenade. Notice the blue-and-white beach house, its portholes and "smokestacks" mimicking an old ocean liner. At the south end of the beach stop by the **chess pavilion** to watch people of all ages engrossed in intellectual combat. The pavilion is 1950s-vintage. Look for the carved reliefs along its base and the king and queen that flank it on either side.

If you don't feel like a walk on the beach, go west from Fullerton Avenue to Stockton Drive and catch the No. 151 bus southbound, which will take you back to Michigan Avenue. The No. 22 and No. 36 buses on Clark Street will also take you back to the Near North or the Loop.

## Tour 7: North Clark Street

A car or bus ride up North Clark Street north of Lincoln Park provides an interesting view of how cities and their ethnic populations grow and change. Before the late 1960s the Clark Street area was solidly white middle class. Andersonville, the Swedish community centered at Foster Avenue (5200 N.) and Clark Street, extended north half a mile and included residential buildings to the east and west as well as a vital shopping strip on Clark Street. Then, in the early 1970s, immigration from the Far East began. Chicago's first Thai restaurant opened at 5000 North Clark Street. (Chicago's Thai population has since dispersed itself throughout the city without establishing a significant concentration here.) The Japanese community, which had shops and restaurants at the northern end of the North 3000s on Clark Street, became more firmly entrenched, joined by substantial Korean immigration. Korean settlement has since grown to the north and west, along north Lincoln Avenue. As the 1970s ended, the Asian immigrants were being joined by newcomers from the Middle East. Together these groups have moved into the neighborhood, in classic fashion, as the old established group (the Swedish community) moved out to the suburbs. Today the shops on North Clark Street bear witness to the process of ethnic transition.

You can board the northbound Clark Street (No. 22) bus on Dearborn Street in the Loop or on Clark Street north of Walton Street. Or you can drive to Clark Street and North Avenue, where we'll begin our ride. North Avenue (1600 N.) is the southern boundary of the Lincoln Park neighborhood, which extends north to Diversey Avenue (2800 N.). The drive through Lincoln Park affords views of handsome renovated housing, housing in the process of being restored, upscale shops, and youthful joggers.

As you cross Belmont (3200 N.), you'll notice that the character of the neighborhood has changed. In the 3300 North block of Clark Street the **Happi-Sushi** restaurant and the **Suehiro** restaurant provide for Japanese tastes in food and are long-time denizens of this strip. You can get all the ingredients for authentic Japanese dishes at **Star Market** (3349 N. Clark St.), including exquisitely fresh (and astronomically expensive) fish to be used raw, sliced thinly, for sashimi.

Continuing north to the intersection with Addison Street, you'll find **Wrigley Field,** the home of the Chicago Cubs. The surrounding neighborhood of Wrigleyville is the last solidly white middle-class neighborhood remaining on this strip. Until

the summer of 1988, area residents were successful in fighting
the installation of lights for night games at Wrigley Field, and
the Cubs played all their home games in the afternoon.

At Clark Street and Irving Park Road (4000 N.), you'll find
**Graceland Cemetery**, the final resting place of many 19th-cen-
tury millionaires and other local luminaries. In the 4500 N.
block are **K-World Trading** and **Bee Tradin' Co.**, and a bit farther north is **Nice Trading Co.** All are East Asian import and
export firms that aren't much to look at—they don't do business with the public—but their names speak volumes.

North of Wilson Avenue, pictures of fish swim across the window of the **Clark St. Fishmarket**, where very little English is
spoken; the customers and the shop owners are Korean immigrants. **Charming Woks** (4628 N. Clark, tel. 312/989–8768) prepares Hunan and Szechuan food. The **Korean Restaurant** (4631
N. Clark, tel. 312/878–2095) advertises carryouts. **Oriental
Food Mart Wholesalers and Importers** is just south of Leland.
**Tokyo Marina** restaurant (5058 N. Clark), comes up on your left
(*see* Chapter 6).

Foster Avenue is the old southern boundary of Andersonville.
Around the corner on Foster Avenue, west of Clark Street, is
the **Middle Eastern Bakery and Grocery** (1512 W. Foster Ave.).
Here are falafel, meat pies, spinach pies, *baba ghannouj* (eggplant puree dip), oil-cured olives, grains, pita bread, and a se-
ductive selection of Middle Eastern sweets—flaky, honey-
dipped, nut-filled delights. In the 5200 North block just north
of Foster Avenue, the **Beirut Restaurant** serves *kifta* kebabs
(grilled meatballs), baba ghannouj, *kibbee* (ground lamb with
bulghur wheat), falafel, meat and spinach pies, and more.
Across the street the original **Ann Sather's** restaurant, with its
white wood on red brick storefront, specializes in Swedish cuisine and generally does a good business. South of Ann Sather
the **Mediterranean Snack Shop and Grill** advertises steak sandwiches, Italian beef, burritos, and tacos; the specials of the day
are potato stew with rice, *kheema* (ground beef) stew with
rice, okra stew with rice, and other traditional dishes of the
Mideast and Indian subcontinent.

Across the street on the same block the **Byblos I Bakery and
Deli** offers Lebanese Middle Eastern bread and groceries. If
you arrive at the right time, you'll see the window filled with
pita breads still puffed. Opposite the bakery, the **Swedish-
American Museum Center** has beautifully decorated papier-
mâché roosters and horses, place mats, craft items, tablecloths, and candelabras. North of the Byblos Bakery is the
**Scandinavian Furniture Center**. The wares of **Nelson's Scandinavian Bakery** are classic European pastries: elephant ears and
petit fours with chocolate, for example. The **Svea Restaurant**
has pretty blue and white tablecloths and a counter. **Erickson's
Delicatessen** has glögg in bottles, crispbreads, Ramlösa, hol-
landaise sauce mix, and homemade herring and imported
cheese.

Just north of Erickson's the **Andersonville Artists Original Arts
and Crafts Display** features the work of local artisans, which includes hand-painted china, small sculptures, and paintings. On
the other side of the street, the shelves of **Wikstrom's Gourmet
Foods** contain Wasa bread, Swedish pancake mix, coffee roll
mix, lingonberries, dilled potatoes, and raspberry dessert.

Just north of Wikstrom's is **G. M. Nordling Jeweler.** At **Reza's Restaurant** (5255 N. Clark) you can dine on kebabs, *must* and *khiyar* (yogurt and cucumber), pomegranate juice, charbroiled ground beef with Persian rice, and other Middle Eastern entrées in an attractive setting.

On the 5400 North block are **Seoul House,** which carries food, groceries, and general merchandise, and the **Kotobuki Japanese Restaurant.** On the 5600 North block are **Gabriel Philippine Food** and the **Korean Chap Chae House.**

**Phil House** (5845 N. Clark) is a Philippine market stocking fresh fish, taro root, fresh shrimp of all sizes, crayfish, langostinos, *longaniza* (Philippine sausage), and a huge selection of spring roll skins. Chicago is home to a very large group of Philippine immigrants, but like the Thais (and unlike the Indians and the Koreans) they have not concentrated in a single area.

Here ends our ride up Clark Street, an urban tour through time and the waves of ethnic migration and replacement. In that respect, Clark—like north Milwaukee Avenue, which has gone from being Polish to Hispanic to Polish again as new immigrants have arrived in the 1980s—is a microcosm of the city of Chicago and the continuing ebb and flow of its populations.

## Tour 8: Argyle Street and Uptown

In many cities, *uptown* suggests an elite residential area, as opposed to *downtown*, the central business district. Something like that must have been in the mind of the Californian who bought Chicago's Uptown National Bank sight unseen a few years ago; ever since he got a look at his property and its neighborhood, he's been trying to sell it. In Chicago, Uptown—an area bounded by Irving Park Road (4000 N.) on the south, Foster Avenue (5200 N.) on the north, the lake on the east, and Clark Street and Ravenswood Avenue (1800 W.) on the west— is the home of the down-and-out: Appalachians who came to Chicago in search of jobs following World War II, blacks, Native Americans, families on welfare, drug addicts, winos, and others of Chicago's most disadvantaged residents live here. The neighborhood is rough, the rents are low.

Given the characteristics of the neighborhood, numerous social service agencies are located here. Because of that, and the low rents, Uptown is where Vietnamese immigrants were placed when they began arriving in Chicago in substantial numbers following the end of the Vietnam War. Hmong refugees from Vietnam likewise joined a polyglot community whose common bond, if any, was a shared destitution.

Yet the arrival of the Vietnamese groups brought interesting developments in Uptown. The first years were difficult: Although some of the families were educated and well-to-do in Vietnam, they came here with no money and no knowledge of English. The Hmong were further disadvantaged by having had no urban experience; these tribal mountain people were transplanted directly from remote, rather primitive villages into the heart of a modern urban slum. Nonetheless, like earlier immigrants who came to America, these people arrived with the determination to make new lives for themselves. They took any job that was offered, no matter how menial or how low the pay, and they worked two jobs when they could find them. From their meager earnings, they saved money. And they did two other important things: They sent their children to school and zealously oversaw their studies, and they formed self-help associations. Through the associations, they used pooled savings as rotating funds to set one, then another, up in business: grocery stores and bakeries to sell the foods that tasted like home, clothing shops and hairdressing salons to fill the needs of the community, and finally restaurants that attracted not only people from the old country who were beginning to have discretionary funds but also Americans from all over the city.

As their businesses prospered, they bought property. And the property they bought was the cheapest they could find, on the most depressed street in this crumbling neighborhood, Argyle Street (5000 N.). Today Argyle Street, a two-block strip between Broadway on the west and Sheridan Road on the east, is thriving. Its commercial buildings have been upgraded, thereby attracting the shops and restaurants of other Asian communities in Chicago, principally the Chinese and Thai. As "New Chinatown" or "Chinatown North," the area became so attractive that the old Chinatown merchant's association, representing the stores along Wentworth Street on the south side, considered relocating there en masse. While that plan fell through, some stores moved on their own. The Argyle Street group has been so successful that there is now a rivalry between the two Chinatowns for the customers of the Asian (and American) communities in Chicago.

If you've never been to Southeast Asia, a walk down Argyle Street is the next best thing. The neighborhood bustles with street traffic, and the stores are crowded with people buying fresh produce, baked goods, kitchen equipment, and 50-pound sacks of rice. Few signs are in English, though merchants know enough English to serve customers who don't speak their native language. Often older children and teenagers who learned English in school are pressed into service to help visitors. If you've been to Southeast Asia and long again for those tastes, smells, and sights, you must visit Argyle Street. Only here will you find, for example, the wonderful, vile-smelling durian fruit—an addiction for many, anathema to some—and other staples of Southeast Asian cuisine. Here, too, you will find many of the best Vietnamese restaurants in the city, including **Mekong** (4953 N. Broadway) and **Hue** (1138 W. Argyle St.; *see* Chapter 6), as well as Chinese restaurants serving noodles and barbecued duck and pork (which you might enjoy munching as you walk).

Today, fueled in part by the success of the Vietnamese and, more generally, the prosperity that that success has brought, Uptown is changing. Renovators are buying once fine old properties and restoring them, and young middle-class folk, driven here by the high prices in such neighborhoods as Lincoln Park to the south, are beginning to move in. The area has become a political battleground between those who claim to represent the poor and downtrodden and those who believe that the undeniable social costs of rehabbing are less than the social costs of allowing the neighborhood to fall further and further into decay.

A walk on Argyle Street is one of the most complex experiences you can have in Chicago. You'll become totally immersed in the tastes and sounds of another culture; you'll see the classic immigrant pattern, the process of successful Americanization; and you'll appreciate the pushes and pulls at work as cities decay, are restored, and grow again.

## Tour 9: Devon Avenue

As immigration laws were made more lenient in the 1970s and 1980s, the number of immigrants arriving in Chicago increased substantially. In the 1970s, newcomers from the Indian subcontinent began to arrive, and in the 1980s they were followed by Asians from Thailand, Korea, the Philippines, and Vietnam; as well as large numbers from the Middle East, including Palestinians, Syrians, Lebanese, and Turks. The Soviet relaxation of restrictions on Jewish emigration shortly before the breakup of the Soviet Union turned many Jewish refuseniks into American residents.

Several of these diverse cultures mingle along a mile-long strip of Devon Avenue between Sacramento and Oakley streets, near the northern edge of the city. A stroll down the strip on any sunny Sunday afternoon or hot summer evening will allow you to appreciate the avenue's variety of cultures. At the eastern end is the hub of the Indian community, with stores catering to both Muslims and Hindus. As you walk west, you will see saree stores give way to Korean restaurants and Russian grocery stores. At the western end is an orthodox Jewish neighborhood, dotted with kosher bakeries and butchers, and religious bookstores.

To get to Devon Avenue (6400 N.), take Lake Shore Drive north to Hollywood Avenue. Stay in one of the left lanes and go west on Hollywood Avenue to Ridge Avenue. Turn right on Ridge Avenue and head north for about a mile to Devon Avenue. Turn left on Devon Avenue, drive about 2 miles west to Oakley Street (2200 W.), and park your car. Your tour will take you down Devon Avenue as far as Sacramento Avenue (3000 W.).

Starting on the south side of Devon Avenue at Oakley Street, you'll see **Suleiman Brother Farm City Meats** (2255 W. Devon Ave.), purveyors of *Halal* meat, from animals slaughtered according to the provisions of Islamic law. The store sells baby goat meat, as well as a large selection of fish. As you walk west, you'll see many stores, such as **Video Palace** (2315 W. Devon Ave.), that sell or rent Indian and Pakistani movies and videotapes.

There are also at least a dozen stores that sell the colorful sarees worn by Indian women, including the **Taj Saree Palace** (2553 W. Devon Ave.), **Sarees Sapne** (2623 W. Devon Ave.), **Sharada Saree Center** (2629 W. Devon Ave.), and **ISP Indian Saree Palace** (2536 W. Devon Ave.).

Numerous grocery stores along your route sell Indian foods, condiments, and kitchenwares; the exotic smells are enticing. Take a look at the **Middle East Trading Co.** (2505 W. Devon Ave.), **Patel Brothers** (with three locations at 2542, 2600, and 2610 W. Devon Ave.), and **Foods of India** (2331 and 2614 W. Devon Ave.).

For a quick snack, try the Indian food at the **Pakistani Indian Chat House** (6357 N. Claremont Ave., at the corner of Devon

Ave.), or **Annapurna Fast Food Vegetarian Snacks and Sweets** (2608 W. Devon Ave.).

Several Indian restaurants along Devon Avenue are good choices for a meal, including **Viceroy of India** (2516 W. Devon Ave.), **Moti Mahal** (2525 W. Devon Ave.), and the vegetarian **Natraj** (2240 W. Devon Ave.). Try the tandoori chicken or fish, which is marinated and grilled, the *sagh paneer* (a creamy mixture of spinach and cheese), or the *dal* (a lentil puree).

Several stores specialize in Russian cuisine and are easily recognized by the signs in Cyrillic writing hanging outside. Among them are **Globus International Foods and Delicatessen** (2837 W. Devon Ave.), **Three Sisters Delicatessen** (2854 W. Devon Ave.), and **Kashtan Deli** (2740 W. Devon Ave.). Three Sisters has a large selection of *matrioshkas* (the popular Russian dolls that are stacked one inside another). At 2845 West Devon Avenue, you'll see the **Croatian Cultural Center.**

When you reach the western end of Devon Avenue, notice the many stores and restaurants catering to the orthodox Jewish community. The restaurants and bakeries are good bets for either a sit-down meal or a snack to eat while you walk. Watch for **Miller's Market** (2527 W. Devon Ave.), **Tel Aviv Kosher Bakery** (2944 W. Devon Ave.), **The Bagel Restaurant** (3000 W. Devon Ave.), **Kosher Karry** (2828 W. Devon Ave.), and **Levinson's Bakery** (2856 W. Devon Ave.). The **Midwest Fish Market** (2942 W. Devon Ave.) has lox and other smoked fish for sale.

Several stores along the way sell Hebrew books and sacramental items, including **Rosenblum's Hebrew Bookstore** (2910 W. Devon Ave.) and the **Chicago Hebrew Bookstore** (2942 W. Devon Ave.). Rosenblum's has a large selection of unusual cookbooks, including several on Yemeni and Sephardic cuisine.

## Chicago for Free

Like all great cities, Chicago offers a wealth of things to see and do that cost no more than the price of transportation to them.

Concerts **Chicago Public Library Cultural Center** (78 E. Washington St., tel. 312/269–2900) presents the Dame Myra Hess Memorial Concert Series Wednesday at 12:15, a program of recitals by rising professional classical musicians.

**Petrillo Bandshell** in Grant Park is the site of summertime concerts sponsored by the Chicago Park District. In mid-June the Jazz Fest and the Gospel Fest are three-day events in which numerous performances take place on several stages. The Grant Park Symphony Orchestra and Chorus perform three to four times a week, late June through August. The Blues Festival comes to town in late August and early September. *The Reader* (free at stores and other locations in The Loop, Near North Side, Lincoln Park, and Hyde Park on Thursday and Friday) gives program details and performance times.

**Daley Plaza** (Washington between Clark and Dearborn Sts.) and **First National Bank of Chicago Plaza** (Dearborn to Clark Sts. between Monroe and Madison Sts.) have performances of light music, including folk and pop, during the noon hour in the summertime.

**Chicago Chamber Orchestra** (tel. 312/922–5570), under the direction of Dieter Koeber, gives free chamber concerts throughout the year at various locations. The performances are funded by corporate and foundation grants and individual memberships; the organization's goal is to bring live performances of fine music to those who cannot afford to pay for them.

Many Chicago churches offer free concerts, frequently organ recitals, choral programs, and gospel music. *The Reader* lists programs and locations.

**Museums**  Several Chicago museums do not charge admission fees, among them: **Chicago Public Library Cultural Center, Czechoslovakian Society of America Heritage Museum and Archives, DuSable Museum of African American History, Mexican Fine Arts Center Museum, Oriental Institute, Polish Museum of America, Telephony Museum.** Of the museums that have admission fees, many of them schedule one day a week when admission is free to all: **Art Institute of Chicago** (Tuesday), **Chicago Academy of Sciences** (Monday), **Chicago Historical Society** (Monday), **Chicago Children's Museum** (Thursday) **Field Museum of Natural History** (Thursday), **Museum of Contemporary Art** (Tuesday), **John G. Shedd Aquarium** (Thursday) and **Museum of Science and Industry** (Thursday). Though there is a fee for the Sky Show, the exhibits are free at the **Adler Planetarium.**

**Music School Programs**  Chicago has several fine music schools and university departments of music, where faculty and students frequently give recitals (public performances are often a part of degree requirements).

**University of Chicago Concert Office** (tel. 312/702–8068) schedules concerts by a number of performing ensembles: the Motet Choir, the University of Chicago Chorus, the University of Chicago Orchestra, and the Collegium Musicum (an instrumental and vocal ensemble that performs music of the Renaissance and Baroque periods).

**American Conservatory of Music** (17 N. State St., tel. 312/263–4161) offers student and faculty recitals, at noon and in the evening, when school is in session. A program is scheduled almost every day except Sunday, and most performances are free.

**DePaul University School of Music** (804 W. Belden Ave., tel. 312/341–8373) has concerts by a chorus, an orchestra, a jazz band, and other performing ensembles as well as recitals. There are daily events throughout the school year.

**Chicago Musical College of Roosevelt University** (Rudolf Ganz Memorial Hall, 430 S. Michigan Ave., tel. 312/341–3787) schedules recitals and orchestral, chamber, woodwind, and jazz concerts. Early in the semester there are two to three events a week; later there's something every day.

**Sherwood Conservatory of Music** (1014 S. Michigan Ave., tel. 312/427–6267) has faculty and student recitals most Sunday afternoons and some Saturdays.

**Picnics**  Between April and October, picnicking can be delightful almost anywhere along the lakefront. Favorite spots include Grant Park and Navy Pier.

**Tours**  Many institutions offer free guided tours of their operations; most require reservations.

**Chicago City Hall** (121 N. La Salle St., tel. 312/744–7774) has one tour daily at 10 AM that takes in the City Council chambers and an exhibit of gifts presented to the late Mayor Harold Washington. City council meetings are open to the public and are famous for their often heated debates. Call 312/744–3081 for meeting times.

The main **U.S. Post Office** in Chicago (433 W. Van Buren St., tel. 312/765–3009), the largest postal facility in the world, offers tours of its mail processing division weekdays at 10:30 and 12:30. Call one week in advance; no children under nine.

**James Jardine Water Purification Plant** (Navy Pier, tel. 312/744–7007), the largest facility of its kind in the world, shows you the entire purification process in tours Tuesday and Thursday at 9:30 and 1:30. Make reservations at least 10 days in advance.

**Federal Reserve Bank** (230 S. La Salle St., tel. 312/322–2386) explains how checks are processed and how money travels; tours are given daily 9–1. Call for reservations.

## What to See and Do with Children

Among the outstanding activities Chicago has in store for family groups are several museums that provide hours of fascination for youngsters, where dozens of exhibits not only don't forbid you to touch them but actually require that you interact with them.

**Adler Planetarium** (*see* Tour 4: South Lake Shore Drive, *above*). The Sky Shows enthrall young and old alike.

**Brookfield Zoo** (*see* Chapter 9: Excursions, *below*). Here are elephants, dolphins, a rain forest, and animals enough to keep you busy all day.

**Chicago Academy of Sciences** (*see* Tour 6: Lincoln Park, *above*) has many exhibits that will fascinate children.

**Chicago Children's Museum** (*see* Tour 5: Near North, *above*). Designed specifically for very young children, this museum at North Pier has many things to see and touch.

**Chicago Public Library Cultural Center** (*see* Tour 1: Downtown, *above*). Programs for youngsters take place throughout the year.

**Children's Bookstore** (2465 N. Lincoln Ave., tel. 312/248–2665). Browsing is encouraged among a superb collection of carefully selected books for children; story hours for children under six are scheduled several times a week.

**Field Museum of Natural History** (*see* Tour 4: South Lake Shore Drive, *above*). Three rooms are filled with the touchy-feely stuff that small folk love, and many of the regular exhibits have considerable appeal for children.

**57th Street Books** (*see* Tour 3: Hyde Park and Kenwood, *above*). In addition to the excellent selection of children's books, the store has a play and reading area where youngsters can browse or grownups can read to them.

**Harold Washington Library Center** (*see* Tour 1: Downtown, *above*) offers a variety of children's activities, including story time for preschoolers, film programs, theater and music performances, and tours.

**Lincoln Park Zoo** (*see* Tour 6: Lincoln Park, *above*). The Children's Zoo, the Farm-in-the-Zoo, and the Kids' Corner Discov-

ery Place are the special attractions prepared just for youngsters.

**Museum of Science and Industry** *(see* Tour 3: Hyde Park and
Kenwood, *above)*. Children and parents may find themselves
competing here to see who gets to use the instruments or take
part in the activities first.

**John G. Shedd Aquarium** *(see* Tour 4: South Lake Shore Drive,
*above)*. The display of sea creatures is guaranteed to captivate
every visitor, regardless of age.

## Off the Beaten Track

If you're at McCormick Place, take a walk on the promenade
that runs between the convention center and the lake. You can
watch small planes take off from and land at tiny Meigs Field
and, in the summer, observe the sailboats as they bob in Burnham Harbor.

The **Trompe l'oeil Building** (1207 W. Division Street) is on the
northeast corner of La Salle and Division streets, but you
should study its appearance from a block east, at Clark and Division Street, or approach it from the south for the full effect of
its rose window, ornate arched doorway, stone steps, columns,
and sculptures. As you move closer to the building, you'll discover that an ordinary high rise has been elaborately painted to
make it look like an entirely different work of architecture.

**Olive Park** juts out into Lake Michigan a block north of Lake
Point Towers (505 N. Lake Shore Dr.); to find it, walk east on
Grand Avenue, pass under Lake Shore Drive, and bear left. It
has no roads, just paved walkways and lots of benches, trees,
shrubs, and grass. The marvelous and unusual views of the city
skyline from here, in addition to the absence of vehicular traffic, make it seem as though you're miles from the city, not just
blocks from the busy Near North side.

Slightly northwest of Hyde Park, at the corner of Drexel Boulevard and 50th Street, is the headquarters of **Operation PUSH**
(930 E. 50th St., tel. 312/373–3366), Jesse Jackson's black self-
help organization. A former synagogue, you'll recognize the
building by its splendid columns before you see its colorful cloth
banner. Three blocks east and one block north you'll find **4995
South Woodlawn Avenue**, the home of the controversial black
leader Louis Farrakhan, who has made it a headquarters of the
Nation of Islam. The great house was built by Elijah Moham-
med, the Nation's founder; its $3 million funding was rumored
to have come from the Libyan despot Muammar Khadafi.

Nearby, at 49th Street and Kenwood Avenue, stand two early
works by Frank Lloyd Wright, **Blossom House** (4858 S.
Kenwood Ave.) and **MacArthur House** (4852 S. Kenwood Ave.),
both built in 1892. Across from Blossom House is **Farmers'
Field**, a park where animals grazed as recently as the 1920s. A
few blocks away, at 49th Street and Ellis Avenue, (4901 S. Ellis
Ave.), is the 22-room Prairie Style **Julius Rosenwald mansion**
built by the Sears Roebuck executive in the early 1900s. After a
stint as a home for boys, followed by years of disuse, the mansion was purchased by a family and extensively restored.

A treeless hill near Lincoln Park's **Montrose Harbor** draws kite-
flying enthusiasts of all ages on sunny weekends. Take Lake
Shore Drive north from the Loop about 5 miles, exit at Mont-

rose, turn right into the park, and look for colorful stunt kites on your left. Windsurfers often practice at nearby **Montrose Beach.**

If you're interested in the social history of the late 19th century, there's no place that exemplifies the era better than the planned community of **Pullman** on the far south side. Built in 1880 by railcar tycoon George M. Pullman for the workers at his Palace Car Company, the town had its own hotel, hospital, library, shopping center, and bank. The styles of the homes reflect the status of their original occupants: Workers' homes are simple, those of skilled craftsmen slightly fancier, and executive housing more elaborate still. The town was the site of the famous Pullman strike of 1894 and also its partial cause, because the company cut wages without reducing the rents for workers in company-owned housing. The factory is closed now, but the houses are occupied and the community is thriving. To get to Pullman, take I–94 (Dan Ryan Expy.) south, exit at 111th Street, and turn right. For more information, call the Historic Pullman Foundation (tel. 312/785–8181).

# Sightseeing Checklists

### Historical Buildings and Sites

This list of Chicago's principal buildings and sites includes both attractions that were covered in the preceding tours and additional attractions that are described here for the first time.

**Amoco Building** (Tour 1. Downtown)

**Art Institute of Chicago** (Tour 1. Downtown)

**Associates Center** (Tour 1. Downtown)

**Auditorium Theatre** (Tour 1. Downtown)

**Biograph Theatre** (Tour 6. Lincoln Park)

**Blackstone Hotel** (Tour 2. Downtown South)

**Blackstone Theatre** (Tour 1. Downtown)

**Buckingham Fountain** (Tour 1. Downtown)

**Carbide and Carbon Building** (Tour 1. Downtown)

**Carson Pirie Scott** (Tour 1. Downtown)

**"Chevrolet" Building** (Tour 3. Hyde Park and Kenwood)

**Chicago Academy of Sciences** (Tour 6. Lincoln Park)

**Chicago Board of Trade** (Tour 1. Downtown)

**Chicago City Hall–Cook County Building** (Tour 1. Downtown)

**Chicago Hilton and Towers** (Tour 2. Downtown South)

**Chicago Historical Society** (Tour 6. Lincoln Park)

**Chicago Mercantile Exchange** (Tour 1. Downtown)

**Chicago Public Library Cultural Center** (Tour 1. Downtown)

**Chicago Temple** (Tour 1. Downtown)

**Chicago Theatre** (Tour 1. Downtown)

# You've Let Your Imagination Go, Now Get Up And Follow Your Dreams.

## For The Vacation You're Dreaming Of, Call American Express® Travel Agency At 1-800-YES-AMEX.*

American Express will send more than your imagination soaring. We'll fly you, sail you, drive you to any Fodor's destination and beyond. Because American Express believes the best vacations happen from Europe to the Orient, Walt Disney® World to Hawaii and everywhere in between.

For dependable service, expert advice, and value wherever your dreams take you, call on American Express. After all, the best traveling companion is a trustworthy friend.

# It's easy to recognize a good place when you see one.

American Express Cardmembers have been doing it for years.

The secret? Instead of just relying on what they see in the window, they look at the door. If there's an American Express Blue Box on it, they know they've found an establishment that cares about high standards.

Whether it's a place to eat, to sleep, to shop, or simply meet, they know they will be warmly welcomed.

So much so, they're rarely taken in by anything else.

## Always a good sign.

**Chicago Theological Seminary** (Tour 3. Hyde Park and Kenwood)

**Civic Opera House** (Tour 1. Downtown)

**Clarke House** (1800 S. Prairie Ave., tel. 312/326–1393). Chicago's oldest building, Clarke House was constructed in 1836 in Greek Revival style. Period furniture enlivens the interior. Part of the Prairie Avenue Historical District. Closed Monday, Tuesday, and Thursday.

**Crilly Court** (Tour 6. Lincoln Park)

**Daley Center** (Tour 1. Downtown)

**Dearborn Park** (Tour 2. Downtown South)

**Dearborn Station** (Tour 2. Downtown South)

**Donohue Building** (Tour 2. Downtown South)

**Drake Hotel** (Tour 5. Near North).

**Federal Center and Plaza** (Tour 1. Downtown)

**Fine Arts Building** (Tour 1. Downtown)

**First National Bank of Chicago** (Tour 1. Downtown)

**Fisher Building** (Tour 1. Downtown)

**Franklin Building** (Tour 2. Downtown South)

**Glessner House** (1801 S. Prairie Ave., tel. 312/326–1393). The only surviving building in Chicago by the architect H. H. Richardson, Glessner House was designed in 1886. Part of the Prairie Avenue Historic District. Closed Monday, Tuesday, and Thursday.

**Heller House** (Tour 3. Hyde Park and Kenwood)

**Hull House** (800 S. Halsted St., tel. 312/413–5353). The columned, redbrick, turn-of-the-century Hull House seems out of place on its site, surrounded by the massive and modern buildings of the University of Illinois campus. Here Jane Addams wrought social work miracles in a neighborhood that was then a slum. Here, too, Benny Goodman learned to play the clarinet. Open to the public at no charge weekdays 10 AM–4 PM, Sunday noon–5. Closed Saturday and most holidays.

**Illinois Institute of Technology** (31st–35th Sts. on S. State St., tel. 312/567–3000). The campus was designed principally by Mies van der Rohe, with participation by Friedman, Alschuler and Sincere; Holabird and Roche; and Pace Associates. Built between 1942 and 1958, the structures have the characteristic box shape that is Mies's trademark. Unlike most of his work, they are low-rise buildings. Crown Hall (3360 S. State St.) is the jewel of the collection; the other buildings have a certain sameness and sterility.

**International House** (Tour 3. Hyde Park and Kenwood)

**John Hancock Center** (Tour 5. Near North)

**Joseph Regenstein Library** (Tour 3. Hyde Park and Kenwood)

**Julius Rosenwald Mansion** (Off the Beaten Track)

**Laird Bell Law Quadrangle** (Tour 3. Hyde Park and Kenwood)

**Lutheran School of Theology** (Tour 3. Hyde Park and Kenwood)

**Main Post Office** (Tour 1. Downtown)

**Marquette Building** (Tour 1. Downtown)

**McCormick Seminary** (Tour 6. Lincoln Park)

**Metropolitan Detention Center** (Tour 1. Downtown)

**Midway Plaisance** (Tour 3. Hyde Park and Kenwood)

**Monadnock Building** (Tour 1. Downtown)

**Moody Bible Institute** (Tour 5. Near North)

**Museum of Science and Industry** (Tour 3. Hyde Park and Kenwood)

**Northwestern Atrium Center** (Tour 1. Downtown)

**One Financial Place** (Tour 1. Downtown)

**Orchestra Hall** (Tour 1. Downtown)

**Oriental Institute** (Tour 3. Hyde Park and Kenwood)

**Page Brothers Building** (Tour 1. Downtown)

**Palmer House** (Tour 1. Downtown)

**Promontory Apartments** (5530 S. South Shore Dr.). The building, designed by Mies van der Rohe in 1949, was named for Promontory Point, which juts out into the lake just east of here.

**Quaker Oats Building** (Tour 5. Near North)

**Railway Exchange Building** (Tour 1. Downtown)

**Reliance Building** (Tour 1. Downtown)

**River City** (Tour 2. Downtown South)

**Robie House** (Tour 3. Hyde Park and Kenwood)

**Rockefeller Memorial Chapel** (Tour 3. Hyde Park and Kenwood)

**The Rookery** (Tour 1. Downtown)

**The Sanctuary** (Tour 6. Lincoln Park)

**Sears Tower** (Tour 1. Downtown)

**State of Illinois Center** (Tour 1. Downtown)

**333 West Wacker Drive** (Tour 1. Downtown)

**Tribune Tower** (Tour 5. Near North)

**Union Station** (Tour 1. Downtown)

**University of Illinois at Chicago** (705 S. Halsted St., tel. 312/996–7000). Designed by Walter Netsch, of Skidmore, Owings, and Merrill, the university buildings seem to surge and weave toward each other.

**Water Tower** (Tour 5. Near North)

**Windermere House** (1642 E. 56th St.). This was designed in 1920 by Rapp and Rapp, known generally for their movie palaces. Notice the grand gatehouse in front of the sweeping semicircular carriage path at the entrance; notice also the heroic scale of the building, with its ornate carvings.

**Wrigley Building** (Tour 5. Near North)

**Xerox Building** (Tour 1. Downtown)

## Museums and Galleries

Museums    **Adler Planetarium.** (Tour 4. South Lake Shore Drive)

**American Police Center and Museum.** The museum's exhibits are concerned with police work and relationships between the police and the public. Safety, crime and punishment, and drugs and alcohol are among the subjects. One exhibit shows how the police communication system works; another details the history of the Haymarket Riot. A memorial gallery is dedicated to policemen who have lost their lives in the line of duty. *1717 S. State St., tel. 312/431–0005. Admission: $2 adults, $1.50 senior citizens, $1 children 6–11. Open weekdays 9–4.*

**Art Institute of Chicago** (Tour 1. Downtown)

**Balzekas Museum of Lithuanian Culture.** The little-known Balzekas Museum offers a taste of 1,000 years of Lithuanian history and culture on its three floors. You'll find exhibits on rural Lithuania; concentration camps; rare maps, stamps, and coins; textiles; and amber. The library can be used for research. *6500 S. Pulaski Rd., tel. 312/582–6500. Admission: $4 adults, $3 students and senior citizens, $1 children under 12; free Mon. Open daily 10–4 (Fri. until 8).*

**Chicago Academy of Sciences** (Tour 6. Lincoln Park)

**Chicago Children's Museum.** (Tour 5. Near North)

**Chicago Historical Society** (Tour 6. Lincoln Park)

**Chicago Public Library Cultural Center** (Tour 1. Downtown)

**Czechoslovakian Society of America Heritage Museum and Archives.** The collections of the Czechoslovakian Society include crystal, marble, dolls, musical instruments, china, ornamented eggs, vases, paintings, and statues. A library is part of the museum. *2701 S. Harlem Ave., Berwyn, tel. 708/795–5800. Admission free. Open weekdays 10–noon and 1–4.*

**David and Alfred Smart Museum of Art** (Tour 3. Hyde Park and Kenwood)

**DuSable Museum of African American History.** A 10-foot mural in the auditorium of the museum, hand-carved by Robert Witt Ames, depicts black history from Africa to the 1960s. Another gallery features great history makers: Martin Luther King, Jr., Rosa Parks, Paul Robeson, Sojourner Truth, and others. Special exhibits change frequently; a recent one on the cultural history of Haiti included paintings, papier-mâché crafts, flags, and other cultural artifacts. *740 E. 56th Pl., tel. 312/947–0600. Admission: free. Open weekdays 9–5, weekends noon–5.*

**Field Museum of Natural History.** (Tour 4. South Lake Shore Drive)

**International Museum of Surgical Sciences.** The surgical sciences museum has medical artifacts from around the world. *1524 N. Lake Shore Dr., tel. 312/642–3555. Admission free. Open Tues.–Sat. 10–4, Sun. 11–5.*

**John G. Shedd Aquarium.** (Tour 4. South Lake Shore Drive)

**May Weber Museum of Cultural Arts** (Tour 5. Near North)

**Mexican Fine Arts Center Museum.** The exhibits of the work of contemporary Mexican artists change every two to three months. *1852 W. 19th St., tel. 312/738–1503. Admission free. Open Tues.–Sun. 10–5.*

**Museum of Broadcast Communications.** Thousands of tapes of old TV and radio programs are collected here, and 10 study bays allow visitors to view or listen to them. Among the exhibits are the original Charlie McCarthy and Mortimer Snerd puppets. A reconstructed WGN radio studio broadcasts Saturday 1–5, and visitors to the museum can attend the broadcasts. Recent special exhibits were "40 Years of WGN-TV" and "A Salute to the TV Western." *800 S. Wells St., tel. 312/987–1500. Admission: $3 adults, $2 students, $1 senior citizens and children under 13. Open Wed.–Sun. 12:30–5, Sat. 10–5.*

**Museum of Contemporary Art.** (Tour 5. Near North)

**Museum of Holography.** Holograms are three-dimensional images produced by lasers. If you have never seen a hologram, consider this museum a must stop; the images seem to leap out at you from their frames. The exhibits of holographic art from around the world include computer-generated holograms, moving holograms, pulsed portraits of people, and color holograms. Two to three special exhibits are mounted annually. *1134 W. Washington Blvd., tel. 312/226–1007. Admission: $2.50. Open Wed.–Sun. 12:30–5.*

**Museum of Science and Industry.** (Tour 3. Hyde Park and Kenwood)

**Newberry Library.** This venerable research institution houses superb book and document collections in many areas and mounts exhibits in a small gallery space. *60 W. Walton Dr., tel. 312/943–9090. Admission free. Closed Sun.*

**Oriental Institute** (Tour 3. Hyde Park and Kenwood)

**Peace Museum** This unconventional museum presents exhibits on themes of war and peace using art, photography, and multimedia shows. *430 W. Erie St., tel. 312/440–1860. Admission: $3.50 adults, $1 children and senior citizens. Open Tues.–Sun. noon–5, Thurs. noon–8.*

**Polish Museum of America.** Dedicated to collecting materials on the history of the Polish people in America, the Polish Museum has an eclectic collection that includes an art gallery, an exhibit on the Shakespearean actress Modjeska, one on the American Revolutionary War hero Tadeusz Koscziusko, and another on the pianist and composer Ignaczi Paderewski that includes the last piano on which he performed and the chair he carried everywhere and without which he could not perform. The Stations of the Cross from the first Polish church in America (which was located in Texas) are on display. A library is available. *984 N. Milwaukee Ave., tel. 312/384–3352. Admission free. Open daily noon–5.*

**Spertus Museum of Judaica** (Tour 2. Downtown South)

**Swedish-American Museum Association of Chicago.** Permanent exhibits here include a history of Swedish immigrant travel to the United States and a survey of the textile arts and industry in Sweden. Special exhibits, often on loan from other museums, come every six weeks. *5211 N. Clark St., tel. 312/728–8111. Admission: $1 adults, 50¢ children and senior citizens. Open Tues.–Fri. 11–4, Sat. 11–3.*

**Terra Museum of American Art.** (Tour 5. Near North)

**Ukrainian Institute of Modern Art.** Located in the heart of Ukrainian Village on the west side, this museum focuses on contemporary paintings and sculpture by artists of Ukrainian descent. *2318 W. Chicago Ave., tel. 312/227–5522. Admission: $2. Open Tues.–Sun. noon–4.*

Galleries    Chicago has more art galleries than any American city after New York. Most galleries are open weekdays and Saturday 10–5 or 11–5 and at other times by appointment. The largest concentrations of galleries are in the River North area and on Superior and Ontario streets east of Michigan Avenue. The Near North tour in this chapter points out many of the buildings that house galleries. Because the galleries and their shows change frequently, the prospective visitor should consult the *Chicago Gallery News* for a full current listing.

## Churches, Temples, and Mosques

For many decades the immigrants who settled in Chicago came principally from Ireland, Germany, Italy, and the Catholic countries of Eastern Europe. They struggled to build temples to their faith in the new neighborhoods, and churches where the faithful could be uplifted and carried away from the often grinding struggles of their daily lives. As new waves of immigrants arrived, the churches became places where the ethnic community gathered to reinforce its cultural and artistic traditions as well as its faith. In this sense, it has been observed that the history of Chicago's churches is the history of the city.

Today many of the exquisite churches and the historical repositories they represent are threatened; indeed, the churches may have fulfilled their function and outlived it, for the communities they were meant to serve are gone. It is rumored that as many as 25 old neighborhood ethnic churches may be demolished over the next 10 years. Ironically, while churches in the ethnic neighborhoods languish, others—the Fourth Presbyterian Church on Michigan Avenue's Magnificent Mile, for example— whose congregations are well able to support them, are threatened because of the tremendous underlying value of the property on which they stand.

Many of Chicago's most beautiful churches may not be around much longer, and the wise visitor will take the opportunity to see these treasures while it is still possible. Always remember to call ahead before planning to visit a church; economic constraints have forced many churches to restrict the hours during which they are open to the public.

**Baha'i House of Worship** (Chapter 9, Excursions from Chicago)

**Bond Chapel** (Tour 3. Hyde Park and Kenwood)

**Fourth Presbyterian Church** (Tour 5. Near North)

**Holy Cross** (4600 S. Hermitage Ave., tel. 312/376–3900). The Lithuanian Holy Cross Church was built in 1913 in Renaissance revival style. Its exterior has columns and twin towers; the interior has an arched ceiling, elaborate altar, and geometric-pattern marble floor.

**Holy Name Cathedral** (Tour 5. Near North)

**Holy Trinity Cathedral** (1121 N. Leavitt Ave., tel. 312/486–6064). This Russian Orthodox church was designed by Louis Sullivan, who also did the Carson Pirie Scott building. It is said that Czar Nicholas of Russia contributed $4,000 to the construction. The interior, elaborately detailed and filled with icons, contains no pews; worshipers stand during the services.

**Midwest Buddhist Temple** (Tour 6. Lincoln Park)

**Moody Memorial Church** (Tour 6. Lincoln Park)

**Nativity of the Blessed Virgin Mary Ukrainian Catholic Church** (4952 S. Paulina St., tel. 312/737–0733). Note the Byzantine domes. The interior is richly ornamented with murals, icons, chandeliers, and stained glass.

**Old St. Patrick Church** (718 W. Adams St., tel. 312/782–6171). This is the oldest church in Chicago; built in 1852–1856, it withstood the Chicago Fire. Located just west of the west Loop redevelopment area and the huge Presidential Towers high-rise development, Old St. Patrick's is in the happy (and unusual) situation of finding its membership increasing. The towers, one Romanesque and one Byzantine, are symbolic of West and East.

**Our Lady of Mt. Carmel Church** (690 W. Belmont Ave., tel. 312/525–0453). Mother church for the north side Catholic parishes, Mt. Carmel is a serene oasis in the midst of urban cacophony.

**Rockefeller Memorial Chapel** (Tour 3. Hyde Park and Kenwood)

**St. Alphonsus Church** (2960 N. Southport Ave., tel. 312/525–0709). Having originally served a German neighborhood, the Gothic St. Alphonsus is now in the heart of the redeveloping Lincoln Park. The beautiful interior has a vaulted ceiling and stained glass.

**St. Basil Church** (1824 W. Garfield Blvd., tel. 312/925–6311). Originally an Irish church, St. Basil's congregation tried unsuccessfully to stave off the white flight that hit this west side neighborhood in the 1960s.

**St. Clement's Church** (642 W. Deming Pl., tel. 312/281–0371). Combining both Roman and Byzantine elements in its design, St. Clement's has beautiful mosaics and lavish stained glass.

**St. Gabriel Church** (4522 S. Wallace, tel. 312/268–9595). Situated in the heart of the Irish Bridgeport neighborhood, St. Gabriel was designed more than 100 years ago by Daniel Burnham and John Root. Unlike many of Chicago's neighborhoods, Bridgeport has remained the Irish community it was 100 years ago, despite expansionist pressures from Hispanic Pilsen to the northwest and Chinatown to the northeast.

**St. James Cathedral** (Tour 5. Near North)

**St. Michael's Church** (Tour 6. Lincoln Park)

**St. Michael's Italian Roman Catholic Church** (2325 W. 24th Pl., tel. 312/847–2727). The beautifully ornate St. Michael's is now in a Hispanic parish in the neighborhood of Pilsen.

**St. Nicholas Ukrainian Catholic Cathedral** (2238 W. Rice St., tel. 312/276–4537). The Byzantine St. Nicholas is situated in the heart of Ukrainian Village, an ethnic enclave in the changing west side. The interior is decorated with mosaics, frescoes, and chandeliers; services are conducted in Ukrainian.

**St. Thomas the Apostle** (Tour 3. Hyde Park and Kenwood)

**Second Presbyterian Church** (1936 S. Michigan Ave., tel. 312/ 225–4951). Located in a black neighborhood just south of Downtown South, this handsome Victorian church endured years of struggles to stay afloat. In recent years, aided by new members from both Hyde Park to the south and Dearborn Park to the north, the congregation has grown and become racially integrated and ethnically diverse. The church has lovely stained glass, and oak is used lavishly throughout the interior.

**Unity Temple.** (Chapter 9)

## Parks and Gardens

Thanks to the Lakefront Protection Ordinance, most of Chicago's more than 20 miles of lakefront is parkland or beach reserved for public use. Visitors to the city tend to concentrate on the lakefront, even though the Chicago Park District maintains hundreds of parks in neighborhoods throughout the city. While all the lakefront land is maintained for park use, several areas have been specifically designated as parks, and these areas offer special delights.

**Chicago Botanic Garden** (Chapter 9, Excursions.)

**Garfield Park Conservatory,** perhaps the largest in the world, keeps more than 5 acres of plants and flowers indoors in near-tropical conditions throughout the year. Here are a palm house, a fern house, an aeroid house (which includes such plants as dieffenbachia and antherium), and others. Like the Lincoln Park Conservatory, Garfield Park does four major shows a year: azaleas and camellias in February, a spring show beginning in mid-March, chrysanthemums in November, and a Christmas show from mid-December. Each year the conservatory honors one nation with displays of the country's typical flowers and plants, from April to November. By car, take I–290 (Eisenhower Expressway) to Independence Boulevard. Turn right onto Independence and go north to Lake Street. Turn right on Lake Street and left at the first traffic light. *300 N. Central Park Blvd., tel. 312/ 533–1281. Admission free. Open daily Sun.–Thurs. 10–6, Fri. 10–9, with extended hours during shows.*

**Grant Park** (Tour 2. Downtown South)

**Jackson Park,** just south of the Museum of Science and Industry, features an island known as Wooded Island and a Japanese Garden with authentic Japanese statuary.

**Lincoln Park** (Tour 6. Lincoln Park)

**Morton Arboretum** (Chapter 9)

## Zoos

**Brookfield Zoo,** (Chapter 9)

**Lincoln Park Zoo** (Tour 6. Lincoln Park)

# 4 Shopping

Chicago shopping is extensive and varied, ranging from elegant department stores, small boutiques, and specialty shops to malls and bargain outlets. Visa, MasterCard, American Express, and most other major credit cards are widely accepted, and traveler's checks are welcome in most establishments throughout the city. An 8.75% state and county sales tax is added to all purchases except groceries and prescription medicines.

Many stores, particularly on north Michigan Avenue and the north side, are open on Sunday; call ahead for Sunday hours.

*The Reader,* a free weekly paper available in stores and restaurants in the downtown, Near North Side, Lincoln Park, and Hyde Park areas, carries ads for smaller shops. Sales at the large department stores are advertised in the *Chicago Tribune* and the *Chicago Sun-Times.*

There are far too many stores in Chicago to attempt a complete or fully descriptive listing here. The following pages offer a general overview of the more popular shopping areas and list some of the stores where certain items can be found. If you're looking for something in particular, check the Yellow Pages classified phone directory, but if you have no concrete shopping goals, simply choose any one of the major shopping districts and browse to your heart's content.

## Major Shopping Districts

**The Loop** is the heart of Chicago business and finance. The city's two largest department stores, Marshall Field & Co. and Carson Pirie Scott, anchor the Loop's State Street–Wabash Avenue area, which has declined since the years when it was known as "State Street, that great street." (Four of State Street's largest retailers—Sears, Montgomery Ward, Wieboldt's, and Goldblatt's—have closed their doors in the last decade.) Several Loop buildings, including the Stevens Building (17 N. State St.) and the Mallers Building (5 S. Wabash Ave.), contain groups of small shops on their upper floors, and there are a number of interesting specialty stores on the west end of the Loop. Most stores in the Loop are closed on Sunday except during the Christmas season.

**The Magnificent Mile,** Chicago's most glamorous shopping district, stretches along Michigan Avenue from the Chicago River (400 N.) to Oak Street (1000 N.). The street is lined on both sides with some of the most sophisticated names in retailing: Tiffany (715 N.), Gucci (900 N.), Chanel (990 N.), and Ralph Lauren (960 N.), to name just a few. Look on the Mag Mile for stores offering clothing, shoes, jewelry, and accessories, as well as for several art galleries.

Aside from dozens of designer shops, Michigan Avenue also features three "vertical malls." **Water Tower Place** (835 N. Michigan Ave.) contains branches of Lord & Taylor and Marshall Field's, as well as seven floors of specialty stores. Branches of national chains, such as The Gap, Banana Republic, The Limited, Casual Corner, Hoffritz for Cutlery, Benetton, and Rizzoli Books are all represented; the Ritz-Carlton Hotel sits atop the entire complex.

The **Avenue Atrium** (900 N. Michigan Ave.) houses the Chicago branches of Bloomingdale's and Henri Bendel, along with doz-

# Shopping North

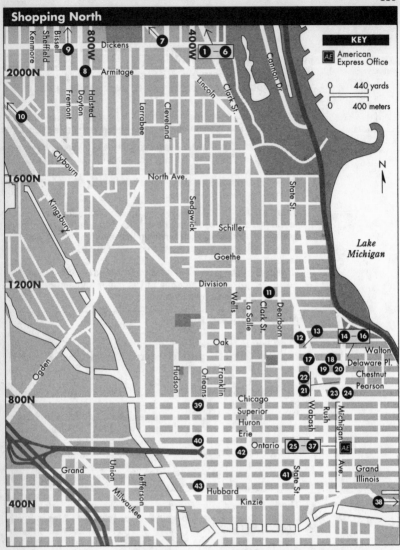

**KEY**

AE American Express Office

0 — 440 yards
0 — 400 meters

800W
400W
2000N
Kenmore
Sheffield
Bissell
Dickens
Armitage
Halsted
Dayton
Fremont
Larrabee
Cleveland
Lincoln
Clark St.
Cannon Dr.
1600N
Clybourn
Kingsbury
North Ave.
Sedgwick
Schiller
Goethe
Division
State St.
1200N
Wells
Clark St.
La Salle
Dearborn
Oak
Lake Michigan
Walton
Delaware Pl.
Chestnut
Pearson
Hudson
Orleans
Franklin
Chicago
Superior
Huron
Erie
Ontario
Wabash
Rush
Michigan Ave.
800N
Ogden
Grand
Illinois
Union
Jefferson
Milwaukee
Grand
Hubbard
Kinzie
State St.
400N

N

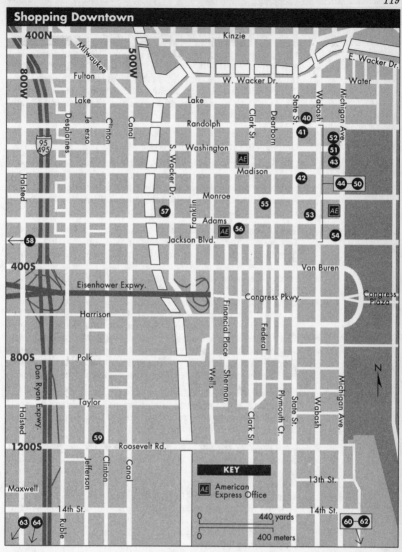

# Shopping Downtown

**KEY**

AE American Express Office

| 0 | 440 yards |
| 0 | 400 meters |

ArchiCenter Store, **54**
Bennett Brothers, **53**
Brooks
Brothers, **43, 56**
Capper & Capper, **46**
Carl Fischer, **50**
Carson Pirie Scott, **42**
Central Camera, **49**
Chernin's, **59**
Crate & Barrel, **45**
Eddie Bauer, **44**
57th Street Books, **60**
Helix, **58**
I Love a Mystery, **51**
Kroch & Brentano, **47**

Marshall Field
& Co., **41**
Powell's, **61**
Rand McNally, **57**
Rose Records, **48**
Savvy Traveller, **52**
Sears, **64**
Seno Formalwear, **40**
The Sharper
Image, **55**
Spiegel, **63**
University of Chicago
Bookstore, **62**

ens of smaller boutiques and specialty stores. Generally, the merchandise found here is more sophisticated, and more expensive, than in Water Tower Place. The Atrium also has a hotel on top—the lavish Four Seasons. The restaurants and movie theaters found in both malls are a good option for entertainment during inclement weather. The third, **Chicago Place** (700 N. Michigan Ave.), has Saks Fifth Avenue, women's clothier Ann Taylor, and jeweler C.D. Peacock, along with many specialty stores and a food court on the top floor.

There's another cluster of shops at the **Merchandise Mart,** including a branch of Carson Pirie Scott.

**Oak Street,** between Michigan Avenue and Rush Street, is populated with stores selling designer clothing and European imports. Designers with Oak Street addresses include Giorgio Armani (113 E. Oak St.), Gianni Versace (101 E. Oak St.), Sonia Rykiel (106 E. Oak St.), and Ultimo (114 E. Oak St.).

The upscale residential neighborhoods of **Lincoln Park and Lakeview** offer several worthwhile shopping strips. **Clark Street** between Armitage (2000 N.) and Diversey (2800 N.) avenues is home to a number of clothing boutiques and specialty stores. The shopping continues north of Diversey Avenue to School Street (3300 N.), with several large antiques stores, more boutiques, and some bookstores. **Broadway** between Diversey Avenue and Addison Street (3600 N.) also offers a variety of shops. The **Century Mall,** in a former movie palace at Clark Street, Broadway, and Diversey Parkway, houses a variety of national outlets and small specialty stores. Take the Clark Street bus (No. 22) at Dearborn Street or the Broadway bus (No. 36) at State Street north to reach this neighborhood.

The **North Pier** development, on the lake, at 435 E. Illinois St. is teeming with fascinating small shops, including a seashell store, a hologram showroom, and a shop that embroiders custom designs on T-shirts and jackets.

Contained by the Chicago River on the south and west, Clark Street on the east, and Oak Street on the north, **River North** boasts a profusion of art galleries, furnishing stores, and boutiques. The *Chicago Gallery News*, available from the tourist information center at the Water Tower (Michigan Ave. and Pearson St.), provides an up-to-date listing of current art gallery exhibits.

## Department Stores

**Marshall Field & Co.** (111 N. State St., at the corner of Randolph St., tel. 312/781–1000). Though there are branches at several other locations in Chicago and its suburbs, the State Street Field's is the granddaddy of them all. Founder Marshall Field's catchphrase was "Give the lady what she wants!" and, for many years both ladies and gentlemen have been able to find everything they want, from furs to riding boots to padded hangers, on one of Field's nine floors. After a period of decline, Field's launched a $110-million-dollar renovation project and is currently restoring the building to its former glory. The bargain basement has been replaced with "Down Under," a series of small boutiques that sell clothing, luggage, picture frames, Chicago memorabilia, and Field's famous Frango mints, which many consider to be Chicago's greatest edible souvenirs. You'll find restaurants on the seventh floor and in the basement. Architecture buffs will admire the Tiffany glass dome that tops the store's southwest atrium. At press time Field's had been acquired by Dayton-Hudson Corp., Minneapolis, but observers of the retail industry don't expect the new owners to tamper with this Chicago tradition.

**Carson Pirie Scott** (1 S. State St., tel. 312/641–7000). Second only to Field's for many years, Carson's was operating at a loss when it was acquired in 1989 by P.A. Bergner, a Milwaukee-based retail chain. At the time there was some question whether it would survive, but so far, it's still in business and carries a full line of clothing, housewares, accessories, cosmetics, and more. The building itself, the work of famed Chicago architect Louis Sullivan, is protected by landmark status. It's worth visiting just to see the northwest door at the corner of State and Madison streets; the iron scrollwork here shows Sullivan at his most ornate.

**Neiman Marcus** (737 N. Michigan Ave., tel. 312/642–5900). Neiman's prices may be steep, but browsing here is fun. Be sure to take a look at the graceful four-story wood sculpture that rises between the escalators of this branch of the famous upscale Dallas department store.

**Bloomingdale's** (900 N. Michigan Ave., tel. 312/440–4460). Unlike both its Michigan Avenue neighbors and its New York City sibling, this branch of Bloomies, built in a clean, airy style that is part Prairie School and part postmodern, gives you plenty of elbow room to sift through its selection of designer labels. The adjacent six-floor Avenue Atrium offers a profusion of specialty stores and boutiques.

**Sak's Fifth Avenue** (700 N. Michigan Ave., tel. 312/944–6500) is a smaller and less elaborate cousin to the original New York store. It offers the same upscale men's and women's clothing.

## Specialty Stores

**Books**
*General Interest*
**Kroch & Brentano** (29 S. Wabash St., tel. 312/332–7500). The most comprehensive branch of this local chain, the Wabash Street flagship store will special-order any book they don't have in stock. The city's largest selection of technical books shares the lower level with an impressive paperback department. Upstairs, Kroch's collection of hardcover books is extensive and includes several sale tables of remaindered and slightly damaged books. There's a foreign-language department on the mezzanine and a large selection of magazines and newspapers.

**Stuart Brent** (670 N. Michigan Ave., tel. 312/337–6357). A Chicago literary landmark, Stuart Brent carries an extensive and tasteful, if sometimes quirky, collection of hardcover and paperback books, as well as a good selection of music and art books. The walls are covered with photographs of well-known authors posing with owner Mr. Brent, who for years has been prominent in the Chicago literary scene.

**57th Street Books** (1301 E. 57th St., tel. 312/684–1300). Wood floors, brick walls, and books from the popular to the esoteric distinguish this Hyde Park institution. An excellent place to while away the hours on a rainy afternoon.

**University of Chicago Bookstore** (970 E. 58th St., tel. 312/702–7712). Aside from the expected selection of textbooks, this bookstore also carries many works of general interest, with an emphasis on cooking and computer books. Closed Sunday.

*Specialty* **Rand McNally Map Stores** (150 S. Wacker Dr., tel. 312/332–2009 and 444 N. Michigan Ave., tel. 312/321–1751). Maps for everywhere from Manhattan to the moon, as well as travel books and globes, are available in abundance here.

**Savvy Traveller** (upstairs at 50 E. Washington St., tel. 312/263–2100). Aside from a full range of travel books, the Savvy Traveller also carries a number of odds and ends that can come in handy on the road.

**I Love a Mystery** (55 E. Washington St., tel. 312/236–1338). This shop specializes in—you guessed it—mysteries.

**Mystery Loves Company** (1114 W. Belmont Ave., tel. 312/935–1000) can provide hardcover and paperback versions of most favorites; it recently moved to expanded quarters.

**Season to Taste** (911 W. School St., tel. 312/327–0210). This homey shop has all manner of cookbooks, as well as an assortment of cooking videocassettes.

**The Stars Our Destination** (1021 W. Belmont Ave., tel. 312/871–2722). Science fiction fans will find a large selection of their favorites, along with the latest news on local sci-fi happenings.

**Le Grand Tour Bookstore** (3229 N. Clark St., tel. 312/929–1836). Foreign-language books are the specialty here, but there's a large selection of English volumes and an eclectic assortment of periodicals, as well.

*Used* **Powell's** (1501 E. 57th St., tel. 312/955–7780). Powell's Hyde Park store has one of the largest and most diverse selections of used books in town.

**Abraham Lincoln Bookstore** (357 W. Chicago Ave., tel. 312/944–3085). Civil War buffs will want to visit this shop, which specializes in Lincolniana and Civil War books.

**Camera and Electronic Equipment** **Central Camera** (230 S. Wabash Ave., tel. 312/427–5580). This store, stocked to the rafters with cameras and darkroom equipment, is a Loop institution.

**Helix** (310 S. Racine St., tel. 312/421–6000). Off the beaten track in a neighborhood west of the Loop, this warehouse store sells and rents all manner of camera and darkroom paraphernalia at competitive prices. A good selection of used equipment is also available. Helix has two smaller branches in the Loop, at 70 West Madison Street (tel. 312/444–9373) and 440 South La Salle Street (tel. 312/663–3650).

**Catalog Stores/ Factory Outlets** **Sony Store** (663 N. Michigan Ave., tel. 312/573–0059) sells electronics in a rarified atmosphere of almost hushed elegance.

**Bennett Brothers** (30 E. Adams St., tel. 312/263–4800). Primarily a catalog store, Bennett's sells jewelry, silverware, kitchen appliances, cameras, and electronic equipment at discount prices. The store's second-floor showroom displays some of the merchandise available in the catalog.

**Spiegel** (1105 W. 35th St., tel. 312/254–0091) and **Sears** (5555 S. Archer Ave., tel. 312/284–3200) both operate warehouse stores on the city's south side. The two famous mail-order establishments have ever-changing inventories of clothing, appliances, and housewares, and can offer fabulous bargains to the sharp-eyed and flexible shopper. Don't expect elegant surroundings or helpful salespeople, and do check your merchandise thoroughly before you take it home.

**Land's End Outlet** (men's, 2241 N. Elston Ave., tel. 312/276–2232; women's, 2317 N. Elston Ave., tel. 312/384–4170). This Wisconsin mail-order firm sells casual and business wear, luggage, housewares, and outdoor gear. The quality of the stock may be inconsistent at these outlet stores, but the discount savings can be considerable.

**Clothing** The major department stores are good sources of mainstream sportswear, and the smaller boutiques of the Avenue Atrium, Water Tower Place, River North, Oak Street, and Lincoln Park can provide you with more unique designer clothing.

*Business Clothing* **Brooks Brothers** (209 S. La Salle St., tel. 312/263–0100 and 713 N. Michigan Ave., tel. 312/915–0060), **Capper & Capper** (1 N. Wabash Ave., tel. 312/236–3800), **Brittany Ltd.** (999 N. Michigan Ave., tel. 312/642–6550), and **Mark Shale** (919 N. Michigan Ave., tel. 312/440–0720): All four of these stores are good sources of high-quality business attire.

*Women's* **Henri Bendel** (900 N. Michigan Ave., tel. 312/642–0140) is an excellent source for high-priced, high-style women's clothes and accessories.

**Ann Taylor** (103 E. Oak St., tel. 312/943–5411 and Chicago Place, 700 N. Michigan Ave., tel. 312/335–0117) offers a selection of classic, upscale womenswear.

*Men's* **Barney's New York** (25 E. Oak St., tel. 312/587–1700) is a smaller version of the New York store that's a paean to high style in men's and women's fashions.

**Seno Formalwear** (6 E. Randolph St., tel. 312/782–1115). This popular store both rents and sells tuxedos.

**Food** **The Chalet** (40 E. Delaware Pl., tel. 312/787–8555). This store is one of a chain that has several branches on the near north and north sides. All stores offer a large selection of wines, beers, cheeses, coffee, and other gourmet items.

**Treasure Island** (75 W. Elm St., tel. 312/440–1144, and 680 N. Lake Shore Dr., tel. 312/664–0400). This Chicago institution is a combination supermarket/gourmet store. Any of its branches is ideal for buying the makings for a gourmet picnic or an elegant, edible house gift.

**Nuts on Clark** (3830 N. Clark St., tel. 312/549–6622). This warehouse, located just a few blocks from Wrigley Field, displays bins full of nuts, as well as an assortment of candies, spices, jams and jellies, coffee, tea, mustards, and other culinary delights.

**Convito Italiano** (11 E. Chestnut St., tel. 312/943–2983). Both a restaurant and an Italian food shop, Convito Italiano sells olive oil in porcelain vessels, an array of wines, Saronno biscuits, cookbooks, an enormous selection of pastas, and ready-to-eat carry-out items. Elegant party trays can be ordered.

**Gifts** Water Tower Place, the Avenue Atrium, Michigan Avenue, and the larger department stores are likely places to find gifts and toys. For artsy gifts with a twist, try the River North art galleries and boutiques.

**The Sharper Image** (55 W. Monroe St., tel. 312/263–4535) and **Hammacher Schlemmer** (618 N. Michigan Ave., tel. 312/664–9292). Both stores are great for browsing and can provide upscale gadgets and unusual gifts.

**Tiffany & Co.** (715 N. Michigan Ave., tel. 312/944–7500) is the spot for impeccably correct crystal, silver, and jewelry.

**Kitchenware** **Crate & Barrel** (101 N. Wabash Ave., tel. 312/372–0100, 646 N. Michigan Ave., tel. 312/787–5900. Warehouse store: 800 W. North Ave., tel. 312/787–4775). One of the first "lifestyle" cookware, glassware, and furniture stores, the Crate remains one of the best. There are large branches on Michigan Avenue and in the Loop and a warehouse store at North Avenue and Halsted Street where you may pick up a good bargain.

**Williams-Sonoma** (17 E. Chestnut St., tel. 312/642–1593). The selection of kitchenware and cookbooks is excellent, and if you're there during an equipment demonstration you get to taste the results.

**Music** **Rose Records** (214 S. Wabash Ave., tel. 312/987–9044). This chain's main store on Wabash Avenue has three floors of records, tapes, and compact discs. If you're looking for movie soundtracks or Broadway musicals, Rose has an exceptionally large selection. One entire floor is devoted to "cut-outs," budget labels, and other bargains.

**Wax Trax** (2449 N. Lincoln Ave., tel. 312/929–0221). This crowded shop is the place to go for the latest rock and other offbeat imports.

**Jazz Record Mart** (11 W. Grand Ave., tel. 312/222–1467). This specialty store stocks one of Chicago's largest collections of records, in addition to compact discs and tapes. Jazz and blues fanciers will be delighted to find many rare historic recordings and obscure imports at the Record Mart.

**Carl Fischer** (312 S. Wabash Ave., tel. 312/427–6652). This venerable store carries the largest selection of piano, vocal, choral, and band sheet music in Chicago.

**Shoes** There are a great many shoe stores along Michigan Avenue, including several in Water Tower Place. Large selections can be found at: **Florsheim** (622 N. Michigan Ave., tel. 312/787–0779), **Florsheim Thayer McNeill** (727 N. Michigan Ave., tel. 312/649–9619), **Hanig** (660 N. Michigan Ave., tel. 312/642–5330), **Bally** (919 N. Michigan Ave., tel. 312/787–8110), and **Cole-Haan** (645 N. Michigan Ave., tel. 312/642–8995).

**Chernin's** (606 W. Roosevelt Rd., tel. 312/922–4545). Chicago's famous bargain shoe outlet is all that remains of a once flourishing Roosevelt Road shopping district. If you're in the market for lots of shoes, it may be worth a trip down here. There's a branch in Lincoln Park at 2665 North Halsted Street (tel. 312/404–0005).

**Lori's Discount Designer Shoes** (808 W. Armitage Ave., tel. 312/281–5655). Located in Lincoln Park, this store offers women's designer shoes below department-store prices.

**Souvenirs**  **The Tourist Information Center** (163 E. Pearson Ave., tel. 312/467–5305). This is an excellent source for postcards and souvenirs, as well as maps and city guides.

**Accent Chicago** (Water Tower Place, 835 N. Michigan Ave., 7th Floor, tel. 312/944–1354) and **Down Under at Marshall Field's** (111 N. State St., basement, tel. 312/781–1000). Both stores are good spots to shop for Chicago memorabilia. Accent Chicago has branches at Sears Tower (tel. 312/993–0499) and the Chicago Hilton (tel. 312/360–0115).

**The ArchiCenter Store** (224 S. Michigan Ave., tel. 312/922–3432). A large selection of books, posters, T-shirts, toys, mugs, and other souvenirs with architectural themes can be found here.

**The City of Chicago Store** (435 E. Illinois St., tel. 312/467–1111). This shop carries merchandise from 35 of the city's cultural institutions and organizations, including the Art Institute and the Lincoln Park Zoo. There's also an eclectic collection of restored artifacts, such as traffic lights, ballot boxes, parking meters, and manhole covers, culled from 12 city departments.

**Sporting Goods**  **MC/Mages Sports** (620 N. La Salle St., tel. 312/337–6151). Be sure to look at the "Wall of Fame" outside the store that shows the handprints of famous Chicago sports figures such as football's Jim McMahon, baseball's Ryne Sandberg, and hockey's Stan Mikita. Inside you will find six floors of reasonably priced sporting and camping equipment, shoes, and clothing.

**Sportmart** (3134 N. Clark St., tel. 312/871–8500 and 440 N. Orleans St., tel. 312/222–0900). These large emporia, one in Lakeview and the other in River North, offer low prices and good selections as long as you're not looking for uncommon sizes.

**Herman's** (111 E. Chicago Ave., tel. 312/951–8282). Part of a national chain, Herman's carries a respectable selection of shoes, tennis rackets, golf clubs, skis, and workout wear.

**Eddie Bauer** (123 N. Wabash Ave., tel. 312/263–6005). You'll find clothing for the outdoors and some camping equipment at this chain's Wabash Avenue store. Another branch at Water Tower Place carries mostly sportswear.

**Erehwon Mountain Outfitters** (644 N. Orleans St., tel. 312/337–6400). For hiking, camping, rock climbing, canoeing, and other rigorous outdoor pursuits, you can probably find clothing and equipment at Erehwon, which has a rough-hewn atmosphere and friendly salespeople.

**Nike Town** (669 N. Michigan Ave., tel. 312/642–6363) glorifies athletic shoes and the people who wear them in a store-as-entertainment setting.

**Toys**  **F.A.O. Schwarz** (840 N. Michigan Ave., tel. 312/587–5000) is a fantasy toy emporium that's only a little smaller than the chain's New York flagship.

# 5  Sports, Fitness, Beaches

**Participant Sports and Fitness**

**Bicycling**   The lakefront bicycle path extends about 20 miles along Chicago's lakefront, offering a variety of scenic views. The prospect of the harbor, created with landfill a few years ago when Lake Shore Drive's notorious S-curve between Monroe Street and Wacker Drive was straightened, is lovely. Be careful: A few blocks to the north, Grand Avenue is one of a few places along the route where the path crosses a city street (two others are parallel to Lake Shore Drive in the downtown area). Rent a bike for the day as you enter Lincoln Park at Fullerton Avenue or from **Village Cycle Center** (1337 N. Wells St., tel. 312/751–2488). **Turin Bicycles** (435 E. Illinois St., tel. 312/923–0100) at North Pier also rents bikes by the hour or the day. There are many other scenic routes in the Chicago area. For information, contact the **Chicagoland Bicycle Federation** (Box 64396, Chicago, IL 60664, tel. 312/427–3325).

**Boating**   Lake Michigan is right here, but those who didn't bring their sailboats or motorized craft with them to Chicago will have to content themselves with renting paddleboats in Lincoln Park or taking sightseeing boat trips. Rentals are located at the lagoon just north of Farm-in-the-Zoo.

**Golfing**   The Chicago Park District (tel. 312/753–8670) maintains six golf courses, five of them with nine holes and one (Jackson Park) with 18, and two driving ranges, one in Jackson Park and one at Lake Shore Drive and Diversey Avenue (where there is a miniature 18-hole course). The Jackson Park facilities are located two and three blocks east of Stony Island Avenue at 63rd Street.

**Ice Skating**   During the winter months there is ice skating at the **Daley Bicentennial Plaza,** Randolph Street at Lake Shore Drive. A small fee is charged, and skate rentals are available (tel. 312/294–4790).

**Jogging**   The lakefront path accommodates both joggers and bicyclists, so you'll need to be attentive. Avoid jogging in areas where there are few other people and after dark. You can pick up the path at Oak Street Beach (across from the Drake Hotel), at Grand Avenue underneath Lake Shore Drive, or by going through Grant Park on Monroe Street or Jackson Boulevard until you reach the lakefront.

**Swimming**   Lake Michigan provides wonderful swimming opportunities between Memorial Day and Labor Day, particularly toward the end of the summer, when the lake has warmed up (*see* Beaches, *below*).

**Tennis**   The Chicago Park District maintains hundreds of tennis courts, most of which can be used free of charge. The facility at the **Daley Bicentennial Plaza,** Randolph Street at Lake Shore Drive, is a lighted facility that can be used at night; there is a modest hourly fee, and reservations are required (tel. 312/294–4790). The **Grant Park** tennis courts, at 9th Street and Columbus Drive (between Michigan Avenue and Lake Shore Drive), are also lighted, and there is a modest fee; reservations are not required.

## Spectator Sports

Chicago's loyal sports fans turn out regularly, year after year, to watch what are not the most winning teams in professional sports (with the exception, in recent years, of the Chicago Bulls). At press time, the Cubs and the White Sox were continuing their standard pattern of mediocrity punctuated by the occasional brief winning streak. The White Sox won a lone division championship during the 1980s, and the Cubs won two, though neither was able to capture a league title.

Other owners have threatened to relocate their teams, most recently the owners of the White Sox, who conducted a lengthy courtship with the city of St. Petersburg, Florida, in 1988; in the end, a deal was made with the State of Illinois. The brand-new stadium opened in 1991 across the street from old Comiskey Park, which is being demolished.

**Baseball**   The **Chicago Cubs** (National League) play at Wrigley Field (1060 W. Addison St., tel. 312/404-2827); the baseball season begins early in April and ends the first weekend in October. Wrigley Field is reached by the Howard Street el line; take the B train to Addison Street. Wrigley Field finally received lights in 1988, the last major-league ballpark in the nation to be lighted for night games. But the Cubs still play most of their home games during the day, and the bleachers are a great place to get a tan while listening to Chicagoans taunt the visiting outfielders. The grandstand offers a more sedate atmosphere. Most games start at 1:20 PM, but call for exact starting times.

The **Chicago White Sox** (American League) play at Comiskey Park (333 W. 35th St., tel. 312/924-1000 or 312/559-1212 for ticket information). Games usually start at 7:30 PM. Take an A or B Dan Ryan el train to 35th Street.

**Basketball**   The **Chicago Bulls** play at the Chicago Stadium (1800 W. Madison St., tel. 312/943-5800); the basketball season extends from November to May, and games usually start at 7:30 PM. Avoid leaving the game early or wandering around this neighborhood at night.

**Football**   The **Chicago Bears** play at Soldier Field (425 E. McFetridge Dr., tel. 312/663-5100) from August (preseason) through January (postseason, if they're lucky). While subscription sales generally account for all tickets, you can sometimes buy the tickets of a subscriber who can't use them at the stadium shortly before game time. To reach Soldier Field, take the Jeffery Express (No. 6) bus to Roosevelt Road and Lake Shore Drive and follow the crowd. The stadium is just south of the Field Museum of Natural History.

**Hockey**   The **Chicago Blackhawks** play at the Chicago Stadium (1800 W. Madison St., tel. 312/733-5300) from October to April. Games usually start at 7:30 PM. Again, avoid leaving the game early or wandering around the neighborhood at night.

**Horse Racing**   Hawthorne Race Course (3501 S. Laramie Ave., tel. 708/780-3700), just beyond the Chicago city limits in Cicero, features **flat racing** October–December.

Arlington Park has **flat racing** May–October (N. Wilke Rd. at West Euclid Ave., Arlington Heights, tel. 708/255-4300). Sportsman's Park (3301 S. Laramie Ave., tel. 312/242-1121) has **flat racing** Feb.–May and **harness racing** May–October.

Maywood Park (North and Fifth Aves. in Maywood, tel. 708/343–4800), has **harness racing** February–May and October–December.

## Beaches

Chicago has some 20 miles of lakefront, most of it sand or rock beach. Beaches are open to the public daily 9 AM–9:30 PM, Memorial Day–Labor Day, and many beaches have changing facilities. The **Chicago Park District** (tel. 312/294-2333) provides lifeguard protection during daylight hours throughout the swimming season. The water is too cold for swimming at other times of the year.

**Oak Street Beach** (600-1600 N.) is probably Chicago's most popular, particularly in the 1000 North area, where the shoreline curves. You can expect it to be mobbed with trendy singles and people-watchers on any warm day in summer. There are bathrooms here, but for changing facilities you'll have to make the walk to the North Avenue Beach bathhouse. The concrete breakwater that makes up the southern part of Oak Street Beach is a popular promenade on hot summer nights. You can walk along the water all the way to Grand Avenue, where you'll find both Navy Pier and Olive Park.

**North Avenue Beach** (1600-2400 N.) is heavily used; the crowd tends to be more family oriented than the crowd at Oak Street Beach. There are bathrooms, changing facilities, and showers. The southern end of this beach features lively volleyball action during the summer and fall.

**South Shore Country Club Beach** (7100 S.), Chicago's newest and one of the nicest beaches, is quite pretty and not overcrowded. There are bathrooms, changing facilities, and showers. Enter through the South Shore Country Club grounds at 71st Street and South Shore Drive; you may see the police training their horses in the entry area.

Other Chicago beaches are:

**Leone/Loyola Beach** (6700-7800 N.), changing facilities.
**Foster Beach** (5200 N.), changing facilities.
**Montrose Beach** (4400 N.), changing facilities.
**12th Street Beach** (1200 S. at 900 E., just south of the planetarium), changing facilities.
**31st Street Beach** (3100 S.), changing facilities.
**Jackson Beach, Central** (5700-5900 S.), changing facilities.

# 6 Dining

*The restaurants were selected by Phil Vettel, restaurant critic of the* Chicago Tribune.

However you judge a city's restaurant scene—by ethnic diversity, breadth and depth of high-quality establishments, nationally prominent chefs—Chicago ranks as one of the nation's finest restaurant towns. Here you'll find innovative hot-spots; lovingly maintained traditional establishments; and everything in between.

Chicago's more than 7,000 restaurants range from those ranked among the best in the nation, and priced accordingly, to simple storefront ethnic eateries (the city has more than 80 Thai restaurants alone) and old-fashioned pubs that offer good food in unpretentious settings at modest prices. Our listing includes the restaurants we recommend as the best within each price range.

It's a good idea to make reservations in advance; many restaurants will not accommodate you without one, and at others, no reservation means a long wait before being seated. (It's also wise to call ahead to be sure the restaurant is open.) Ordinarily, reservations can be made a day or two in advance, or even on the afternoon of the same day, but securing a table at the more popular restaurants may take more planning, requiring reservations a week or two (in extreme cases, a month or more) in advance, especially on weekend evenings. Some of the trendiest restaurants do not accept reservations at all; at such places, a wait of an hour or more on weekends is commonplace. For some people, waiting in a crowded bar area is all part of the show.

As a general rule, you should expect to tip 15% in restaurants in the Inexpensive and Moderate price categories. The Chicago meal tax is 8½%, and you can double that amount for a 17% tip when you feel generous and don't want to have to do higher math. Expensive and Very Expensive restaurants have more service personnel per table who must divide the tip, so it's appropriate to leave 20%, depending on the quality of the service. An especially helpful wine steward should be acknowledged with $2 or $3.

This guide divides the restaurants of Chicago into three areas, each with its own dining map locating the restaurants: (1) Near North, River North, and Lincoln Park; (2) North; (3) Downtown and South. Several noteworthy suburban restaurants appear at the end, with no map. Within each area, the restaurants are grouped by type of cuisine. Restaurants serve lunch and dinner daily except where noted. Casual attire is appropriate at most restaurants, except where noted.

The restaurant price categories are based on the average cost of a dinner that includes appetizer, entrée, salad, and dessert (except as noted). Prices are for one person, food alone, not including alcoholic beverages, tax, and tip.

The following credit card abbreviations are used: AE, American Express; D, Discover; DC, Diners Club; MC, MasterCard; V, Visa.

Highly recommended restaurants are indicated by a star ★.

# Dining *(Boxes Refer to Detail Maps)*

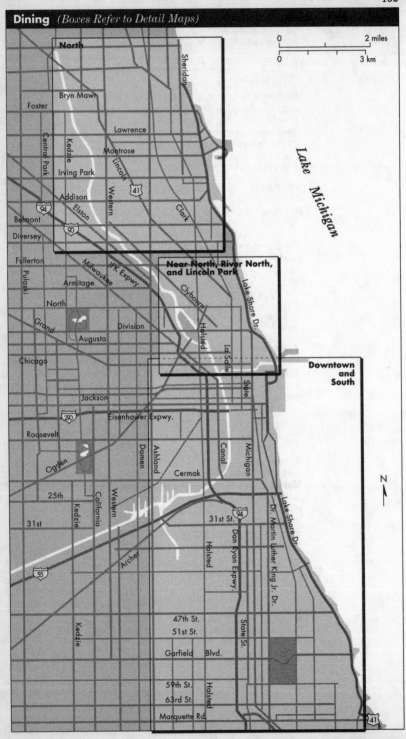

North

Near North, River North, and Lincoln Park

Downtown and South

Lake Michigan

0        2 miles
0        3 km

N

| Category | Cost* |
|---|---|
| Very Expensive | over $45 |
| Expensive | $30–$45 |
| Moderate | $18–$30 |
| Inexpensive | under $18 |

*per person, excluding drinks, service, and sales tax (8½%)*

### Near North, River North, and Lincoln Park

**American**  **The 95th.** At the top of the third-tallest building in the world sits this elaborately elegant restaurant, which commands spectacular lake and city views. The regional American menu changes seasonally but many include such specialties as smoked duck breast with onion and raisin relish, and sautéed veal chop with morel mushrooms and roasted garlic sauce. Desserts, such as chocolate fondue with Grand Marnier, are a particular strength. The wine list, while pricey, is splendid. The restaurant puts on an elaborate buffet for Sunday brunch, and the view is every bit as impressive in daytime as in the evening. At press time there was talk that The 95th might close its doors in 1993, so call before you go. *John Hancock Center, 875 N. Michigan Ave., tel. 312/787–9596. Jacket required at dinner. Weekend reservations required. AE, D, DC, MC, V. Very Expensive.*

**Seasons.** This hotel restaurant has become a stop on the gourmet circuit, thanks to the creativity of executive chef Mark Baker. New England and Asian influences give the creations here, such as papardelle with grilled Maine lobster and pesto-crusted rack of lamb, a distinct spark. The opulent dining room offers unmatched comfort and plenty of room to relax. Seasons also produces Chicago's best (and most expensive) Sunday brunch. *Four Seasons Hotel, 120 E. Delaware Pl., tel. 312/280–8800. Reservations strongly advised. AE, D, DC, MC, V. Very Expensive.*

★ **Charlie Trotter's.** This tastefully renovated town house accommodates only 20 closely spaced tables, serving many fewer people than would like to eat here. The owner and chef Charlie Trotter prepares the newest of new American cuisine with hints of Asian flavors incorporated into classic European dishes. Menus, which change daily, have included such appetizers as red snapper carpaccio with Asian noodle salad and sesame mayonnaise, and foie gras ravioli with mango and lemongrass sauce. Entrées have included mahimahi with leek and sorrel sauce and mushroom ravioli, garlic-laced veal chop with wild mushrooms and eggplant tartlet, and lasagna of sea scallops with squid-ink pasta and saffron sauce. It's a good idea to make reservations well in advance. *816 W. Armitage Ave., tel. 312/248–6228. Jacket required. Reservations required. AE, DC, MC, V. No lunch. Closed Sun., Mon. Expensive–Very Expensive.*

**Arnie's.** Stained glass, Tiffany lamps, and Art Deco accents are highlights of this venerable restaurant's decor. Various ethnic influences determine the appetizer and soup offerings; entrées are more dependably American, and beef dishes are always a good bet. Live music, from casual piano music to more complex acts, is a daily feature. *1030 N. State St., tel. 312/266–4800.*

Al's Italian Beef, **49**
Ambria, **1**
Arnie's, **23**
Avanzare, **58**
Bangkok Cafe, **68**
Benkay, **72**
Bice, **61**
Billy Goat Tavern, **66**
Bistro 110, **32**
Blackhawk Lodge, **35**
Boulevard, **65**
Bub City Crabshack
and Barb-B-Q, **14**
Bukhara, **53**
Busy Bee, **12**
Cafe Ba-Ba-Reeba!, **5**
Centro, **37**
Catch Thirty Five, **73**
Charlie Trotter's, **6**
Coco Pazzo, **45**
Cuisines, **74**
The Dining Room, **30**
Eccentric, **50**
Ed Debevic's, **48**
Eli's The Place for
Steak, **34**
Frontera Grill, **67**
Galans, **16**
Gene & Georgetti, **46**
Gibson's, **25**
The Golden Ox, **15**
Gordon, **51**
Gypsy, **60**
Hard Rock Cafe, **52**
Harry Caray's, **71**
Hat Dance, **42**
Hatsuhana, **62**
Home, **36**
Honda, **47**
House of Hunan, **64**
Jackie's, **3**
Jaxx, **57**
Jimo's Cafe, **13**
Kiki's Bistro, **19**
Kiki's Bistro, **19**
Klay Oven, **44**
L'Angolo di Roma, **2**
La Locanda, **40**
La Tour, **33**
Le Mikado, **20**
L'Escargot, **38**
Metropolis 1800, **11**
Mirador, **17**
Morton's of
Chicago, **24**
The 95th, **29**
Old Carolina Crab
House, **59**
Papagus, **54**
Pattaya, **39**
Pizzeria Due, **56**
Pizzeria Uno, **55**

## Dining Near North, River North, and Lincoln Park

The Pump Room, **18**

Relish, **4**

Robinson's No. 1
Ribs, **9**

Scoozi!, **41**

Seasons, **28**

Shaw's Crab House
and Blue Crab
Lounge, **70**

Sole Mio, **7**

Spiaggia, **27**

Szechwan House, **63**

Tang Dynasty, **26**

Topolobampo, **67**

Toulouse, **22**

Trattoria Gianni, **10**

Trattoria Convito, **31**

Tucci Benucch, **28**

Tucci Milan, **69**

Tuttaposto, **43**

Un Grand Cafe, **1**

Vinci, **8**

Yvette, **21**

*Jacket and tie required. Reservations advised. AE, D, DC, MC, V. Closed Mon., Sat. lunch. Expensive.*

★ **Boulevard.** This imaginatively restored hotel dining room offers skillful interesting cuisine and impeccable service. The menu features low-fat and low-cholesterol selections; if you're exempt from such concerns, the dessert soufflés are not to be missed. The prix-fixe lunch is an outstanding bargain. *Hotel InterContinental, 505 N. Michigan Ave., tel. 312/944–4100. Reservations recommended. AE, DC, MC, V. Expensive.*

★ **Gordon.** For more than 16 years this has been one of the most innovative restaurants in Chicago. Gordon's kitchen features a light, uncomplicated cooking style, revealed in such dishes as crispy shallot ravioli and sherry-vinegar jus. The four-course prix-fixe dinner is a very good value. Desserts are outstanding, ranging far beyond the usual chocoholics-only selection. Half-size portions are also available. The restaurant's decor is rococo, with Oriental rugs, swag curtains alongside each table, and dark wood surrounding tables set with white cloths and centerpieces of fresh flowers. Service is exceptional here, and on Friday and Saturday evening you can dance as well as dine. *500 N. Clark St., tel. 312/467–9780. Jackets required. Reservations required. AE, DC, MC, V. Closed holidays. Expensive.*

**The Pump Room.** Probably Chicago's most famous restaurant name among out-of-towners, the Pump Room has in recent years augmented its traditional menu with dishes representing a fresh, new style of cooking. The years-loyal clientele keeps coming back for the steaks and baked Alaska, while a newer breed of customer enjoys such dishes as pine-nut-breaded sole with infused oils. Celebrity photos still line the walls. *Omni Ambassador East, 1301 N. State Pkwy., tel. 312/266–0360. Reservations strongly recommended. AE, D, MC, V. Expensive.*

**The Eccentric.** Restaurateur Richard Melman has teamed with talk-show star Oprah Winfrey to open this aptly named adventure in dining. The combination French café/Italian coffeehouse/English pub can seat 400 diners and is decorated with the works of local artists. The food is surprisingly good, given the novelty of the enterprise. Don't miss the excellent steaks and chops, as well as Oprah's mashed potatoes with horseradish. And keep an eye out for Oprah. *159 W. Erie St., tel. 312/787–8390. Reservations accepted for 6 or more. AE, D, DC, MC, V. No lunch weekends. Moderate–Expensive.*

★ **Blackhawk Lodge.** Rustic, vacation-lodge decor sets this American regional restaurant apart. Hickory-smoked cuisine is something of a specialty—the ribs are particularly good—and the aromas coming from the kitchen are just about irresistible. *41 E. Superior St., tel. 312/280–4080. Reservations accepted. AE, D, DC, MC, V. Moderate.*

**Gypsy.** The Mediterranean influences abound in the decor and menu of this eclectic American restaurant. Potatoes and smoked salmon head the list of intriguing pizza toppings, and a roasted artichoke stuffed with Brie makes a great shared appetizer. Chicken cacciatore with whole-wheat pasta and grilled tuna with Mediterranean vegetables are representative entrées. Portions are very large, making this one of the most value-conscious restaurants in town. Sunday brunch is very good, too. *215 E. Ohio St., tel. 312/644–9779. Reservations advised. AE, D, DC, MC, V. Moderate.*

**Hard Rock Cafe.** Street signs, musical instruments, and posters adorn this branch of the London-based Hard Rock Cafe chain. Music blares over the din of 275 diners (or is it 1,000?). Hamburgers, lime-barbecued chicken, and Texas-style barbecued ribs are among the house specialties, but does anyone come to the Hard Rock Cafe for the food? *63 W. Ontario St., tel. 312/943–2252. Reservations accepted Mon.–Thurs. for lunch only. No reservations other times; the wait can be substantial. AE, MC, V. Closed some holidays. Moderate.*

**Home.** Not quite as traditional as the name suggests, Home is a comfortable neighborhood place, with cooking that makes use of traditional elements but goes beyond them: At least our Mom never fixed grilled pompano with grapefruit-cilantro-tomatilla sauce. *733 N. Wells St., tel. 312/951–7350. Reservations advised. AE, MC, V. Closed Sun. Moderate.*

**Jaxx.** This American restaurant delights with occasional British influences. Wood-grilled and -roasted meats and fish are the specialties, but don't forget the side dishes, notably the sinfully rich mashed potatoes. Small pizzas, great salade Niçoise, and steak-and-kidney pies help make Jaxx a popular lunch spot. *Hyatt Regency Suites, 676 N. Michigan Ave., tel. 312/266–3020. Reservations recommended. AE, D, MC, V. Moderate.*

**Jimo's Cafe.** Live music, long hours, and a melting-pot clientele help make this energetic café popular. The menu is eclectic—expect anything from Cajun chicken salad to sautéed soft-shell crab—and so are the customers; expect everything from shorts with cowboy boots to jacket-and-tie. *1576 N. Milwaukee Ave., tel. 312/278–2424. Reservations for parties of 6 or more. AE, MC, V. Moderate.*

**Metropolis 1800.** This very sophisticated restaurant successfully blends a casual atmosphere with serious cooking. Offerings change daily. The emphasis is on light, healthful, contemporary fare: fresh seafood, pastas, and such vegetarian dishes as the seasonal vegetable pie. However, those who wish to indulge themselves will find an occasional hearty pâté or sinfully rich sauce. And save room for the desserts—baked on the premises, they're killers. *1800 N. Clybourn, tel. 312/642–6400. Reservations recommended. AE, DC, MC, V. Closed Sun. Moderate.*

**Relish.** The important thing to remember here is to save room for dessert. It's wonderful, even if you find it awkward ordering something like the Very Chocolate Orgasm. (If you do, stick to the free-form ice-cream sandwich.) The wide-ranging American menu offers plenty of pre-dessert temptations as well. Sunday brunch is very pleasant in this airy, open dining room. *2044 N. Halsted St., tel. 312/868–9034. Reservations advised. AE, DC, MC, V. No lunch. Moderate.*

**Robinson's No. 1 Ribs.** Just about everything in this tiny restaurant is barbecued or deep fried. Ribs (baby backs, tips) head the menu, followed by barbecued chicken, hot links, jumbo shrimp, pork and beef, cracklin' Louisiana catfish, and batter-dipped shrimp. Choose from side orders of natural cut fries, coleslaw, baked beans, and corn on the cob. A spinach salad and Robinson's No. 1 salad (a chef's salad) are offered for militant cholesterol watchers. *655 W. Armitage Ave., tel. 312/337–1399. AE, MC, V. No lunch weekends. Inexpensive–Moderate.*

**Al's Italian Beef.** This tiny spot on busy Ontario Street is one of the best in Chicago for those two local delicacies, "Italian beef" (thinly sliced, well-done beef, served on a bun with its juice and as many toppings—hot peppers, onions, ketchup, mustard—as you like), and the Chicago-style hot dog (hot dog with toppings in the same manner). You can get Italian sausage and meatball sandwiches here, too, as well as fries, sweet peppers, hot peppers, and chili. Eat at one of the tiny, cramped tables or order carry-out. *169 W. Ontario St., tel. 312/943–3222. No credit cards. Inexpensive.*

**Billy Goat Tavern.** A favorite hangout for reporters, this self-service bar and grill just across the street and down the stairs is the columnist Mike Royko's second office. Don't come here if you're watching your cholesterol level: The famed "chizboogers" are held together with grease. Do come for the atmosphere, a quick bite, and a cold one that won't set you back a day's pay. *430 N. Michigan Ave. (lower level), tel. 312/222–1525. No credit cards. Inexpensive.*

★ **Ed Debevic's.** Half serious, half tongue-in-cheek, this imitation 1950s diner packs them in from morning till midnight. The signs are an important part of the decor: "If you don't like the way I do things—buy me out"; "If you're not served in 5 minutes—you'll get served in 8 or 9. Maybe 12 minutes. Relax." The menu features eight types of hamburger; a sandwich selection that includes tuna salad, chicken salad, chicken BLT, and Sloppy Joe; four chili preparations (plain, with macaroni and cheese, the same plus onion, and with onion and beans); five hot dog offerings; and a selection of "deluxe plates": meat loaf, pot roast, breaded pork loin, and chicken pot pie, all served with bread, butter, and choice of soup, slaw, or salad. The banana cream pie, coconut cream pie, and pecan pie are homemade. Unlike the real 1950s diner, Ed's has a selection of cocktails, wines, and Ed Debevic's Beer, Aged in its Own Bottle. *640 N. Wells St., tel. 312/664–1707. No reservations; the wait may be substantial. No credit cards. Closed some holidays. Inexpensive.*

**Chinese** **Tang Dynasty.** Lavishly appointed Tang Dynasty is the best-looking Chinese restaurant in the area. It also offers some of the best cooking. Alongside the usual pot stickers, wonton soup, and hacked chicken are many innovative dishes that change at the chef's whim. All are carefully prepared and professionally served. *100 E. Walton St., tel. 312/664–8688. Reservations advised. AE, DC, MC, V. Closed Sun. lunch. Expensive.*

★ **House of Hunan.** The original Magnificent Mile Chinese restaurant, House of Hunan continues to please. The large, elegantly decorated dining area is appointed with porcelains and carvings. With offerings from the four principal Chinese culinary regions—Mandarin (from Beijing), Hunan, Szechuan, and Canton—the enormous menu offers a satisfying dinner to anyone who enjoys Chinese food. Spicy hot dishes are plentiful, but so are mild ones. Pot stickers, scallop roll, satay beef, buns filled with minced pork and crabmeat, and stuffed crab claws are among the more than a dozen appetizers; cold dishes include drunken chicken, abalone salad, and jellyfish. Noodles, fish, shellfish, pork, duck, chicken, lamb, beef, vegetable, and mu shu (pancake-wrapped) specialties make up the remaining hundred or so preparations. *535 N. Michigan Ave., tel. 312/329–9494. AE, D, DC, MC, V. Moderate–Expensive.*

**Szechwan House.** Oriental paintings adorn the walls here, carpets on parquet floors soften the sound, and the service is attentive. The menu is nicely balanced; highly seasoned and spicy hot dishes are plentiful, as one would expect from a Szechuan restaurant, yet there are plenty of choices for diners who prefer milder food. Try the pot stickers or the wonton to start; both dumplings are filled with meat, and the wonton come with